A Perfect Dwelling Place

Janice Reed Cobb

WestBow Press books may be ordered through booksellers or by contacting:

WestBow Press
A Division of Thomas Nelson
1663 Liberty Drive
Bloomington, IN 47403
www.westbowpress.com
1-(866) 928-1240

ISBN: 978-1-4497-2159-6 (sc)
ISBN: 978-1-4497-2160-2 (hc)
ISBN: 978-1-4497-2158-9 (e)

Library of Congress Control Number: 2011911726

Printed in the United States of America

WestBow Press rev. date: 10/24/2011

In loving memory of my parents, Mabel and Terry Cobb;
my brother, Tommy; and in honor of my family.

Foreword

In *A Perfect Dwelling Place,* Janice Cobb has captured the essence of Narrative, and with that as her starting point, she takes us, as her readers, on a fantastical journey that explores the importance of family and its power to change lives.

Having read the book and after multiple discussions on its promise and purpose, I have discovered that in addition to a fascinating tale set in the Deep South in the early 1900s, it proceeds to be more than just an engaging and educational experience for the reader. Although the reader is caught in a tale told by the narrator's mother, recently deceased, set in dreamlike fashion, the characters brought forth are those who inhabited an era and place that no longer exist in reality. The times and incidents set down here are also of periods, places, and events that lie buried in the culture of the South, which was often seen as fixed in racism and poverty.

A Perfect Dwelling Place opens the reader to a family that lived both within and outside of the accepted mores during a time of great strife. It is laced with a true family feeling, with characters who love and support one another, and parents who see it as their main goal to pass along their wisdom to their children. They do it with love, discipline, and understanding. They are often in need of an explanation for which there are no easy words. They are respectful of all and are religious without being zealots. They tackle issues like racism, the Klan, relationships, the loss of loved ones, the need for privacy, and when necessary, secrecy to live within the culture that surrounds them. There is ready evidence of the need for courage as well when events demand it.

What resonates most powerfully in this book, however, is the simple truth spoken, which makes it an excellent example of the teaching power of the Narrative process. Long ago, it was not thought unusual for folklore to be passed from one generation to the next by way of storytelling, of both fiction and nonfiction. This book is a series of folklore stories and real-life stories being passed from one generation to another and then again. The stories are based on fact and experience, and the loving telling that goes on in genuinely skillful parenting. Using authentic relational characters adds to the charm and strength of the stories and allows them to become incorporated into an experiential learning process.

It is no accident that Janice Cobb has been able to accomplish so much in this, her first and hopefully not her last, book based loosely on her own mother's reflections. Janice Cobb has been a teacher and mentor throughout her professional career. Her techniques, especially those encompassing Narrative principles, speak to the need for encouragement and exposure to kindness and compassion, empathy and advocacy for all children, regardless of talent or ability. *A Perfect Dwelling Place* might serve as a powerful teaching tool for stimulating ideas in the training of parents, teachers, students, and mentors of learning from the Narrative example.

A Perfect Dwelling Place, a skillfully crafted work of fictionalized nonfiction, will occupy a place on my bookshelf of references both for the strength of Narrative practice as well as for those who seek to educate and advise. It is easy to see an evil, a weakness, or even a mistake; it is quite another thing altogether to make it recognizable, understandable, and remediable. This book goes a long way in that direction.

Dana Gage, MD
Masters Candidate, Narrative Medicine
Columbia University

A Personal Note

As a child, I sat in fascinated wonder as I listened to the stories my parents shared about their childhoods. Through their detailed accounts, I came to understand where our family's belief structure and traditions originated. I learned that God and His teachings are the foundation for all decision making. I learned too that devotion to family, after God, comes before all else; and that honesty is the key to healthy relationships. These elements became the underpinning for our family code of honor.

When I became an educator, I quite naturally carried a sense of my family's foundational principles to the classroom. As a teacher, I acted *in loco parentis*, in place of the parent. Looking into those curious little faces every day gave me a true sense of my responsibility to them as well as their parents. Like any parent, I found things to love in every child I taught.

In the winter of my mother's life, we traveled back in time through her narrative. Though bedridden, she remained bright, witty, conversant, and positive throughout her illness. Our focus became her stories—recording them, reviewing them, and enjoying them together. She never complained about her illness or her condition. My mother set a positive example even in dying.

A Perfect Dwelling Place is a compilation of her stories and the learning that evolved from them. Because of the need to create and extend characters, conversations, situations, and outcomes, *A Perfect Dwelling Place* falls under the fictionalized nonfiction genre.

I hope that parents will gain an insight into the importance of the circle of influence in their child's life. It really matters who and what your child interacts with in their daily lives. Face-to-face interaction with people—not things—continues to be what is most important in your child's development as a valued contributor to society.

For my colleagues in the teaching profession, I encourage you to use this book as a personal springboard to generate ideas for subjects that can be taught in the classroom. Some of the subjects covered may lead to the study of genealogy, World War I, hydroelectric power, oral histories, the Civil War, the Corps of Engineers, creative writing, racial segregation and integration, historical figures of the early 1900s, the history of medicine, and creative problem solving.

For those who are interested in Narrative Medicine, *A Perfect Dwelling Place* is the direct result of the Narrative process. Owen Flanagan of Duke University, a leading consciousness researcher, said, "Evidence strongly suggests that humans in all cultures come to cast their own identity in some sort of narrative form. We are inveterate storytellers" (*Consciousness Reconsidered* 198). Through my mother's narrative, she and I, her caregiver, had our burdens lightened by focusing on life as opposed to illness, pain, and death. My mother, Mabel, became the narrator and I recorded her accounts of her early life. I cannot adequately describe the joy this process brought to my mother. I personally carry a particularly rich learning experience from listening to the details of her history.

My mother took the most devastating experience known to mankind and turned it into a positive. What a blessing!

Acknowledgments

My heartfelt thanks go out to those who supported and encouraged me throughout the writing process:

To Patty O'Brien Fallon, Mabel's only surviving sibling, who talked through many of the personal qualities of the characters and provided a sense of the history of northern Alabama.

To Mickey Cobb, Mabel's son, his wife, Celia, and Mabel's beloved granddaughter, Catherine Cobb, for their ongoing support and encouragement. My deepest appreciation to Allison Cobb Marks, Mabel's dearly loved granddaughter, who provided excellent feedback regarding transitional phases in *A Perfect Dwelling Place* and offered her support.

To Alexis Bond, Mabel's adored great-granddaughter, for her opinions regarding the readability and flow of the book.

To Teri Riley Bond, Mabel's beloved granddaughter, for her constant support and encouragement.

To Dr. Dana Gage who encouraged and supported this project from its inception. She was an invaluable resource for working through historical events and their applicability, southern culture, and the history of medical practice. Dr. Gage provided constructive criticism and kept me moving forward. Her input regarding Narrative Medicine and the Narrative process afforded me the opportunity to gain new learning and insights into the value of listening to those who need to be heard.

Janice Cobb
Nashville, Tennessee
janicercobb@comcast.net

Chapter 1

THE BUTTERFLIES OF ANTICIPATION IN MY stomach contradict my outward calm. I am going to visit my mother, Mabel, for the first time since her death some years ago. I stroll along the sidewalk and lean into the steep incline. When I glance back slightly to the right, I notice a stranger. He is wearing a grayish tweed suit with a matching vest, a starched white shirt, a black tie, and a black felt hat. Based on his clothing, he seems to be from another time—a time I have never experienced. His face is not visible, but I sense his kindness and somehow know that he is escorting me to see my mother.

When the stranger and I reach a succession of brick row houses, he begins to explain his presence through his thoughts. "I'm taking you to your family; they have chosen to dwell above an elegant museum. After you enter the building, go up the marble staircase. The committee decided to keep the museum open so there is a constant flow of museum patrons; however, they cannot enter the living quarters until their hearts change as directed. Here it is." He does not pause and quickly fades away into the distance.

My eyes move from the stranger's path to the wide steps leading up to an elaborately etched glass door. Sitting on each side of the steps, two stately lions, chiseled from white marble, seem to announce the importance of things to come. Their massive heads stare forward as their manes lie in gentle tresses and stream down toward their gigantic paws.

My anticipation increases as I climb the front steps and turn the bronze doorknob. Stepping into the grand foyer, I am greeted by a gloved attendant who nods and touches the bill of his black cap. I attempt to see his face, but I can't. His face is obscured like the stranger who escorted me up the sidewalk. He extends his right arm toward a larger adjoining room, indicating that I should keep moving forward. Without exchanging words, I tentatively maneuver into what appears to be the main room of the museum. Finely dressed people stand in small clusters in front of enormous paintings hanging throughout the room. The golden frames surrounding the paintings emit a shimmer that makes the room appear to sparkle. Scanning across the room, my eyes search for a familiar face, but light and shadows distort their features. Although I am aware of the crowd, the paintings, and the beauty of the museum, nothing seems familiar. Everything seems vague, indistinct.

With only one goal in mind, I drift across the floor and begin to ascend the white marble staircase as the stranger outside had directed. My heart pounds with excitement, but confusion about this place makes my head reel. The higher I climb, the more the crowd of art lovers turns to watch me go up the elegant stairway. When I reach the landing at the top of the stairs, I slowly twist around and look down at them—their awe fills the air. I hear their thoughts rather than their voices and learn that my presence does not create their wonder. It's my ability to enter the living quarters that astounds them. As I stand there, in a state of uncertainty and with multiple voices in my head, I begin to realize that this must be a dream.

It all makes sense as a dream: a nameless place, unknown date, faceless people, blurry artwork, and my ability to hear the thoughts of others. My rapid heartbeat turns into breathlessness. I begin to question if I should continue my dream or turn away. Then I doubt myself. *Did I die? No, I couldn't have—this is just a dream. Should I go back down the stairs and return to my life or walk into my mother's presence? Stay calm.* Somehow, my uncertainty doesn't discourage me. I take a deep breath, turn from the crowd, and walk toward the entrance to Mabel's divine world. A feeling of peace falls over me the instant I seemingly float through the archway.

Entering the living quarters, I feel overwhelmed and surrounded by love—the same love I sensed as a child in the safety of our family and home. As I wander through what appears to be a long hallway, I notice a succession of windows along the left wall. The brilliance of the white light coming through the windows causes me to look away. My eyes seek out and find my mother, Mabel, in the distance; she is sitting on a long settee beside my living brother. Because they appear so happy and seem to be deeply involved in conversation, I know I should not interrupt their time together.

Patiently, I wait for my turn to be with her. My brother eventually stands and walks away. Clothed in a white, flowing, sari-like garment, Mabel stands when she sees me. "There you are; I'm so happy you came for a visit. Come here and let me look at you." I hear her voice in my mind, but know that she is not communicating as she did before she left: her lips are not moving. I'm listening to her thoughts.

Transfixed for only a moment, I begin moving toward her. The strength of her voice in my consciousness shocks me. Mabel's hair looks as white as the light shining through the windows in the hallway. She wears it pulled straight back and rolled into a bun, like the picture of her sitting on my dresser, when her hair was chestnut brown. I can see that the beauty of her youth has returned to her eyes and skin. Her welcoming smile, as always, curves softly across her face. Mabel's hands seem transformed to a more youthful time and show no signs of the tremors she suffered when I last saw her. The most astounding thing is her ability to stand; she is no longer stooped from the ravages of sickness. I stop in astonishment as I observe her gliding toward me. In our delight to be together once again, we begin rapidly exchanging thoughts. "You look incredible, Mabel."

"Things are much better here. I've been waiting for your visit; I have so much to show you." It's as though our spirits intertwine and there is no separation—there's no need to touch. She motions me toward the sitting area. "Your brother had to go back to his family. That's as it should be; he's devoted to them. He escorted me here from the hospital, you know."

Seemingly exhilarated, she doesn't wait for my response. "We don't have enough of your earthly time to talk about a lot of things. For those who live here, there is no time—light, joy, and blessings fill every moment. I know that you must have a lot of questions." We laugh at her dry sense of humor. "We are free from the burdens of our earthly lives because only healed souls live here. No tears or pains exist now. It's such a joyous relief. This is truly a perfect dwelling place. The rewards of being here far exceed what one can imagine on earth."

Feeling her peace, I sit back and listen.

"The brightness of the light is constant. It's the light of God; there's never a moment of darkness. There are no negative thoughts or deeds here. Everything is as it should be."

I watch her face as she continues to explain why I'm here with her.

"Now for the reason I called you to come for a visit. Do you remember how you could take a crystal, hold it just right in the sunlight, and see all the colors of the rainbow?"

I nod my head showing her that I remember.

"That always fascinated you kids, but what we have here is far more astonishing. Come with me. I'm going to take you to the place where I spend most of my time reviewing my life." We get up as she points to a massive door. "Follow me."

As we walk, the nimbleness of her movement fascinates me. Because I fully understand that her new life is far better than anything she has ever experienced, a smile edges across my face. I become conscious of why she left. When we reach the door, I run my hand over its smoothness. My eyes question her as I think, "This door is beautiful, Mabel. Can you believe this?"

"Oh yes, I can believe it," says Mabel. "When you come back to stay, you'll learn that all things here are made of the finest materials. Even the streets reflect the beauty of God's love. The only rule here is the Golden Rule. It's also the only rule needed on earth." Her serenity fills the room. She's finally in the place she described to me all of my life: her mansion on the hilltop.

She rests her hand on the knob of the beautiful door. "Now, close your eyes. The light in here is intense. It doesn't bother me, but we'll have to allow time for your eyes to adjust."

I close my eyes. Standing in the doorway beside her, I sense that the brightness of the room is beyond anything I have ever experienced. And I ask, "Are you sure my eyes will be able to adjust to the light?"

"Yes, just open them very slowly. Let your eyes get use to it; then open them a bit more." We step forward and I hear the door close behind us. Ever the trusting child, I must rely on her completely. "We're going to sit in two chairs that are across the room. Feel my presence and move with me. Are you beginning to get use to the light?"

"Yes, ma'am. It's much better than it was at first. I should be fine by the time we sit down," I respond as the light wraps around us. Everything appears to be varying shades of white. When we finally reach the chairs, my eyes are completely open. A sense of uneasiness begins to creep into my being. My mind tells me that even though

I am here, I don't belong—not yet. I turn toward Mabel and look into her pale blue eyes.

With her reassurance, I calm down and listen to her voice in my mind. The comfort of her presence erases my momentary fear. "Stop worrying; everything's fine. You're free to return to your life the instant you want to leave. You aren't finished on earth. It's unusual that you were given this opportunity to visit."

As Mabel predicted, I have many questions. "Who are all those people in that museum-type room below the staircase?" Mabel leans back and rests her head against the softness of the chair.

A gentle smile brushes over her face as her thoughts begin to flow. "Those people are the ones who cannot yet enter the divine world. You saw all the gold, the glitter, and the elaborate clothing. On their way up here, those worldly things and the people they saw distracted them. As I always told you, God doesn't allow people to bring one material thing up here. The break from earthly things is absolute. The people you saw will not gain entry until they stop clinging to the temporary things of the world from which they came."

I send her another question, "How long will they stay down there?"

"Each person will remain there until they fully understand the worthlessness of worldly things. The only possession you can bring here is your soul."

"How did I manage to get up here?"

Mabel turns her eyes toward me and responds, "I called to you because I want you to fully understand my new life as well as my past life. You came with one purpose: to see me. You set your goal and did not allow any distractions. That's how single-minded all people must be to gain entry."

"When they do gain entry, do they all come to where you are?"

"No, they go to where the souls of their loved ones reside. Just like you, they will long to see their families. There are many rooms here."

"Are you allowed to visit with friends?"

A smile comes across her face as she answers, "Oh, yes. You can move about freely here. We tend to remain close to those we loved on earth, but we are also free to form new circles of friends. Jealousy, envy, and social class do not exist here. All souls here are true equals—intellectually and socially. You see, all those false faces we wear on earth are worthless in the end."

"Sorry to ask so many questions."

"Your curiosity is perfectly normal," says Mabel.

She gets up and stands in front of me. The surrounding light brings out the magnitude of her physical beauty. Goodness pours from her being. She gestures in a sweeping motion and says, "I do most of my thinking in here. This is the place where I can review my life. All people here have the same power because looking back is important. It enables us to understand ourselves. Though you can never go back, you can learn from the past and move forward with what you learn. Past events and the people who touch our lives influence who we become. Parents carry their life experiences forward to their children. Through understanding my life, you will be able to better understand who you are and why you have become the person you are."

"How does being in this room allow you to review your life?" I ask.

"White light fills the window behind me, just like the crystals you use to play with in the sunshine. In this light, however, and only in this room, we can look into the light and see my past. This light separates into my chosen memories. All I have to do is think of an age, a year, or an event, and it reveals itself in front of us."

I struggle to take in the complexity of her explanation. "Do you mean that all those stories about your childhood will come to life right here in front of us?"

"That's exactly what will happen," answers Mabel. "Over the years, I tried to give you a feel for what life was like for me as a child. Until I could actually review my life when I came here, I never realized the hardships my family went through. As a child, I thought the world around me was a glorious adventure. Therefore, quite naturally, I left out a lot of the people and events that influenced my life."

Her thoughts begin carrying me back to her childhood. "When I was five years old, our country became involved in World War I; new diseases threatened our daily lives; doctors, if you could find them, had few cures; and the Klan was rearing its ugly head. It amazes me that so many of us survived all the troubles of 1918."

She continues to remember as I take in her thoughts. "I now understand how hard Mama and Papa worked for our family. We kids had no idea how poor we were in those days. As you and I look into the light, we'll be able to see the town, our home, Mama and Papa, Grandpa, and everything we discussed over the years. The most extraordinary part is that we'll be able to hear what I was thinking as a child. The voice of the storyteller will tell you everything you need to know."

"This is unimaginable, Mabel. We're going into the past." She sits back down beside me, smiles, and stares at the window of light. My eyes move to the window. Like a kaleidoscope, colors begin to entwine and shift into shapes. The shapes become recognizable objects. Within seconds, we look down on the small town where Mabel was born. The image moves to street level and begins to walk us along the main road. The voice of the storyteller mystically begins to relate Mabel's world as a child....

—

The town of Shoal Crossing, Alabama, stands inconspicuously on the bank of Shoal Creek. Major flooding can occur when the smaller creeks in the region swell and cannot empty fast enough into the Tennessee River. When the surrounding soil is oversaturated, locals know that these bodies of water can become destructive to buildings, bridges, and even perilous for people.

The horse-drawn wagons traveling through or into Shoal Crossing have carved deep ruts in the red clay road. In a downpour, the road turns to red mush and it's impassable. With fewer than one thousand men, women, and children living in the town and on the surrounding farmland, the settlement is small. On both sides of the main road, white clapboard homes with covered front porches proudly rest among the flowers planted by the owners.

Glancing at the side yards, you can see that nearly every one of the homes has some form of a barn and a small vegetable garden. The Army Corps of Engineers employs almost all of the men in Shoal Crossing. They moved here to work at Lock 6 which is used to control the Tennessee River, but that changed when President Wilson declared war on Germany in 1917. The president selected the Shoals area of northwest Alabama as the site for two nitrate plants and the construction of a dam across the Tennessee River for power. Some of the men within the community leave for military duty every day, but hundreds more have construction jobs throughout the area.

In 1918, the only businesses in Shoal Crossing are two stores and a barbershop. The general stores stand in the middle of town, across the road from each other. Mr. Stevens and Mr. Bicknell, the storeowners, have an ongoing competition for the best prices and the variety of things they sell. In-town people can take a short walk to either store, while the farmers typically come into town on their wagons. For the convenience of their riding customers, each business has a hitching post along the storefront where their horses can be safely tied. The stores are surprisingly similar. As long as there's money to pay in advance, either owner can order whatever a customer needs.

Customers can select from the folded stacks of work shirts and trousers, boots and shoes lining the wooden floor, and bolts of cloth or yarn from behind the counter. Foodstuffs like flour, cornmeal, crackers, and hoops of hard cheese are stored in wooden barrels with heavy lids sitting on top. Smaller items like needles, thread, candy, billfolds, and coin purses rest inside the glass display case. By a certain date each month, trusted customers who maintain a running tab must pay their balance in full or risk losing their credit in the store. Neither storeowner allows customers to graze as they shop. Regulars have learned that those few grapes or peanuts they choose to slyly taste always show up on their tickets at the front counter.

Next door to Mr. Stevens's store, Ed Smithers runs a one-chair barbershop called Ed's Haircuts. The barbershop is so small that only two waiting customers have chairs to sit on inside the shop. The rest must wait outside the door. Since there is no electricity, all haircuts are done with scissors and hand razors in front of the window where there is more light. Farmers load their families in wagons for the ride into town, where they stand around Ed's place to wait their turn for their fifteen-cent scalping.

Mr. Smithers only charges ten cents to cut the hair of a woman or a child under the age of twelve. Locals aren't sure if Ed has any special training for his business. Nobody really knows anything about him. He just showed up one day and hung his sign. Most of Ed's customers look like he sat a bowl on their head and simply cut away any hair that extended below the bowl's rim. The men and boys describe it as "getting their ears lowered," especially when it appears that Ed used a shallow bowl.

The churches and schools are the centers of activity for the townspeople. There are two churches for the white families and one for the coloreds. Traveling preachers provide the white churches with their sermons. Roving the countryside, the preachers accept the kindness of the church families for their food and shelter on a rotating schedule. The host families in turn feel honored to have the preacher in their home or, if there is no room, in their barn. The colored church has a permanent preacher who lives in a one-room shanty built by the members on the church property.

The white children go to Shoal Crossing Elementary, but the coloreds' school doesn't have a name. On school days, the colored preacher becomes the principal of their one-room school in the church. One teacher works with all ages in her classroom and they don't have many textbooks—just the ones the white children have worn out.

A number of the children in both schools in town sometimes have to miss school days so that they can work in the fields or help at home. Most children must walk to and from school, some traveling over an hour each way. A few of the lucky ones can ride a horse or hitch a ride in a wagon. Those who make it to high school have to go to Florence, just across Shoal Creek, for classes.

Turning off the main road, within eyeshot of Mr. Stevens's store, sits Mabel O'Brien's birthplace and home. The house faces west and the evening sun reflects the brightness of the white exterior. Along the white picket fence, rose bushes are sprouting their earliest leaves, announcing another year of the perfumed aroma of deep red roses. Thick Bermuda grass blankets the yard and shows its first hint of the deep green that matches the shutters and roof of the house. An unpainted boardwalk leads to the three front steps and the slatted front porch that stretches across the width of the house.

The narrow balusters that support the handrails around the perimeter of the porch cast faint shadows on the porch's floor.

Standing between the porch and picket fence is a large oak tree that provides shade for the dining room side of the house. Beneath the shadow of the tree sits a sandbox with imprints of small feet in the sand. A galvanized bucket lies on its side with an old split wooden spoon resting on top of one of the unpainted side boards. A thin tuft of fur from a shedding dog clings to the outside rim of one of the edges of the sandbox.

Chapter 2

THE SCREECH OF THE DOOR SPRING echoes in Mabel's ears as she steps out on the front porch. She holds the brass handle as she lets the door shut, not making a sound. Mabel knows not to make any noise in the afternoons after school because, Bubba, who is eleven, and Sister, who is eight, do their homework at the dining room table. Brother, five months old, is sleeping in his baby bed in Mama's room.

Mabel is going on six, but can't go to school with her brother and sister until she is seven years old. As she walks across the porch to the top step, Mabel's blue eyes search the front of Mr. Stevens's store to see if her papa is close to home. Not seeing him, she sits down and rests her back against the corner post. Mabel puts her legs out flat in front of her and pulls her pale blue cotton dress over her legs so that it touches the tops of her white knee socks. Reaching up, she rubs the back of her head to feel the prickly stubs of hair.

Mabel doesn't like her hair and wishes for it to be long again. *I can't stand the way that old barber cut my hair; he calls it a bob. Mama paid him a whole ten cents just to whack it off like Bubba's hair. She just had it cut off because she can't curl it like Sister's hair. She says that mine's too thick to wrap around the curling rags.* Mabel feels tears beginning to well up in her eyes again. *It didn't hurt, but I don't like to look like a silly boy.* Mabel puckers her lips in contempt for what the barber did to her. When she thinks about her papa, she remembers that he told her that it would grow out soon. *I hope it'll grow out before I start school.*

The sound of Mama's footsteps coming up the hall causes Mabel to turn and watch for her face through the screen door. *Mama's coming out here. It must be time for Papa to get home.* She sees the tray Mama is carrying as she balances three glasses of iced tea with lemon slices. "Come open the door, Mabel. I made us some tea." Mabel opens the door for her mama. "I thought this would taste good while we wait for your papa." The chunks of ice melodiously jingle inside the glasses as Mama walks over to place the tray on the black table that stands between two wooden rocking chairs. "This will taste good to your papa when he gets home from that hot foundry." She hands Mabel a glass of tea.

"Thank you, Mama," says Mabel. She feels the cool dampness of the glass in her hand and takes a sip. "It sure is good. Did you give Bubba and Sister a glass?"

"Sister didn't want anything to drink, but Bubba drank his down and asked for another glass," says Mama. "They've got enough schoolwork to keep them busy until supper, poor things."

Walking over to the to the red clay flower pot sitting on the porch, Mama wishes out loud, "I sure hope this ivy goes where I want it to go." Then she sets her glass of tea on the railing and begins to wrap the new growth around the string she attached to the ceiling. Reaching her finger down into her glass of tea, she pulls out a piece of ice. Mabel watches as Mama puts the ice on the dirt surrounding the plant.

"Why'd you do that?" asks Mabel. "Won't that be too cold for the ivy?" Before Mama has a chance to answer, Mabel sticks her finger down in her own glass of tea. "May I put a piece of my ice in there too?" She slides a piece of ice up the side of the glass and into her hand.

"Put that one piece in there, but no more," says Mama. Her brown eyes, outlined by her dark brown hair, smile down at Mabel. "That ice will turn to water in no time in this heat. It's too early for it to be this hot. I hope we'll get a few more days of cool air before the heat sets in for the summer."

Mama picks up her glass of tea from the railing, walks over to her rocking chair, and sits down. Mabel gazes at the circle of water left by Mama's glass. She then turns to watch Mama's sitting-down ritual. She pulls her black skirt up over her black shoes and scoots back in the chair. As Mabel watches, Mama begins to rock with the rhythmic touching of her toes to the floor.

Going back to the top step, Mabel positions herself so she can gaze at her mother. *Mama fixes herself up before Papa comes home from work. She brushes her hair, fixes the sleeves of her white blouse, puts on a tinge of lipstick, and rouges her pale cheeks. Today she added a small brooch at the neck of her blouse.* "I think I hear Papa's whistle," says Mabel. She stands and walks along the boardwalk to the front gate. She looks up into her papa's blue eyes just as he reaches his arm over to unlock the gate.

"Afternoon, Mrs. O'Brien." He reaches down and takes Mabel's hand as they walk toward the porch. "How's my Mabel doing today?" He heads straight for his rocker and sits down. "Is this glass of tea for me, Lizbeth? You look mighty pretty this afternoon."

"Thank you, Mr. O'Brien. I knew you'd be burning up by the time you walked home," says Mama. "I felt sorry for you all day long because I knew you were about to suffocate in that foundry."

"It sure did get hot in there today. Turning that brass to liquid takes more heat than a human can stand, but it's what we need to do to keep things going for all the fittings for the dam. Even though it's hot as the dickens outside, it feels cool when you walk out of the furnace area. This tea is mighty good." Papa removes his denim cap and leans back with his eyes closed.

"Mabel, bring me your glass. I've got to go in and get things ready for supper," says Mama. She gets up and picks up the tray. "Do me a favor and open the door for me one more time." Mabel goes over to the door and holds it open.

Returning to her spot on the step, Mabel watches as Papa sleeps in the rocker. *Poor Papa—he's always so tired when he comes home. Mama says that the heat in the foundry makes him extra tired. His hair is still wet from sweating—Bubba looks just like Papa. They have different kinds of hair, but they both have blue eyes, a big smile, and big ears (what Papa calls their "Irish ears"). Papa's taller and doesn't have freckles like Bubba. He's stronger too.*

Mama interrupts Mabel's thoughts when she comes to the door. "Mabel, wake your papa up so y'all can wash your hands for supper."

Papa's gonna be surprised when he sees what we're having for supper. Mama fixed us some stew with carrots, potatoes, and chunks of meat. It's one of Papa's favorite things to eat. Mabel walks over to Papa, places her hand on his arm, and gives him a gentle pat. "Time to eat supper, Papa." He opens his eyes and smiles at Mabel. Holding onto his hand, Mabel and Papa walk into the house in silence.

Across from the dining room are two glass-paned doors that open into the parlor where the O'Brien family gathers in the evening after supper. Furnished with a long velvet settee along the front wall and three overstuffed red velvet chairs, the one coal-oil lamp casts a soft light across the room. Bubba, Sister, and Mabel usually sit on the large woolen rug that decorates the deeply oiled plank floor. At this time, on most nights, Brother is asleep in his baby bed. Mama and Papa prefer to sit on the two chairs that flank the lamp sitting on the small mahogany table.

Mama lifts her black Bible from the side table. Before she says a word, Mabel knows that their story time is about to begin. "Would you children like for me to read the newspaper article from the *Princeton Leader* about your papa and me getting married?"

As they nod their heads in pleased agreement, Mama unfolds the tattered newspaper. So they can immerse themselves in the coming story time, all three children scoot closer to their parents and look up at their faces "You remember that I lived in Princeton, Kentucky when I met your papa, and my best friend sent me this article from my hometown paper." Again, the three nod in agreement.

> *The announcement of the marriage of Miss Elizabeth Hood and Mr. Tom O'Brien at Florence, Alabama, Sunday evening was received here by Mr. and Mrs. T. J. Hood the early part of the week.*
>
> *After attending the Confederate reunion in Nashville, in the spring, in company with her father and several Princeton friends, Miss Elizabeth left for Florence, Alabama for a visit to her sister with the avowed intention of returning to Princeton, but Cupid would not have it so, hence her marriage, which is received here with much surprise by her many friends. She was one of Princeton's most beautiful young women and very attractive. Mr. O'Brien is a promising young businessman of Florence and is highly spoken of by the home papers.*
>
> *They will make Florence their home and it is to be hoped that they will ever be happy and contented. Miss Hood, born and raised in Kentucky, lived in Cadiz when a little girl and has many relatives in the county.*

"Your papa and I got our marriage license on the first Saturday in November; we got married the next day. That was on Sunday,

November 6, 1904." She refolds the article and places it back in her Bible.

Mabel's gaze moves from her mama's face to Sister's silhouette. *I can see gold in Sister's long curls. People say that we look like twins, but I think she's prettier than me. Our blue eyes look the very same. Sister's what Mama calls prissy. She's older than me and thinks that makes her smarter. We can wear some of the same clothes, but she's getting a lot taller than I am. We like to play house and school together. She always gets to be the mother and the teacher.*

Bubba interrupts Mabel's thoughts by asking, "Where'd y'all live in Florence?"

Papa leans forward and rests his arms on his legs. "We were as poor as church mice, Son. We found us a little rental house near my job at the ironworks. Your mama and me had to learn how to live on next to nothing," says Papa. "But we were happy, weren't we Lizbeth?"

Mama nods her head in agreement. "Yes, times weren't easy, but we had each other. That's about all we had." She pauses and seems to consider how to put her words together. "I think the hardest thing for me was that I moved away from all my family and friends in Princeton. My friends meant the world to me. Of course, having one sister in Florence helped, but I constantly mourned for my home. Time took care of my sadness but, to this day, I have my memories of my friends in Kentucky. Your papa's brothers and sisters were good to me. One of them usually came calling most every day."

Sister rises to her knees and then sits back down, leaning against Mabel. "Tell us about the time you went to the train station, Papa," begs Sister. "That day you went with your daddy." Knowing how much they both like the story about their grandfather, Mabel looks into Sister's eyes and smiles.

"I had no idea what would happen to Mother and us nine kids when we went with Daddy that day, Sister. My parents had moved to Florence from Cincinnati, Ohio," says Papa. "Times were so bad that it was next to impossible for Daddy to make a living for all of us. Mother had a severe case of ague. It kept her flat on her back most of the time. Her fever would shoot up so high that her clothes would get sopping wet, but then she'd turn around and have chills that'd make her whole body shiver. It drained all of her strength."

Papa leans back and grasps the arms of his chair. "Everything looked bleak at home. There was no money for food. All of us boys took odd jobs here and there. One day Daddy heard about some jobs down in Birmingham. He told us that he had to go for the family. My daddy promised us that he'd mail Mother his pay for our rent and food."

Mabel feels the sting of tears. "How old were you?" asks Bubba. Mabel doesn't have to look at Bubba. She knows he is about to cry too.

"I was twelve years old; about your size, Bubba. Anyway, Daddy wanted my brother and me to walk to the train station with him so he could buy Mother some oranges. They only cost a few cents. He wanted her to have them to make her stronger. My brother and me stood there with those oranges until the train pulled away. Tears rolled down our cheeks. Until that day, we'd never known life without Daddy. That's the last time we saw him."

Mama reaches over and pats Papa's knee. "Your papa never got to go to school another day. At the age of twelve, he had to work like a grown man."

Papa's eyes water as he rubs his hands together. "That's when I started learning about working with metals in the foundry at the ironworks. I started out sweeping floors. They slowly let me do more. My older sisters stayed home and took care of Mother. All of us older boys had to work to make money for food, clothes, and rent. The younger ones went to school. We never found out for a certainty what happened to Daddy. The rumor is that a terrible storm blew through Birmingham and killed him. Another story is that he made some money, flashed it around, and someone murdered him to get his cash. I reckon we'll never know. That was in 1886."

"Tell us about Ireland," encourages Sister.

"Daddy was born in Dublin and my mother was born in Galway. My daddy's name was Edward O'Brien; and mother's name was Cecelia Welsh. They both came to America on a ship with their families; they were immigrants. I don't believe they knew each other until they moved to Cincinnati. After they got up older, they took a liking to each other, married, and moved to Florence, about five miles west of here. Now, your mama's ancestors came from Holland. They settled in Tennessee, but her daddy eventually moved to Kentucky where she was born. That makes the three of you Dutch-Irish."

Mama shifts as she places her Bible back on the table beside her. "I hate to break up such a nice conversation, but there's school tomorrow and you early birds have to go to bed. We'll have another story time real soon."

Mabel raises her hand to draw attention. "I didn't get to ask my question, Papa."

Smiling, Papa looks down at Mabel. "What would you like to hear about, Mabel?"

"Can you tell us about when you and Mama moved to Shoal Crossing?" Mabel looks at Bubba and Sister for approval. When they nod their heads, she knows they want to hear that story too. Mabel scoots closer to Papa and looks straight up into his handsome face. The furrows in his forehead shift closer together when he looks back down at her.

"We moved here in the late summer of 1910. Your mama and I liked Shoal Crossing. It was small, had a good school, a nice church for us, and put me within walking distance of the Corps of Engineers. Bubba, back then you were the only child, because little John died before we left Florence." Papa looks over at Mama and she looks down at her lap. "He was a fine boy, but his tiny body couldn't handle the problems caused from his drinking that kerosene."

"I remember John," says Bubba. "He looked like you, Mama. He had your brown eyes and dark hair." Bubba's brown knickers slide up above his socks as he sits up on his knees. "Didn't y'all bring everything over here in just one trip?"

"We hauled everything we owned plus the three of us in one wagonload. That should tell you how little we accumulated. We did okay until we got to Shoal Creek. The bridge was out, so we had to ford it. We literally bounced across those shoals. I didn't know if we were gonna sink down in the silt or tip over from the stones. It felt like we were hitting one rock after another. That poor old mare just about tuckered out on us. Do you remember how tired we were, Lizbeth?"

"I'll never forget that ride—we were filthy, hungry, and exhausted. When we finally got to this house, your papa and me just took what we needed out of the wagon, tied the horse to the oak tree out front, and fell asleep on this parlor floor. Sister, you were born almost two months from the day we got here. Getting the government job made us feel like it was a new beginning. So you see, children, your papa having to work at such an early age turned out to be what was best for him for his future. It turned out to be best for all of us." Mama leans back and nods in agreement with herself.

"I don't remember it, Papa, but I like to hear about our wagon ride," says Bubba.

"You don't remember it because you slept all the way over here. You've always been an ole sleepyhead." Papa reaches over and tousles Bubba's curly red hair. Bubba smiles and looks at Sister and Mabel.

"Okay, kiddoes, it really is time to go to bed," says Papa. As he rises from his chair, Papa stretches his arms toward the ceiling. "Bubba, you should be able to finish digging the storm cellar when you get home from school tomorrow. We'll make the cut-out in the floor Saturday. After that, your mama won't have to worry about the storms."

When Mabel crawls into bed, she begins to think about the story time with Mama and Papa. She stares into the darkness. *My favorite storytellers are Papa and Grandpa. Josie tells me stories too when she comes to work for Mama. I wonder what it would have been like to live in Florence and know little John. Mama says that Shoal Crossing has just about everything Florence has—only closer together. She says that we might move again someday. I hope not—I want to go to school in Shoal Crossing.* Mabel turns her pillow over to find a cooler spot. *That hole Bubba and Papa are digging under the house sounds scary to me.* Then she drifts off to sleep.

After school the next day, Bubba wastes no time getting to work on the cellar, while Sister does her homework at the dining room table. Mabel decides to go outside to see if she can watch Bubba working. She gets down on all fours and ducks under the back porch. Feeling her way to some concrete block supports, she looks around and sees Snooks, Bubba's general-mixture dog, over by the pile of dirt. "Bubba, are you under here? Where are you, Bubba?"

"Here I am, Mabel. What you want?" Bubba's blue eyes peek over the dirt. "Papa said that you girls shouldn't come up under here. You'd better get gone."

"I ain't over there with you. He never said that I couldn't come up under the porch," retorts Mabel. She feels proud of her boldness. *He can't get at me from down in that hole.*

"Mabel O'Brien, you know good an' well what he meant. You can see the hole tomorrow when Papa cuts the floor. I'm gonna tell him to make you and Sister sleep down here—go on, I've got work to do."

Mabel tries to use her distraction skills on Bubba by ignoring what he said and asking a new question. "Are you standing on something?"

Bubba stares at her over the heap of dirt. "That's dumb, Mabel. I'm standing on two concrete blocks. You know I ain't this tall. This thing is deep—it's taller than Papa is. It has dirt steps that go up to the house. Bye, Mabel." His eyes disappear.

Beginning to fear that Papa might really make her sleep in the hole, Mabel decides to let Bubba have his way. "I reckon I'll mosey back into the house. It ain't no fun up under here anyway." Bubba doesn't utter a sound, but Mabel hears the shovel cut through the dirt once again.

When she gets to the edge of the house, she looks back at Snooks and he wags his tail at her. "See if you can hear me walking through the house, Bubba." Mabel wriggles out from under the porch and stomps up the steps. She opens the back screen door, stomps across the screened porch, opens the kitchen door, and stomps into the house. Continuing her stomps, Mabel makes her way across the kitchen into the hallway leading to her room.

Mama steps out of her bedroom with her hands on her hips. Mabel knows that's a bad sign. "What in the world is all that racket about, Mabel? Don't you know how to walk like a lady? You're gonna wake up Brother."

"Yessum, I just want to see if Bubba can hear me walking. I'm sorry, Mama." Mabel tiptoes down the hallway and walks into her room.

—

Early Saturday morning, Bubba and Papa make many trips back and forth from the kitchen to the hole under the house. Papa finally brings in his hand drill and begins twisting it through the kitchen floor. He cuts several holes close together and makes a place big enough for him to fit his handsaw down into the floor. When he finishes sawing, Papa builds a frame around the hole and places a smooth wooden door over it. He attaches one side of the door to the frame with hinges.

"Watch this, Lizbeth," says Papa. "Here's how you can lift the door up so you can get down to the cellar." Papa smiles as he opens the door out of the floor and leans it back against the kitchen wall. "You see? The last person can simply walk down holding the door and close it." Papa vanishes under the kitchen floor and closes the door on top of himself. Mama and the kids crane their necks to search for any hint of Papa pushing on the door. When the door starts coming open, they all take a step back and watch how Papa walks the door back to the wall.

"Well, I sure am proud of that, Mr. O'Brien," says Mama. "We won't have to go to the neighbor's house to find a storm cellar ever again."

"I thought maybe you'd like it," beams Papa. *When Papa's proud, he can't keep from smiling.* "Now, I'll hold the door and y'all practice how you can get down in there." Mabel can hear the excitement in Papa's voice. "I'll go last this time, Lizbeth, but Bubba should go last if I'm not here." They all line up behind Mama.

When Mabel steps on the top step, she feels the coolness of the cellar air on her legs. From the daylight in the kitchen, she can see how Papa put up boards around the cellar. "Your papa put those boards there to brace the walls. Didn't he and Bubba do a good job?" says Mama.

"Yes, ma'am. How long do we have to stay down here? I don't like it, do you, Sister?" says Mabel.

"No, I don't. I'd rather get in the kitchen pantry or hide under our bed during a storm."

"Okay, here I come down and I'm going to close the door," says Papa.

Mabel reaches for Mama's hand as the cellar darkens. Papa sits down on the second step and the door shuts. As she tries to find Sister's face, Mabel squirms closer to Mama.

"Can we go back to the kitchen now, Papa?" says Sister, who seems overly anxious to get back up to the kitchen.

Papa laughs and starts pushing the door open. "You shouldn't be afraid down here, girls. This little cellar might save your lives one day."

"I'm pleased with the nice job you and Bubba did," says Mama, "but I do think we need to light a lantern when we come down here. We need to be able to see what we're walking into."

That night, when Sister and Mabel get into their bed, Sister says, "I don't like that dark old storm cellar and I ain't going down there again—are you? Maybe we won't have any storms this year."

"I think we'll have to go in there if a storm comes, Sister, but it's the scariest place I've ever been."

Sometimes the two use bedtime to talk themselves into being afraid. Mabel closes her eyes to the darkness of the bedroom. "You don't reckon there's a spook down there, do you?" says Mabel. Their giggles fill the room.

From the next room, they hear Papa call out, "You girls need to quiet down in there."

Mabel puts her hand over her mouth and Sister turns her face into her pillow. For the second time, Mabel goes to sleep thinking about the hole under the kitchen.

Chapter 3

MONDAY MORNING STARTS MABEL'S WEEKLY ROUTINE of watching everyone but Mama leave the house. These mornings seem to be the loneliest time for Mabel because Papa leaves for work while Bubba and Sister disappear up the road for another day in school. Brother sleeps most of the time. Mama won't let her play with him when he's in his bed. After their good-byes, Mabel and Mama walk straight down the hall to the kitchen at the rear of the house. While Mama pours water into her dishpan, Mabel sits down at the kitchen table.

"Mama," asks Mabel, "is Josie your maid like all the other white ladies talk about their maids?"

Mama turns around and looks at Mabel. "I don't really think of her as a maid. She's more of a friend who helps me," says Mama. "She's probably the person I'm closest to in this whole town. You know that I can't afford to pay her like the other ladies."

"What time is Josie coming today?" asks Mabel.

"She should be here in just a few minutes. She's walking Drella to school all this week, so you're going to have to play by yourself. Josie's trying to make certain that her daughter gets an education."

"Why's she going to school every day this week? Drella didn't go one single day last week."

"Oh, you know how Josie changes her mind about their school. This week she says that Drella needs her education. Last week she wanted Drella to learn how to work. Josie says they only learn how to count money and print their names. I'm afraid not much learning goes on down there," says Mama. "It's better than nothing, I suppose."

Mabel leans forward and rests her chin in her cupped hands. *Maybe Josie will change her mind about Drella's school this week. We have fun playing outside. Josie says that I'm a good helper too, except when she's cooking. She shoos us out when she and Mama are busy in the kitchen.*

"I think I hear Josie coming in now," says Mama.

Mabel looks up and sees Josie's deep brown face looking through the back door. Josie flashes a big smile at Mabel and walks into the kitchen. "Good morning ladies. It's already hot out there. How are you, Miss Lizbeth?"

"Good morning, Josie. I'm just fine. Did you get Drella to school?"

"Sure did. They's about twenty up there today. Drella wanted to come over here with me. I told her that she'd better learn everything she can before she starts to working and making her some money. That seem to satisfy her, leastways for now," says Josie with a sigh.

Mabel walks over to Josie and reaches her arms out for a hug. "Morning, Josie. I wish Drella could be here. Guess I'll have to help you today."

"I can't think of anyone who can help me any better than you, Miss Mabel." Josie runs her long fingers over Mabel's back and pulls her close. "Now, you go on and sit back down at that table. I don't want you to stand up here and fall to sleep," says Josie.

Josie reaches into the front pocket of her dress and pulls out a folded envelope. "Drella tried to read this writing, Miss Lizbeth, but she can't read nothing 'cept print. Can you read this to me?"

Mama dries her hands on her apron as she walks over to Josie and reaches out for the envelope. "You know I'm happy to help you any way I can, Josie." Mama opens the envelope and pulls out one sheet of paper. She sits down at the table and quickly looks over the letter. "This is signed by a Mrs. Winton Taylor and is written for your sister, Gladys. The date is Saturday, April 6, 1918. Come over here and sit down with us, Josie." Josie steps away from the cabinet and quietly pulls out a chair, and then she slides herself into the seat.

> *My Dear Josie,*
>
> *Times are better for me up here in Detroit. I work for a lady who pays me very nicely for doing the same work we did in Alabama. There are jobs up here and Mrs. Taylor says that she can help you find a good job. There are a lot of stores and factories that are hiring too. I live in a nice apartment on the third floor of a brick building. The people who live in my building are good folks and it's on the bus line. I have plenty of room for you and Drella. Drella can walk to school. Please save your money and come up here to live with me. I can meet you at the train station because Mrs. Taylor will let me use her driver. There are days that I miss Shoal Crossing, but life is better up here. It will be better for you and Drella too.*
>
> *With love,*
> *Gladys*
> *Written by the hand of*
> *Mrs. Winton Taylor*

Mama folds the letter, puts it back into the envelope, and slides it over to Josie. "She sure does want you and Drella to come to Detroit. Do you think you'll go?" asks Mama.

"I ain't studyin' going way up yonder to work. It's too cold up there for me and I don't think Drella would like it neither. Make me shiver just thinking about it. Gladys done told us about all that snow 'n ice."

Josie stands up, scoots the chair back to the table, and rests her hands on the back of the chair. "We'd have to go up there for a visit for me to decide to move away from Shoal Crossing. Anyways, I ain't moving just 'cause Gladys likes it. I like being right here with you folks, my friends, and my church."

"She just wants you with her, Josie," says Mama. "I imagine she's pretty lonely up there." Mama stands up and walks over to Josie. Putting her arms around Josie, she continues, "Mabel and I sure would miss you and Drella. You're just like family to us."

"I'm glad you don't want to move away," says Mabel. Josie acknowledges Mabel's comment by smiling at her. Mabel watches Mama and Josie as they continue talking about the letter.

"Can you write a letter for me one day this week, Miss Lizbeth? I needs to answer her," says Josie.

"I sure will," says Mama. "We can write her this afternoon before you leave. I have some nice stationary. I even have postage stamps. It's nice for two sisters to stay in touch when so many miles separate them. I know you miss her. You be thinking about what you want to say and we'll write it."

"Oh, I pretty well knows what I wants to say—just like I told you, Miss Lizbeth. That's enough about that letter. I'll take over in here. You said Friday that you wanted to work in the parlor today."

"That I did. I'll check back on you two in a little while. I've got to check on Brother first." Mama leaves the kitchen with her dust rag.

Mabel watches as Josie goes over to the pantry and takes out her white apron. Josie ducks her head and lowers the apron around her neck. Then she reaches around and ties a bow in the back. *Josie has big feet. She's wearing some of Papa's old shoes. Papa says that she has to have big feet to hold up her big frame. She slides her feet inside and mashes the back of the shoes down with her heels. Josie is a lot darker than Drella and her eyes are brown. Drella has greenish eyes.*

As Josie adds wood to the firebox in the stove, Mabel's eyes continue to follow her. *She already has beads of sweat popping out on her face. I like the way Josie slicks her black hair back. She says the oil she puts on it makes it shiny.*

"I've got to do a little ironing. Glad this firebox still has a nice glow to it. Won't take so long to get the iron hot." Josie stoops over and picks up the iron from beside the stove; she places it on the hot stove top. She slides her feet out onto the screened porch and brings in the ironing board.

"Your mama wants me to press a tablecloth or two. Won't take long." She unfolds the ironing board and stands it just to the side of the stove. "Sure is warm over here."

Josie wads the tablecloths into two piles and lays them on the kitchen table. She pours some water from the pitcher into a pan, dips her hand into the water, and flicks the water on the dry cloths. "If I don't put this water on these things, it won't do me one bit o' good to iron them. Dry things needs a little drink of water. You wants to help me, Mabel?"

Nodding her head, Mabel moves around to the pan of water. "I helped Mama do this one time when she ironed Papa's work pants." Mabel reaches her hands into the water, cups them together, and tries to flick the water like Josie.

"I can tell that you know how to do this. You're gonna be a fine lady of the house one of these days. Just like your mama." Josie reaches over and pats Mabel's head. A satisfied smile crosses Mabel's face. "I think we's about got them damp enough. You gonna stay in here with me?"

"Yessum," answers Mabel. "And can you tell me the story about your little finger, Josie? The one that's crooked and stiff." Mabel gazes at the pink skin on Josie's heels as she walks over to the ironing board. "I like that story."

"Well, when I's a little girl, just about your age, my daddy, sister, and me lived out in the woods. We lived in a one-room house 'bout the size of mine and Drella's." Josie picks up the iron from the stove top, licks her finger, and taps it on the iron. The quick hiss informs Josie that the iron is hot enough to press the tablecloth. "Don't take me long to know when a iron's hot," Josie says with a laugh in her voice.

Searching for wrinkles as she irons, Josie leans her weight into the ironing board. As Mabel watches Josie, she notices the steam coming up from the dampened tablecloth. She breathes in the heaviness of the warm moisture in the kitchen. "The steam smells clean." Josie looks up from her ironing and nods in agreement. "Tell me the story, Josie."

"My mother died when I's born, so Daddy, Gladys, and me was as close as three peas in a pod. One day I followed him out to gather some firewood. Gladys was cleaning the house. Anyway, he always carry him a hatchet and trim the wood as he found it."

Josie pulls the tablecloth this way and that way as she irons each section of it. She continues, "We'd stack what we found over by a log. When we had enough, he'd cut it to the right size. I held the wood steady on the log while he swung the ax. On this day I made a bad mistake—I moved my little finger right where he come down with that hatchet." Josie finishes ironing the first cloth. After admiring her work, she gently folds the tablecloth. She walks over to the table, lays down the tablecloth, and selects the next one to iron.

"Did it hurt, Josie?"

"Why sure it did, Mabel. I didn't feel much of anything because it went numb. All I saw was the blood. Poor ole Daddy acted like he's gonna fall out right there, but he didn't. My finger was hanging on by the skin. Daddy reached down and stuck my finger back on—right back where it bends to this day. He pulled out his handkerchief and wrapped it all around my finger and hand. Daddy carried me back to the house and poured coal oil over the bandage. We soaked it good. Child, I can still feel that sting. We didn't take that handkerchief off for a long ole time. When we did take it off, my finger had growed together just like it is now. The middle joint is where he cut it. It's a wonder it ever stayed there."

"Did you help him chop wood anymore?"

"Sure did." Josie starts humming and then stops. "My daddy felt bad about it, but we had to have our wood for cooking and heat. We were a lot more watchful after that day though. My sister didn't like to go into the woods, but I did. Any time I could help my daddy, I did."

Mama walks into the kitchen. "Oh, Josie, I'm so glad you remembered the tablecloths. Do you think you could make us some biscuits while the stove's hot? We can have some for tonight's supper and in the morning for breakfast," she says. "Wait. Maybe you could make us some hot water cornbread for tonight and we'll save the biscuits for later. We can crumble the cornbread into the soup we're having tonight for super."

"If you will, Miss Lizbeth, you can fix us a pan of water and set it on the stove. About four cups'll do us. It'll take a while to heat up to boiling." Josie folds another tablecloth and continues to give directions. "Mabel, you go get me the cornmeal, flour, and box of salt. Cornmeal and flour's in the icebox. The salt's in the pantry. Set it all on the table, please. Do you want this cloth on the dining room table, Miss Lizbeth?"

"Yes, Josie, I'll help you spread it," says Mama.

Mabel is surprised that Josie includes her in getting things ready for cooking. She walks out onto the screened porch where the icebox sits. *I like to watch the iceman bring in the big block of ice on Fridays. He carries it with big tongs. Papa says that the ice weighs more than I do. The iceman swings it back and forth like it's pulling him to make his next step.*

When Mabel opens the icebox door, she sees the pot of soup they will have for supper. She gets down on her knees and reaches past the sugar for the sack of cornmeal and the sack of flour. Mabel decides to carry one at a time and takes the cornmeal to the kitchen table. After she brings in the flour, she goes to the pantry and gets out the box of salt. She sits back down at the table, ready to watch Josie mix the cornbread ingredients.

Mabel hears Josie's shoes sliding across the floor as she enters the kitchen. "Is it okay if I stay in here while you make the cornbread and biscuits? I promise I won't bother you."

"Since it's just you, Mabel, I reckon it'll be all right. I just don't like it when all you flittin' 'round girls come in the kitchen—special when I's trying to do my work," says Josie.

"I'll be good, I promise. Mama and Papa say that you're the best cook in Shoal Crossing. I want to be able to cook like you when I grow up."

"It's gonna be a long old time before you grows up, Mabel, but I hopes you can learn how to cook and clean really good."

Josie pulls Mama's biggest green mixing bowl from the cupboard and sets it on the table. With a practiced hand, Josie measures out two cups of cornmeal, a dash of salt, and three tablespoons of flour. She blends them together in the glass bowl with a dark stained wooden spoon.

Going over to the pantry, Josie pulls out a can of lard. Using the same wooden spoon, she digs out a dollop of lard and slaps it into the black iron skillet. Holding onto the skillet handle, Josie rolls the lard from side to side until it's melted. After that, she brings the boiling water to the table and carefully pours it into the mixture. As Josie stirs the mixture, she begins to hum.

"That should be just about right," says Josie as she takes the hot pan to the dishpan. Josie brings the skillet to the table and pours some of the grease into the cornmeal mixture. Mabel listens as Josie's humming gets louder. She watches her return the skillet to the stove. Josie comes back to the table to get the cornmeal mixture and carries it to the stove. She spoons out the thin liquid into the hot skillet and it begins to crackle.

The aroma quickly fills the kitchen. "That smells good," Mabel says as she breathes in the wonderful smell.

"I know you like this, child. If you'll get you a saucer, you can eat the special piece I's gonna make for you. We'll put you some maple syrup on it. Don't you think that'll be good?" asks Josie.

"Yessum. That's my favorite thing to eat. I like your corncakes because they're crunchy. Are you gonna eat some too?"

"Go ask Miss Lizbeth if she wants a corncake. I think I'll eat one with you. Gotta heat the syrup just a bit. I never did know why folks pour cold syrup over they hot food."

Mabel walks into the parlor where her mama is sweeping the rug. "Josie fixed us a corn cake and is heating the syrup. Do you want some?"

"I surely do. That'll hold us over until supper. Tell her that I'll be right there," says Mama.

Mabel and Josie sit down at the kitchen table. She gazes at the syrup seeping into the corn cake; Mabel looks up at Josie as she cuts herself a bite. Putting the first bite into her mouth, Mabel savors the flavors. "Mmmm, this is good, Josie. Mine's crispy around the edges. Do you like it?"

"I sure do. My daddy taught me how to make hot water cornbread. We had it most every day." Josie smiles at Mabel. "You sure have been a lot of help today, plus you've kept me company." Josie mops up the last bit of syrup with her corn cake and puts it in her mouth. "Don't you reckon you need to go outside in the fresh air for a while? Bubba and Sister will be coming home from school soon. I've got to get y'all's biscuits made, write that letter, and go meet Drella."

"Can I walk with you to get Drella? That would be a surprise for her."

"Sure would, child. Be a surprise to all them children. I'll ask your mama when she come back in here," says Josie. "You go on out front. Your mama will let you know if it all right."

Mabel feels full and satisfied from her corn cake. She walks out to her sandbox and begins scooping sand into her bucket. *I love Josie. She's taught me how to do lots of things and she likes to talk to me. Mama says that Josie is more like a friend than someone who works for her. Mama likes to talk to her too. She says that Josie is smart because she knows how to do so many things. She can even wring a chicken's neck.* Mabel watches the sparkling sand as she slowly pours it from her bucket.

She walks over to the tree and boosts herself up from the edge of the sandbox. Her feet move skillfully as she wedges them between the huge limbs and climbs to the spot where she likes to sit. *Those men sitting on the porch of Stevens's store don't know I'm watching them. Wonder where they live. Bet they're talking about the horses out front. Papa says they sit out there and tell tales all day long. He says they need to be working. I hope Mama lets me walk with Josie.* Mabel rests her head on the limb, closes her eyes, and listens to the chirping birds.

"Mabel? Where are you?" calls out Mama. Carrying Brother in her arms, she walks out on the front porch and looks around. Mabel watches Mama crane her neck back and forth with her brown eyes searching the yard. *Brother's got more golden curls than any girl—he's prettier too. His head doesn't bobble around as much as it use to.*

Mabel's giggle causes Mama to look up. "Aren't you just like a bird sitting up in that tree?" Mama leans on the handrail and Brother's blue eyes stare down at the ground. "If you want to walk with Josie, you'd better get down from there. She's waiting for you out back." Mama goes over and sits down in her rocker. "I'm gonna rock Brother for a few minutes, but I'll be in the house when you come home."

Mabel is surprised because her mama doesn't usually let her go off with someone else. Climbing down from her perch, she finally reaches the branch she can use to lower herself to the sandbox. She wipes her hands on the sides of her blue gingham dress and takes off running for the back steps where Josie is sitting. Gasping, she smiles up at Josie and says, "Mama says that I can go with you to get Drella."

"Child, I's about to have to leave you. Pull my hand and help old Josie up." Mabel braces her foot on the bottom step and pulls Josie's hand. "We'll cut back by y'all's barn and walk over to the road. That'll save us some steps."

Mabel and Josie walk hand in hand across the backyard. Her eyes glance over at Josie's hand clinging to hers. *It's pink inside, just like the bottoms of her feet.* Mabel pulls Josie's hand to her cheek and holds it there for a moment. "I sure do love you, my Josie. When I grow up, you're not ever gonna have to work. I'm gonna take care of you. Did Mama write your letter for you?"

"Your mama wrote my letter just like I asked her—I'll mail it in the morning. I ain't leaving Alabama," says Josie with determination. Josie rolls her eyes down at Mabel. "Won't that be nice for you to take care of me?" says Josie with a smile. "Old Josie will be mighty tired by the time you grow up and get rich. I'll need for somebody to take care of me." Josie squeezes Mabel's hand a little tighter. Mabel senses that Josie loves her just like she loves Mama. "You and Drella can take care of me. Yes, that'll be real nice."

When they reach the road, Mabel notices the red dust collecting on Josie's shoes. "Where's your daddy now, Josie?"

Josie keeps her head held high and looks off into the distance. "My daddy died when I's about fourteen years old. He got down with something about his heart and never could regain his strength. It about killed me when he passed. Gladys and me sat right by his side until the very end."

"What was his name?"

"My daddy's name was Nickelberry. Nicodemos Nickelberry was his full given name. Everybody call him NickNick. You see, he had two Nicks in his name. One in the first and one in the last—that made him NickNick. He was a good man. Never liked his name much, but there weren't anything he could do about that. Always said he liked NickNick better than his full name." Josie looks down at Mabel.

"Do you think your daddy's in heaven?"

"Why, yes I do, Mabel. My daddy was a fine man. He stayed right there at that old house and raised two girls all by hisself. Daddy loved our church and doing good for peoples in need. He helped lots of folks, but never asked for nothing in return. My daddy prayed down on his knees every day and every night he lived. He carried his Bible most ever place he went. Couldn't read a word, but said he hoped the good book would soak into his skin. He was as honest as the day is long."

"What's heaven like?"

"I ain't never been up there, but I hears it's a peaceful place. You gets to meet back up with all those who go before you. Just think, Mabel, I's gonna be able to see my mama and my daddy. I ain't never seen my mama. I'll be able to watch over Drella, you, and Miss Lizbeth from up there. I'll be y'all's angel." Josie slows their pace and looks down into Mabel's blue eyes. Mabel senses that Josie's about to cry. "It's good to know that you's interested in me, child. I knows you're gonna take good care of me when I gets old. That's another reason for me not to move up north. Yes ma'am—I sure wants you and Drella to take care of me."

"Yessum, I'll take real good care of you all right." A strong sense of pride wells up in Mabel as she thinks of herself as a grown-up. "You can be the boss of the people who work for me. You won't have to do anything but tell them other folks what to do."

They walk off the side of the road, down a small hill, and onto the grounds of Drella's school. "Is this where you come to church too, Josie?"

"Yes ma'am, Miss Mabel. I've walked these roads many a time to come to this church and to this school."

Mabel looks at the steps leading up to the front door of the church. The white paint on the siding has chips of paint missing across the front. "This old building need for the mens to work on it, don't it?" says Josie. "Look like the preacher'd put them to work; maybe they'll do it this spring." Josie seems irritated to Mabel. "Beats anything I've ever seen. Let's just stand here by this tree and wait for Drella. She'll come down those front steps directly."

This is the church Mama and I hear the angels singing from every Sunday morning. I sit out on the front steps and listen to them. Mama hears them through her bedroom window. Mama says that she calls them angels because their voices floating through the trees sound pretty. They are still singing when we get home from our church. She says that one day we'll come to the coloreds' church. Papa says that some of the men at work are deacons here. "Do you and Drella sing on Sundays?"

"Yes we do, child. We sings and sways. You know I's gonna sing any time I gets the chance. Ain't nothing like singing in my church. It always make me feel close to the Lord." Josie begins humming and then interrupts herself. "My favorite song is 'Amazing Grace.' It was my daddy's favorite too."

The double doors slowly swing out and two boys, dressed in overalls, stand beside the doors to hold them open. The teacher walks to the middle of the opened doors and holds her arm up in the air. The skirt of her long black dress catches the slight breeze from the outside air. Drella stands at the front of the girls' line and she spots Josie and Mabel waiting beside the tree. Mabel smiles up at Josie while the students descend the steps in silence. When Drella reaches the bottom step, she runs toward her mother and Mabel.

Josie bends down and hugs Drella and Mabel waits for her hug. *Drella is so pretty. That yellow dress makes her green eyes sparkle against her light-brown skin. She doesn't have pink on her hands like Josie. Hers are just a lighter brown. Wish I could wear my hair in pigtails. Josie put those yellow bows in her hair to match her dress. Mama says that Drella is lean and beautiful—just like a willow tree.*

"Hi, Mabel," says Drella. She quickly gives Mabel a hug. "I'm glad you could come to school with Mama Josie." They begin their climb up the hill to the road. Josie reaches out a hand to each girl and they start walking back toward the O'Brien house. "School was good today. We did arithmetic, some writing, and the teacher read to us. I want to learn how to read like her."

"You will, Drella," says Josie. "You just needs to go to school every time you can and you'll learn how to be smarter than your teacher."

"Bubba and Sister know how to read," says Mabel. "I know some words, but not as many as Sister. I could read "flour" and "cornmeal" today, Josie."

Just before they turn off the road to cut across to Mabel's house, two colored boys run past them. They turn and run backwards to look at the unusual sight of Mabel walking with Josie and Drella. They slide their feet in the dust as they rapidly step backwards. Mabel notices the red dust powdering up around their bare feet.

"You boys stop your staring at these girls. Gwan home," says Josie. "Your mama shouldn't send you to school without a shirt for those overalls and no shoes on your feet. Gwan now. You're the kind that the Klan will get after one of these days." Looking frightened by Josie's boldness, the boys turn around and speed away, disappearing as they turn up the road beside Stevens's store. "They ain't got no sense. Bet neither one can write a word by hisself."

They continue to walk in silence, but Mabel has a question. "What's the Klan, Josie?"

"Oh, it's just a group of white mens, dressed in white sheets and carrying torches. They don't like no colored folks. They don't like much of anybody, lessen they're of their own kind and their own thinking. They'll kill a colored man in a second. Hang 'em from a tree—just like we hang up chickens to bleed every drop from their bodies. They'll whoop a white man to death for helping us too. They ain't done much around here, but they's in this town. Far as I know, they's in most every town. That Klan don't want no colored man getting ahead of them neither. There's a lot of things they don't like."

"Teacher had one of those boys standing in the corner most of the day. She told both of them not to come back to school until they want to learn something," says Drella. She switches over so she can hold Mabel's other hand. "You don't have to worry about those mean boys, Mabel. Mama Josie and me ain't gonna let nobody hurt you. They're just acting silly, aren't they, Mama Josie?"

"Oh, those boys ain't nothing to worry 'bout. They's just curious about us being out here together, that's all. Reckon they never been taught about curiosity killing the cat. Here's your yard, Mabel. We'll stand here and watch you until you open the back door. We'll see you soon. I love you." She bends down and hugs Mabel. "Thank you for walking with Drella and me. You're very nice company. Why you looking so fretful, child?"

A deep sense of sadness enters Mabel's heart and she feels the threat of tears stinging her eyes. "It scares me for us because those old Klan people are gonna get me and you. That's not fair. You're my friend. You're Mama's friend. She told me that she likes you better than anybody in Shoal Crossing. We like for you to be at our house."

Josie gets down on her knees and looks Mabel squarely in the face. "Wait, child. Them mens ain't gonna come after you and me. They know I works for your mama. That make it all right for us to be friends. Peoples respect Mr. O'Brien in this town. They ain't studyin' little folks like you and me."

Josie pulls Mabel to her. Mabel rests her head on Josie's shoulder. She smells the hint of vanilla that Josie puts on her neck combined with the sweat from the afternoon sun. "Now, don't you worry no more about the Klan. I's just tellin' them boys they's gonna get into trouble. That's all. I's trying to scare them. We ain't did nothing wrong 'cept love one another like the good Lord want us to."

Accepting Josie's explanation, Mabel feels calmness slipping back into her body. *Josie always makes things better.*

"Ain't nobody gonna hurt you; ain't gonna hurt Drella; and they ain't gonna hurt Josie." Mabel forces a smile and watches Josie as she unfolds her long body to rise to her feet. Josie brushes the red dust from the skirt of her dress. "Don't you worry about no Klan. You ain't got no reason at all to worry your pretty little head about them. I ain't either—we ain't did nothing wrong. You need to remember that I love you just like you's my own child—ain't nobody ever gonna harm you. Now, you go on home. We'll watch you run."

"Okay. Bye, Drella. Bye, Josie." Mabel spins around and runs across the yard. Passing beside the O'Brien barn, Mabel looks small. When she reaches the top of the back porch steps, she turns and waves to Josie and Drella. She opens the back door and enters the kitchen where her mama is talking to Sister and Bubba.

Chapter 4
Reflections

THE WHITE LIGHT WASHES OVER US as the picture stays focused on the back of Mabel's house. Sitting next to me, Mabel continues to gaze at the huge picture. Her thoughts begin pouring into my mind. "I'll stop my review from time to time because I want us to talk about a few things." I look at her, but she continues staring into the light.

"When I was small, I thought our house was a mansion. It's amusing how I thought it was the perfect place to live—just as any child or adult, I had no idea what heaven held in store. Mama and Papa looked so young back then. Funny how we remember people as we last saw them. Even Bubba and Sister look different than I remember them. When I was five, they seemed so much older to me. As you can see, I tried every way I could think of to be as grown up as I thought they were."

I listen to her thoughts, but my fascination with what we had just watched overpowers me. "Everything looks so realistic."

Just as soon as I complete my thought, Mabel responds. "It is lifelike. The reviews astound everyone who decides to use them. We are almost too close to the things going on around us on earth to understand them when they occur. The reviews allow you to look at the people and situations that have touched your life on earth. Some don't seem important at the time, but when you come here, you can see how your character develops through the years. It reinforces the fact that nothing happens in our earthly lives without purpose."

"Mabel, would you agree that character development is an ongoing process—even into adulthood?"

She smiles and shares her thoughts. "Yes, it lasts a lifetime. I am still experiencing development. Through seeing how a child develops, we can see that same sort of development in adults who are turning away from things of the world. All of us, regardless of age, are children of God. God's grace allows us to make mistakes and redeem ourselves. Every single day brings new hope and the opportunity to begin anew. That's the miracle of God's grace. God doesn't turn away from any child—young or old."

"Your thoughts are comforting, Mabel. Looking back at your review, it's easy to see how different your lives were in 1918," I think.

Mabel's thoughts respond quickly to mine. "Yes, our lives were different and, I believe, much better than today in many ways. Children spent a large part of their lives focusing on family instead of things. When you think about it, all we really had available to learn from was each other. Families today don't seem as close as they were in 1918. We worked together, learned together, played together, and we prayed together. The family was the center of a child's life. Today there are too many outside influences in homes and in all lives in general.

"How did sitting in the parlor in the evenings play a role in shaping your life?"

"It's essential for every child to understand and appreciate their family ancestry. It builds a foundation and an understanding of how their family has evolved. Our family history was an important part of our simple lives. Talking to each other was our family's entertainment. Mama must have read their marriage announcement to us a hundred times."

Mabel stands and walks over to the picture. "If you'll remember, your daddy and I talked about our childhood memories at the dinner table. I never knew why I did that as a parent—until now. Do you remember how we use to tell y'all stories? "

My thoughts agree with Mabel. "Yes, ma'am, I remember those yarns. We learned a lot by listening to them." Mabel continues to stare at the back of their house. I go on, "I think the account Papa shared about his life is very interesting. It must have been quite a blow to his family when his daddy never came back home."

As Mabel takes a few steps toward me, I am reminded of her beauty. Her thoughts flow smoothly into my mind. "Yes, it was hard on his whole family. Every time he told us that story about his sick mother, going to the train station with his daddy, and having to work at such an early age, it brought tears to my eyes."

Mabel gets a wistful look in her eyes as her thoughts continue. "Papa was so proud of his Irish heritage. He always seemed happy with the way his life turned out. The joy in his heart came through every single day. That joy was a reflection of his devotion to God and his family. He was also proud of his work with the Corps of Engineers. Back then, men were considered fortunate when they worked for the government. He didn't make a lot of money—maybe thirty-five dollars a month. Some families had to survive on literally pennies a week—or nothing at all. Some survived only on what the land gave back to them."

Looking past Mabel, I see the still picture of the back of the O'Brien home; I am reminded of the day she went up under the house. "That's where you crawled under the porch when Bubba was working on the storm cellar, isn't it?"

Mabel laughs at her thoughts about the storm cellar. "Yes, right there beside the steps is where I scooted under the house that day. Old Snooks stayed underneath there most of the time—in the winter, it kept him warm, and in the summer, it kept him cool. He was like Bubba's shadow."

"Did y'all ever use the storm cellar?"

A smile lights up Mabel's face. "Once—and only once." Her thoughts continue as she turns back toward the picture. "Not long after they finished it, Mama gathered all of us up to go down there during a storm. Storms really seemed to upset her. Anyway, Bubba went down first with a lantern, while the rest of us waited in the kitchen. He shot up out of there a whole lot faster than he went in. I'll never forget the look on his face."

"What was wrong?"

"He said that he was about to set the lantern down when he looked over in one corner and saw several snakes slithering around." Mabel laughs at her thoughts. "When Papa got home that afternoon, he promised Mama that he would replace the flooring—sealing off the storm cellar. Mama never mentioned wanting a storm cellar again. Sister and I were happy to see that floor put back down."

"It was scary looking when y'all went down in there the day they finished it." My mind changes over to thoughts about Josie. "Josie was really an important part of your life, wasn't she?"

"Oh, yes. She taught me so much during that time I spent with her. Mama loved her just about as much as I did." Mabel's thoughts continue as she walks back to the chair to sit down. "After she told me about the Klan that day, I was scared to death of them. Mama and Papa seldom spoke a word about the Klan. Back then, parents didn't believe in telling worldly things in front of their children. They didn't even tell us when Brother was about to be born. We woke up on the first day of November in 1917 and there he was. He was a beautiful baby—golden ringlets all over his head." She smiles as she continues to think. "Anyway, Josie didn't seem to mind talking to me about things I didn't hear from Mama and Papa. She made me feel special that way."

My mind goes back to my childhood. "Children like for people to talk to them—to include them, don't they? You always talked to us about almost everything."

"I now realize that my openness as a parent came from the way I liked to be treated as a child. I can also see that I was drawn to those people who shared their beliefs about life. They had the greatest influence on my daily growth and development. Life on earth would certainly be far less complicated if we had the power to review our lives as we can in heaven. Many people have very little to guide them through their daily lives on earth. It seems that it all depends upon one's circumstances—who and what's in one's life."

"That's true, Mabel. All we really have available on earth are our memories, families, churches, schools, and friends to review the rightness or wrongness of our acts. The key to a child's character development is having people around them who are positive role models—people who are available and can talk through their questions."

Even as she sits in her chair, Mabel continues to stare at the image of her house. "That's definitely true. The reviews are far more vivid than our minds and, of course, there's the advantage of being able to evaluate them from a different perspective. For instance, Drella was about four years older than me, but she never treated me like Sister and Bubba did. They always seemed to treat me like I was a baby. That's why I loved those days when Drella came to work with Josie. Just like any child, I wanted to be accepted—those who accepted me were the ones I clung to. That's why it's so important for parents to surround their families with goodness and with people who have gentle spirits."

"I'm happy that you had Drella for a friend. She was pretty, wasn't she?"

"Yes, it's easy to see that Drella was beautiful. Her heart was just as pretty."

Leaning her head against the back of the chair, Mabel's thoughts begin flowing once again. "I wanted you to see this part of my review so that you could understand what my family life was like. You've seen the most important people—my family, plus Josie and Drella."

Mabel's thoughts continue as she runs her hand back and forth on the chair arm. "Those are the ones who had the greatest impact on me at the age of five. Josie took so much time with me. She talked to me and explained things about everyday living. She was such a good soul—she lived what we learned in church. Josie demonstrated her love for all people—she was totally at peace. She brought her peace to those she knew. I'll always be thankful for my time with her. I never fully realized her importance until I came here. I thought of her often over the years, but now I can see how much I loved her. Being mindful of things helps to a certain extent, but the reviews enable us to see the love and goodness of someone like Josie."

My eyes move from the picture to Mabel's profile. Her thoughts come quickly as I try to take in what she's explaining. "Every person has a circle of influence that begins at birth. Because we carry the spirits of those we love and admire in our hearts, parents should be keenly aware of that circle surrounding their children."

"Yes," I interject, "you always used caution about who you allowed in our home."

Mabel acknowledges my comment by nodding and continues her thoughts. "Children become like those in their lives—a blending so to speak. Just outside of the family core, there is usually another, less powerful, circle of influence. So, before all of this can come together, you need to see a few more people who touched my life. Through this, I believe you will be able to grasp the importance of people and our surroundings in our earthly lives. It all affects who we become as adults. If you will remember, about a month before I left you, you asked me who I would most like to talk to from my past. Do you remember who I named?" Mabel turns her face toward me, waiting for my thoughts.

"Yes, ma'am. You said that it would be Grandpa and your Uncle Sam."

Smiling and nodding her head in agreement, Mabel shares her thoughts. "When I was five, Grandpa and Uncle Sam weren't in my life as regularly as my immediate family, Josie, and Drella, but they were always in the background. They lived out in the country. When they came to visit, it was a very happy time for me. You'll see why I adored Grandpa and Uncle Sam. They were different from our family, but I loved them just the same. Through being with them from time to time, I learned many valuable life lessons."

Resting her head against the chair, she stares once again at the picture. "From them I learned that all people are not entirely good. It's probably where I started seeing that some people, though good in many ways, had faults. Like you said earlier, the secret to successfully analyzing negative behaviors for a child is to have an adult available who can explain it. Let's watch this next part of the review."

I focus my eyes back on the picture in front of us. The bright light twists, spins, and refocuses on the front of Mabel's childhood home. The storyteller begins once again.

Chapter 5

As the April days move closer to May, they get warmer. Mabel spends as much time as she can out in her sandbox or up in the tree. Both places are cooler than inside the house. It's late in the afternoon and Mabel is sitting in her favorite spot in the tree. She sees a familiar wagon coming up the road. She watches closely as the gray horse pulls a two-wheeled cart past the front gate. Leaning toward the road, Mabel sees her grandfather heading toward the side gate. She stands and waves. "Grandpa, I'm up in the tree! Grandpa!" As Mabel scurries down the tree and lands on the ground, she hears the roar of his laughter. Laughter fills her own throat. She loves the music of his happiness.

"Meet me at the barn, Mabel," shouts Grandpa. "Tell your mama that her daddy's here."

Mabel springs into the house. "Mama! Mama! Grandpa's here!" She runs into Mama's bedroom—out of breath. She announces to her mother, "Grandpa's here, Mama! I've gotta go help him!"

Without waiting for a reply, Mabel runs down the hall. She makes a quick turn through the kitchen and rushes out onto the screened porch. Bounding over the steps and into the backyard, the chickens in the coop flap their wings in excitement and scurry to hide. She gets to the barn just in time to open the doors for him. Panting for air, she waits for him to step from the cart onto the dirt floor. "Did you come to take me back to the farm, Grandpa?"

A strapping man, Grandpa smiles broadly as his brown eyes look down at his younger granddaughter. "I sure did, Mabel. That is, if it's okay with your mama and papa." Mabel takes his large hand and feels its roughness as they walk toward Mama on the back steps. "Afternoon, Elizabeth. I need me an extra farmhand for several days. Do you know where I might find one?"

"It looks to me like you're holding on to one, Daddy." Mabel's delight shows in her face. There's no one Mabel gets more excited about seeing than her grandpa. Going to the farm means she'll also get to see her Uncle Sam. *They are two of my favorite people. Grandma and Aunt Nell will be there too; all of them are fun to visit. There's always lots of new things to do at the farm—they let me help.*

That night at supper, Grandpa's laughter fills the house as he and Papa swap stories. "Who in the world made these corncakes, Elizabeth? I think they might be better than your mother's. No need to tell her I said that, mind you."

"Those are Josie's specialty. I've never tasted any better in my life," says Mama. She looks around at Mabel and they share a knowing smile. "Josie's just a fine woman. Mabel and I love her very much, don't we, Mabel?"

"Yessum, Josie can make everything taste good."

"Did she make this soup? It's delicious," says Grandpa.

"No, I made that, Daddy, but Josie told me how to flavor it up a bit. Glad you like it. Tom got the meat for us from one of his farmer friends. The meat wagon doesn't carry meat this good."

"He gave me the meat as trade for me helping him clean up his barn and loft. Bubba and I spent one whole Saturday out there. I've never seen such a mess in my life," says Papa. "He'd started it back in the winter, but took sick and couldn't finish the work by himself." Papa leans back in his chair. "I didn't intend for him to pay us anything, but he insisted that we take the meat. We've enjoyed it."

"He's such a nice man," says Mama. "We talk to him at church every week." She reaches for the dishes and starts making a stack for cleaning. "Sister, Mabel and I've got to get her things ready for her trip to the farm. You and Bubba need to wash and put away the dishes by yourselves tonight. We all have an early day tomorrow."

"Wish I didn't have to go to school. I could go with Mabel and Grandpa out to the farm," says Sister. Mabel recognizes Sister's annoyed look because she can't go with Grandpa.

"Mabel's gonna be out there until next week, Sister. I don't reckon your teacher would approve of that," says Grandpa. "You and Bubba can come out there this summer. We'd love to have you visit." He looks at Mama and Papa. "If it's okay with your mama and papa, I need for Bubba to come work for pay. Your Aunt Bennie wants you to come visit her. Maybe you can make a little extra money too, Sister," says Grandpa.

"I think that will be mighty nice for the two of them," says Papa. "Times are hard and every red cent counts."

Bubba and Sister take on looks of satisfaction at the prospect of being able to work for pay. Grandpa scoots his chair back and stands up. "Times sure are hard. President Wilson's upped the draft age to forty-five. If a man doesn't have a job, he'll be going off to war. I'm hearing more and more about that flu too. Eventually, you know it'll be down south. We'll all be lucky if none of those troubles touch us. Tom, walk out to the barn with me. I need to check on Smoke and make sure she's down for the night." Grandpa and Papa walk through the kitchen and out the back door.

Mama and Mabel go to the bedroom to turn down the bed for Grandpa. They begin selecting Mabel's clothes for her trip to the farm. "Your grandpa looks like he's been working too hard.

He seems to have more gray in his hair every time I see him," says Mama. They continue to move about the room. "I'm surprised he ate that cornbread after he found out Josie made it."

"Why, Mama?" says Mabel. "Doesn't he like Josie?"

"It's not Josie, Mabel. It's just that he doesn't take to colored people—no matter who they are," says Mama. "He fought in the Civil War, got captured, and somehow figures he was wronged. I don't know—maybe he's changing for the better. That war's over and all of those men need to just forget about it."

Later, lying in bed, with Sister already sound asleep, Mabel thinks about the farm. *I can't wait to get out to the farm with Uncle Sam and Grandpa. They'll let me walk with them out to the pasture. Grandpa has more than twenty cows, and Grandma churns butter from their milk. They have laying hens and we can eat all the eggs we want. And Grandpa and Uncle Sam grow so many kinds of crops that they don't have to go to the store to buy them. I like their corn best of all. I like the way Grandma cooks the green beans too.*

Mabel visualizes the one hundred acres of land with the dirt road fronting the log house, splitting the land almost in half. *Wonder if Uncle Sam still has Aunt Mabel buried across the road from the house. She's who Mama named me for when I was born. He built him a bench and goes to visit her every day. There's so many pretty flowers and trees out there. I like to hear all the birds singing, cows mooing, and chickens cackling. There's a lot of work to do outside.* Content with her thoughts, Mabel drifts into a peaceful night's sleep.

The next morning, not long after everyone leaves for the day, Mabel and Grandpa take their places up in the seat of the two-wheeled cart that he parked out in front of the house for them to load. Holding Brother, Mama stands at the gate to see them off for their long ride. "Mabel, you mind your grandpa and grandma. In fact, you mind all of your elders," says Mama with firmness. "I sure will miss you. Tell Sam and Nell hello for me. I hope to be out there for a visit real soon."

Mabel, wearing a pale yellow dress, white knee socks, and her black Easter shoes, blows a kiss to Mama. "Yessum. Tell Josie and Drella that I'll see them when I get home. Bye, bye, Brother." Mama lifts Brother's hand and waves it at them. Mabel reaches over and feels for the bow Mama put on the side of her hair. Grandpa clicks his tongue and Smoke begins to jerk the cart up the road. "Bye Mama, I love you." Mabel watches as Grandpa's dark-brown mustache moves from side to side with each *click*.

The cart wobbles over the ruts as Smoke pulls them out onto the main road. The men sitting on the front porch of Stevens's store gawk as the stranger's cart passes in review. Grandpa nods at them and touches the brim of his tan fedora. Mabel knows how proud Grandpa is of the Confederate insignia he has pinned to the center of his hat. *He doesn't talk about the war. Mama says that the Yankees put him in prison, held him until the end of the war, and finally let him come back home. When they let him go, he had to walk and hitch rides to get back down south. She tells us not to ever ask him about the prison. Poor Grandpa; he still doesn't have much use for Yankees.* Mabel leans her head against his arm.

"Well, here we go, Mabel," says Grandpa. "Now we've got to cross this confounded bridge." His deep-brown eyes dart around. "It looks like it's safe enough." Grandpa often speaks of his dislike for the Shoal Creek Bridge. "It won't surprise me at all for this thing to collapse and drop us right into the water. I'd much rather walk Smoke across the shoals. At least we'd be on the ground." Mabel begins to feel Grandpa's fear of falling. She wants him to talk about something else.

"Tell me about the Indian scout while we ride, Grandpa. What's his name?"

"Magi was his name. He was a Cherokee and his name means 'Michael'. I'll never forget his name because he moved and thought like he had a special magic—he could find any direction by looking at the sun, moon, and stars. He was quick, crafty, and very smart. Magi wore a leather over shirt and leather britches. Even wore them moccasin shoes like you see in the pictures in the books."

Grandpa settles back in the cart seat, lifts his left leg, and props his hard-toe boot on the front board. "That's one of my favorite tales," says Grandpa. "Ole Grandpa wouldn't be here if it hadn't been for Magi's keen eyesight and quick thinking." Grandpa reaches down and picks up his leather whip. "Giddy up there, Smoke; don't make me snap you with this strap. We need to hurry up and get across this worthless bridge."

The rumbling of the wheels on the bridge sounds loud to Mabel. She looks down beside the cart and sees the water from Shoal Creek peeking between the wooden slats. When the cart wheel gets in one of the ridges of the boards, the wagon jerks itself straight. Mabel enjoys the echo of the rhythmic *clippity-clop* coming from Smoke's hooves on the wood. *Grandpa must have forgotten about his story.* She looks up at her grandpa. "Are you gonna tell me the story?"

After clearing his throat, Grandpa starts talking. "Well, one evening, just before sundown, our company commander told Magi to scout out several miles ahead of our camp. Magi usually plotted several escape plans just in case them Union soldiers showed up." Grandpa lowers his voice as though he's telling Mabel a secret. She leans closer.

"On this particular evening, I happened to be standing there, so the commander ordered me to go along with the scout. It suited me fine. Camp was boring. Anyway, Magi and me headed deep into the woods. We had to keep our cover, look for Yankee tracks, smell the air, and pick out our unit's best route. Leaving the safety of all the guns and men kinda gave me the heebie-jeebies."

Smoke lowers her head, gaining more strength, and pulls them over the last board of the bridge. "We made it across, Grandpa." Mabel can see that he's relieved to have the bridge ordeal behind them. Grandpa ignores Mabel's comment.

"Well, Magi and me got about as far as we could go before dark. We needed to get back to camp and report. Being a scout, he slowed us down a lot because he whittled cuts into trees and snapped branches along the way. Know why he did that?" Mabel looks up into his face. "That was his way of marking the path we would need to follow the next morning at sunup. We even had to use them marks when we's going back to camp."

"That's smart, isn't it, Grandpa?"

"Sure. Magi was just as smart as they came. He walked me that evening until I was about out of breath. I can still see him, about five paces in front of me, looking back, and pointing ahead to the old rail fence where he said we could turn back toward camp. Just before we got to the fence, Magi stopped, but smart me walked past him and jumped up on the bottom rail. I's about to throw my leg over the top rail to get to the other side when I felt Magi grab the nape of my neck, telling me, without saying a word, to stop right there."

"What was wrong, Grandpa?" asks Mabel.

"Hold on, I'm gonna tell you," says Grandpa. "As quick as a flash of lightning, Magi snapped his Bowie knife past my ear and out about two feet in front of me. He nailed a rattlesnake to the ground perfectly, right through its head. I ain't ever shook as much in my life. Magi waited for the snake to stop its writhing and rattling, picked it up, and carried it back to camp. I never touched it. Commander said that it must have been at least six foot long. That rattler was bigger around than your leg, Mabel."

"That's the scariest story I've ever heard, Grandpa." Mabel leans closer to him and hugs his muscular arm. "Do you think you'll ever see Magi again?"

"Probably not, but I do keep a lookout for him. If I ever see him, I'm gonna give him a big ole hug to thank him for saving my life. I'd sure like to sit down with him and tell him much obliged. I'd just like to talk to him for a while. Ain't much telling where he is today. As far as I know, he might not even be alive."

Mabel watches as the wagons and a few automobiles move along the road into Florence. "Look at them flivvers, Grandpa. Papa says he'll never ride in one. He says that he sees too many of them cars off the side of the road."

"I don't have no use for them neither. Your papa's right. Folks can hardly hold them things on the road. They can scare the devil out of a man's horse." Grandpa pulls back on the reins to slow Smoke's pace. "These city folks like all that fancy stuff. Not me."

He tugs on the right rein, telling Smoke to make a turn away from the main road and onto the last long stretch leading to the farm. Grandpa points to the northern sky. "Look yonder, Mabel. Them's some bad storms moving straight toward us out of the northwest. You can see what a big sheet of rain those clouds hold. It's moving fast and it's gonna come down this road. Reach in the back and get the bumbershoot. Probably won't help much because there's too much wind. You can try it anyway. Giddy up, Smoke." Smoke breaks into a fast trot.

As Mabel balances herself on her knees to reach back and get the umbrella, the red dust starts swirling and blowing into their faces. She tries to open the umbrella, but like Grandpa said, there is too much wind. He can't help her because he's using all of his strength to keep the cart on the dirt road. Just when Mabel gets the umbrella to open a bit, the wind snatches it out of her hands. "Don't worry about that, Mabel," shouts Grandpa, "it's older than Methuselah."

The cart's screeching springs turn to a higher pitch. Mabel senses the danger of being out in the middle of nowhere in a storm. Grandpa pulls his hat on tighter and hunches down. His head bows against the wind. The sand and dirt sting Mabel's face and legs. "Here she comes, Mabel. We're gonna get drenched. Glad I put the blinders on Smoke. Hold on to my arm so you don't get thrown out." He puts his arm across her chest and holds on to her leg, pulling her closer.

The rain feels like rocks of ice pelting Mabel's skin. She locks both of her arms around Grandpa's right arm. "Don't know if we can make it through this." Grandpa raises his voice to be heard over the wind and the thunder. "The road's already turning into mush." Smoke struggles against the wind and rain to move forward through the mud. "Don't want to run us off the road." Mabel's skin feels numb from the pellets of rain. She begins to shiver.

"The lightning's too close, Grandpa. The thunder's booming," shouts Mabel. "I'm cold!"

"Yonder's a house. I don't know who lives there, but we've got to stop. We'll both have pneumonia—if the lightning don't kill us first." Grandpa pulls back hard on the reins, almost causing Smoke to stop; he tugs the rein hard to the left. Smoke slowly walks down into a swale of rushing water. Through squinting eyes, Mabel watches in horror as the cart teeters from side to side. Smoke lowers her haunches to maintain control as she expertly chooses her steps. With Grandpa coaxing her toward the farmhouse, Smoke struggles through tall, slippery weeds and up the far side of the hill.

Mabel's pretty Easter dress is soaked and clings to her frigid body. She watches as Grandpa works to get Smoke up close to the shanty-like house. The bare wood walls look almost black in their wetness. Water noisily erupts from the mottled, rust-covered tin roof, and pounds the ground into a muddy trench. The rain continues to pummel their bodies as the stormy darkness surrounds the cart. Mabel moves closer to Grandpa. She snuggles into his safety and warmth.

"Hello, the house!" Grandpa cups his hands around his mouth again, takes a deep breath, and bellows out at the house's unknown occupants. "Hello, the house! Hello, the house!"

The wooden door opens slowly. A man in ragged overalls steps out on the porch; the butt of his shotgun rests on the porch beside his muddy boots. The stranger's whiskered face slowly breaks into a snaggle-toothed grin. The tan on his forehead stops at his hat line fading into an almost milky white. Mabel stares at the peculiar looking man and focuses her attention on his disheveled black hair. Its greasiness appears to hold his hair in little clumps all over his head.

"You folks need some hep?" calls out the stranger. "Y'all cain't get nowhere in this storm. It's a sittin'-in storm too. Hitch your horse to that thar railin' and come on in the house. You're soppin' wet." Spellbound by the stranger's drawl, Mabel feels a sense of leeriness about what they'll find on the other side of the door.

Grandpa gets out of the cart and stands on the steps. He reaches his arms out to Mabel. She scoots across the seat into his arms, burrows her face into his shoulder, and feels his hurried movement up to the porch. After he puts Mabel down, Grandpa removes his hat and slaps it against his leg, knocking out the wetness it holds. Even with his hat removed, he stands a full head taller than the tousled man. "Much obliged, neighbor," says Grandpa. They shake hands and the man motions them inside. Shivering from the cold rain, Mabel clings to Grandpa's hand and walks slightly behind him.

Inside, it takes a minute for Mabel's eyes to adjust to the deeper darkness. Her eyes sweep around the one-room house, seeking familiar sights of a home. She feels the plank floors, slick from seasons of oil rubbings, give beneath Grandpa's weight as they walk toward a slatted table surrounded by rickety chairs. Mabel breathes in the stuffiness in the room caused by the pots of steaming food sitting on the wood-burning stove. Continuing to search the room, she notices that each wall serves as the backdrop for beds—unmade, with some of the striped ticking showing beneath the crumpled covers. Over by the stone fireplace stand four boys and a frail girl. Each has blondish-red hair, shabby overalls, and bare feet.

"This here's my missus, Lucretia, 'n my name's Early, Early Watson." Grandpa nods and looks at the five children standing and staring. He flashes a smile.

"These here are our children, Matthew, Luke, John, James, and the girl's name is Ruth." Each steps forward and then steps back into line, waiting for the next name. Their expressionless faces don't provide a hint of what they are thinking. "The missus named them after folks she learnt about in the Bible."

"I recognize those names from the Bible," says Grandpa. "It's mighty nice to meet you folks." He places his hand behind Mabel's head and gently nudges her forward. "This is my granddaughter, Mabel. She's from Shoal Crossing. My name's T. J. Hood and I have a farm with my son, just a ways down the road. It's not far from the crossroad north of here."

"I go to the store down thar ever now 'n then," says Mrs. Watson. "Early, get a par of your clean overalls for Mr. Hood. Ruth, get out a clean par of overalls for Mabel. Looks like yours will be a mite short, Mr. Hood. Yours should be just about right, Mabel." Mr. Watson and Ruth walk to the rear left corner of the house and pull back some flour sack curtains. Each selects a pair of overalls from the neat stacks of folded clothes.

For the first time, Mabel focuses on Mrs. Watson. *She's what Mama calls stout. Her lips move when she's not even talking. She curls her lips inward and they disappear as they cling to her gums. She licks her lips before and after each curl. I can't see any teeth in her mouth. Wonder how she eats.* "You folks just go over thar behind them curtains yonder and change out of them wet clothes into them dungarees. They'll warm ya'll up in no time. I'll hang yer wet clothes up to dry. Ruth'll set y'all a place at the table. We ain't got much, but it'll do for a rainy day." Mrs. Watson rolls her lips into a smile as she enjoys her own humor.

Ruth hands Mabel some overalls and a boy's shirt. Mr. Watson hands Grandpa his fresh clothes. "You go on behind there and change first, Mabel," says Grandpa. "I'll wait right out here for you and then I'll change." Mabel closes the curtain and quickly peels off her soggy dress, socks, and shoes. The dry clothing makes her feel warm for the first time since the storm. She pulls the bow from her hair, folds her socks, and rests them on top of her wet dress. Barefooted, she walks back out into the large room.

"Here's my clothes, Mrs. Watson," says Mabel in a quiet voice. By the time Grandpa comes from behind the curtains, Mrs. Watson has supper on the table. *Grandpa looks funny in those overalls. They come up above his ankles, almost like Bubba's knickers. Mrs. Watson was right—they are a mite short.* Mabel tries to keep from laughing as she spies the Watson boys watching her grandpa; they quietly nudge their elbows into each other to make sure everyone sees the sight.

Mrs. Watson serves all the children and herself some mashed potatoes, stewed tomatoes, and lima beans. Mr. Watson and Grandpa have a slice of salt pork to go with their food. The men pay little attention to anyone else at the table as they talk about the weather and farming. Mabel hears the wind howling and rain pounding the tin roof. She pretends to be interested in her food, but doesn't like the bland taste. *Mama and Josie wouldn't ever cook our food like this.*

"Reckon you two needs to sleep on a pallet here with us," says Mr. Watson. "Ain't no sense in y'all gettin' killed out thar. Don't thank that horse of yours can pull you through it, much less see. I'll wake you at sunup and you can be on your way. We go to bed with the chickens, so it won't be no problem to get y'all up."

Grandpa and Mr. Watson go outside to take Smoke to the barn. Mabel waits for her grandpa at the table. Ruth comes over and sits down across from Mabel. Mrs. Watson washes the dishes. "Didn't your daddy say that your name's Ruth?" asks Mabel.

Ruth looks down at the table and shyly nods yes. "Bet you ain't never worn a par of overalls. You're a city girl," says Ruth. She peeks up into Mabel's eyes. Mabel shakes her head no. They timidly smile at each other. *She has pretty teeth. She's got more freckles than Bubba. Wonder why she acts like she's scared to talk out loud.* While Mabel is staring at Ruth, she notices that her face is turning red and her freckles are disappearing.

"I don't have a solitary dress. Maw says I'll have one sooner or later." Mrs. Watson walks over and hands Ruth a wet dishrag. Ruth stands and begins wiping down the table. "Anyway, reckon I don't need one out here on the farm," says Ruth. Grandpa and Mr. Watson come back from the barn, ending Mabel's brief encounter with Ruth.

Mrs. Watson shows Grandpa and Mabel where they should make their pallet. She gives them two blankets for the floor and one extra for cover. Mabel is so tired that the pallet feels like a soft mattress to her body. As she lies there, she notices that she can feel the outside air coming up through the cracks in the floor. *I haven't ever gone to bed in overalls. They feel nice and warm. Wonder why Mr. Watson's getting his shotgun.*

She watches as Early Watson carries his gun to his bed and props it against the wall. "I ain't looking for no trouble, but you cain't never tell what might break through that door in the dark of night," says Mr. Watson. Mabel firmly locks her arm around Grandpa's arm and holds on tight. She falls to sleep listening to his snore.

At sunup, Mabel goes behind the curtains to put on her dress. *It looks like it just came out of the wash. Mama would think my Easter dress looks tacky.* Mabel presses her hands into the wrinkles and tries to push them out. *That doesn't help one bit.* Knowing they will hurt her feet, she decides not to wear her stiff shoes. She stuffs her socks in one shoe and her ribbon in the other. As she walks out from behind the flour sacks, Mrs. Watson says, "Your grandpa's gone to hitch up the cart. Here's some breakfast I fixed for the two of you. Reckon y'all can eat while you ride." She slides her lips into a toothless smile and hands Mabel a box with a string bow tied around it.

"Thank you, ma'am. Me and my grandpa are much obliged for your kindness." As Mabel wonders if she's used Grandpa's "much obliged" correctly, she feels a powerful blush crawling up her neck. Embarrassed and unsure, she scurries out the front door and waits on the steps for Grandpa and Smoke.

Before they come into sight, Mabel can hear Grandpa's booming voice talking to Mr. Watson. *Mama says that he can't hear thunder and that's why he talks so loud.* As soon as he sees Mabel, Grandpa waves at her. After he maneuvers the cart up to the steps, Mr. Watson steps down from the cart. Grandpa motions for Mabel to get into the cart. Mabel places her shoes under the seat, holds out the boxed breakfast for Grandpa, and slides onto the seat.

"Sure hope you folks don't have no trouble. The road's gonna be a mess," says Mr. Watson. "Just stay in them shaller ruts and you should do all right. They's usually not too deep out this way. The water soaks up fast. Ain't many wagons out this way neither." He takes off his hat and rubs his sweaty head with a kerchief. "Gonna be a scorcher. Feels like pure steam coming up from the ground."

"We're much obliged for your family's hospitality, Mr. Watson. Tell the wife that we appreciate this fine boxed breakfast," says Grandpa with a grateful smile. All the Watson kids come out, line up side by side, and lean on the porch railing. *They look like a row of birds sitting on Mama's clothesline,* thinks Mabel. None of them says a word as they gaze at Grandpa smoothing out his mustache. Ruth and Mabel exchange smiles. "We'd best be on our way," says Grandpa. "Thanks again for the night's stay. Giddy up, Smoke." Mr. Watson tips his hat.

Grandpa pulls the reins to the left and the cart slowly rolls away. The big spoke wheels slurp through the mud and slap it against the cart. As Mabel begins to fidget with the string bow, she wonders if Grandpa is as glad to leave as she is. Smoke takes her time going back down into the swale and up to the main road. "You ready for some breakfast, Grandpa?" He reaches over and lifts the lid from the box. They both look down at four golden biscuits. Mabel lifts out one of the biscuits and opens it. "Looks like salt pork and sorghum molasses." She hands one to Grandpa and takes one out for herself.

He takes a bite of his biscuit. "That's a good biscuit. Mrs. Watson's nice to have fixed these for us. I know that she can't really afford to give away their food. Hope you never have to live like them kids back there, Mabel. We're all poor these days, but the Watsons are having a hard time of it. Don't get me wrong, being poor's no disgrace. All those kids, just a bit of land, and no steady job is cause to wonder how they're making it. I reckon the good Lord provides for them, but it hurts my heart to see folks suffer."

"Papa says we're poor. He says that he and Mama were as poor as church mice in Florence. He says that things are better now, but he's always worried about losing his job or the government shutting down."

"Your papa's always provided for his family. He's a hard worker and it shows. Working for the government is just about the best thing a man can do these days. When everything else goes, the government will still be in business—the politicians will see to that." Grandpa surveys the countryside. "That foundry is hot and it's hard on his back," says Grandpa. "Let me have one more of those biscuits. Why don't you eat just the top of the last one? Your grandma and aunt will have dinner ready when we get home. Uncle Sam's gonna be one happy soul when he sees that I brought you back home with me."

Chapter 6

I LIKE HEARING UNCLE SAM'S NAME. His eyes are as brown as chocolate. His blondish hair has waves running through it. Uncle Sam is shorter than Grandpa and Papa, but he's funnier than anybody I know. Ever since I can remember, Mama's read me his letters. Mama once told Mabel that Uncle Sam was a black-faced comedian with different vaudeville shows. She said that Grandpa doesn't approve of his son's stage character, especially when he entertains Yankees. *Mama says that Grandpa thinks like that because of the war. She says that it doesn't take much to get them crossways of each other. Uncle Sam doesn't sing and dance anymore, so he doesn't travel up North for work.*

"You know your mama named you after Sam's wife, don't you?" Without waiting for an answer, Grandpa continues to talk. "She was a pretty thing and could sing like nobody I've ever heard," says Grandpa. "Newspapers called her a nightingale. Sam had everything planned out for his life with her. He came out here and bought this land for him and Mabel to have as a retreat of sorts. Sam wanted all of us to live out on the farm."

"Did Aunt Mabel ever see the farm?"

"She saw the land. They decided to build a log house for their retirement. After they found the land, I remember them leaving Florence for what they called the last time. Sam had some shows to do and she went to visit her ailing brother over in Missouri. Sam went up to Illinois. He also planned to go select the logs and then meet Mabel. They wanted to ride back on the train to Florence together."

Mabel listens closely to Grandpa. She curls her legs up under her wrinkled dress and turns to look at Grandpa. *He seems sad talking about Uncle Sam and Aunt Mabel.*

"Sam had about a week's worth of shows to do, but along about Wednesday he got a telegram telling him to rush to Missouri. Mabel didn't live through whatever struck her. Unfortunately, she died before he got to her. Sam brought her back to Florence as they planned, but he brought her in a casket instead. Saddest thing I've ever seen. He mourns every day. Reckon that's why he buried her out on the farm."

"That's a sad story, Grandpa. Mama says that Uncle Sam never has been the same."

"Nope, he changed all right. You've always been extra special to Sam because of your name. I sure hate it all happened that way. It seemed to suck the life right out of Sam."

"There's the store, Grandpa," says Mabel. "And there's y'all's church."

"I see that they got the grape arbor finished yesterday. We're gonna have our Sunday church under the arbor. Preacher says that it's getting too hot in the church," says Grandpa. He pats Mabel's knee. "And I'm gonna have my granddaughter with me at the next gathering."

Mabel looks at the arbor as he talks about it. She's never been to a preaching on the grounds. They have picnics on the grounds at her church. "That'll be fun, Grandpa."

"Reckon your grandma has been worried about our whereabouts." He guides Smoke to turn right. They finally reach the country lane that runs through the center of the farm. It's just as Mabel remembered it. She takes a deep breath of the fresh air and watches the sunshine dance between the massive trees. Rail fences line the land as they pass in front of Aunt Bennie's house. Up ahead she sees Uncle Sam crossing the road toward the house. He stops and waves, waiting for them to reach his side. Mabel waves, stands up, and broadly smiles at the sight of him.

"You two took your sweet time getting back. Did y'all decide to go to Memphis and shop?" teases Uncle Sam.

"Shop my eye," says Grandpa. "Yesterday's storm stopped us dead in our tracks."

"Me-oh-my, look at that beautiful little girl there with you, Daddy." Uncle Sam turns Mabel's arrival into a magical fantasy. "Come down, my princess, and sashay to the castle in yon woods with me." Mabel laughs with her uncle as he lets out a guffaw. "The maiden woman and her mother are about to serve our midday feast." Mabel offers him her hand and he helps her step down from the cart. Uncle Sam bows. Grandpa pulls the cart forward. Uncle Sam closes the gate after the cart passes through. He stops and looks down at Mabel.

"My dress is wrinkled, Uncle Sam. It got wet in the storm."

"I wondered who ironed your dress, milady. And where have your shoes gone?"

"It was pouring rain with lots of lightning and thundering—and the mud was knee-deep. We had to stop and spend the night with a farm family. My shoes are stiff as boards from the water." He throws his head back and laughs. They begin running through the thick carpet of grass toward the house. When they reach the steps, he stops. "So, I take it that you and your grandpa had an adventure. You're sure it wasn't marauders that chased you off the road?" Uncle Sam laughs again. They walk up the stone steps, cross the porch, open the screen door, and walk into the house. Mabel takes a deep breath of the aroma filling the air from Grandma's cooking.

The hugeness of the front room seems to overwhelm Mabel. She takes in the beauty of the log walls, the stone fireplace, and mantel. Mabel glances over at the dining room table with its white tablecloth and the pretty dishes placed in front of each mahogany chair. Noticing some fresh-cut flowers beside the settee, Mabel sniffs their sweet scent.

The log house doesn't have walls separating the rooms like the O'Brien house in Shoal Crossing. The living room, dining room, and kitchen are in full view when you walk in the front door. Mabel looks up the staircase that Uncle Sam built. *Mama told me that Uncle Sam cut the wood for the steps. He made them smooth and stained them a deep brown.* The stairs lead up to the bedrooms. *Wonder if I'm gonna have to sleep in Aunt Nell's room. I hope Grandma lets me have a room by myself.*

"My goodness gracious, look how you've grown, Mabel," exclaims Aunt Nell. "Come here and let me hug you. We're so happy to have you out here with us." Aunt Nell kneels down and wraps her long arms around Mabel. "What in the world happened to your pretty dress, child? Where are your shoes?" Her deep-brown eyes search Mabel from head to toe causing Mabel's face to redden. Aunt Nell's almost-black hair clings tightly to her head and falls just below her ears. She scrunches her eyebrows together as she waits for the answer. Mabel notices the powder on Aunt Nell's face.

"She got soaked to the bone, that's what happened to her dress and shoes," says Grandpa as he steps inside from the back doorway. "I've already got the cart emptied and Smoke's in a stall."

"Come here, Mabel. Grandma needs a hug too. It makes no difference to me that you have on a wrinkled dress. I love the girl inside that dress." Grandma's smile tenderly welcomes Mabel. As she kisses her Grandma on the cheek, Mabel can feel the moistness of Grandma's kiss on her forehead. She doesn't appear to be much taller than Mabel is—"petite" is how Mama describes it to Mabel. She has on a white cotton blouse with a long black skirt that stops just above her shiny black shoes. The sleeves of the blouse are long and puffy. A crocheted collar circles the neck of her blouse; a single pearl button holds it together. Grandma's strikingly white hair, pulled back in a bun, perfectly matches her silvery blue eyes and wire-rimmed glasses.

"I'm sure hungry for some of your cooking," says Grandpa.

"Go out to the washstand, Mabel, and rinse your little hands for dinner. I know you must feel dirty from those roads," says Grandma. "I'll empty the washbowl after we eat. We're thrilled to have you here with us, Mabel." Mabel feels the touch of another kiss from Grandma on the top of her head.

Mabel's spirits are teeming with excitement as she walks through the kitchen to the washstand. Her Grandma has a special way of making her feel good about herself. Mabel selects the smaller pitcher Grandma has in place for the ladies of the house. The porcelain pitcher has dainty pink roses, surrounded by tiny green leaves that wind around its base. She feels the coolness of the water trickling through her fingers. Mabel picks up the damp bar of soap and jiggles it in the water. *I love the smell of Grandma's soap.* After she rinses her hands, Mabel dries them on Grandma's embroidered towel. Mabel refolds the towel and places it beside the washbowl.

As soon as Mabel sits down at the table and places her napkin in her lap, Grandpa begins to pray. He prays for every living person, animal, and plant in his life. When he finally says amen, Grandma begins passing around the blue willow dishes. She's prepared sliced boiled ham, fresh green beans with tiny carrots, mashed potatoes with red-eye gravy, iced tea with lemon, and some of Aunt Nell's special rolls. The food is so tasty that there isn't much talking at the table. Grandma finally breaks the silence. "Who were the folks you stayed with last night, T.J.?"

"The man's name is Early Watson," says Grandpa. "Mighty nice of them to take in two strangers." He leans back in his chair. "Them folks are having a time of it. They didn't poormouth, but you can tell just by looking. It made me feel guilty to eat their food. I reckon he didn't fully trust me, because he slept with a loaded shotgun by his side."

"Lord have mercy," says Grandma. "I would have slept with one eye open." Everyone laughs when Grandma closes one eye to show how she'd sleep in the Watsons' house.

"Maybe we can fix them up some food or something," says Aunt Nell. "You know, a little remembrance that tells them how appreciative we are for what they done for y'all."

After Mabel folds her white cloth napkin and places it beside her plate, she says, "I know something we can do, Aunt Nell. Mama says that you are a fine seamstress. All the ladies loved the dresses you made for us for Christmas and Easter." Mabel stares into Aunt Nell's eyes and notices how she drinks up her compliments. "The Watsons have a daughter named Ruth. She's about my size around the waist, but she's just a little taller than I am—kinda like Sister. Ruth told me that she doesn't have a single dress. Maybe you could make her a dress. If it fits me, it will fit her. Just make it longer, I reckon." Mabel waits for Aunt Nell's answer to her idea. She shifts in her chair, unsure that Aunt Nell will consider a little girl's suggestion.

Aunt Nell straightens herself in her chair. She takes her napkin, slightly opens her mouth, and dabs at the two corners of her lips. Aunt Nell pauses so long that Mabel fears that she doesn't like her suggestion. "Why, yes, Mabel, that's a very nice plan. I still have some pieces left from that dress you have on today. Think she'd like that pale yellow?" Mabel's gape shows her surprise.

"I think she'd like the yellow a lot." *I wish Bubba and Sister could hear how Aunt Nell likes my idea. They say that nobody listens to me.* "She only has overalls to wear, but even they look like hand-me-downs. The dress will make her happy."

"Speaking of overalls, Mabel," says Uncle Sam. He gets up and walks to the stairs. "Here's a pair of overalls for you to wear when you're working with us out here. I think you'll find them more comfortable than a dress."

"Oh, thank you, Uncle Sam. I've always wanted a pair of these. Bubba has some. I slept in some of Ruth's last night and they felt good." Uncle Sam gives Mabel a wink as he sits back down.

Aunt Nell darts one of her looks of disgust at Uncle Sam and Mabel. After she clicks her tongue, showing her disapproval, she picks up her thoughts about the Watsons' gifts. "Then that's just what we'll do. When are y'all going back that way, Daddy?"

"I reckon we'll go back toward the middle of next week. You ladies just fix whatever you think they'll appreciate. Mabel and I will deliver it on our way back to Shoal Crossing," says Grandpa. "Good Lord willing, we won't need to spend the night again."

When Uncle Sam leans back in his chair, Mabel senses that he's ready to say something funny. "Suppose you might want to be making that dress the best one you've ever made, Nell. We don't want Daddy having to run from buckshot." Mabel searches each face for a smile. No one sees any humor in it. Uncle Sam quickly changes the subject. "I want to play some music out on the front porch. I'm gonna get my banjo. Do you want your concertina, Nell?"

"That sounds like fun, Sam, but we've got to get these dishes done first or we'll be cleaning until suppertime."

"It won't take us long, Nell," says Grandma. "We'll just clean the plates and silverware. We'll have leftovers late this evening."

Grandpa ambles toward the front porch and his rocking chair, while Grandma, Aunt Nell, and Mabel start clearing the table. Uncle

Sam races up the stairs to get the instruments. In just a few minutes, he hurries back down the stairs and out to the porch. By the time the dishes are finished, Uncle Sam is well into his third song. They all end up on the front porch. Mabel snuggles close to her grandma on the swing. They all sing along as Uncle Sam and Aunt Nell play hymns.

"Josie's favorite song is 'Amazing Grace,'" says Mabel. "Do you know how to play that, Uncle Sam?"

He starts humming and playing the song. Aunt Nell pats her foot and plays along with him. Mabel gets up and walks over to Uncle Sam. "I wish you'd sing it for us, Mabel," says Uncle Sam. "When you stumble, we'll help you with the words."

"I'm gonna sing it like Josie does," says Mabel. "Amazing grace, how sweet the sound, that saved a wretch like me. I once was lost, but now am found...." They sing along, guiding Mabel through the verses. Mabel keeps perfect time with the *plinkety-plank* of the banjo. When she finishes, they all applaud. "Josie sways while she sings. She has a pretty voice," says Mabel.

"Well, you ain't too shabby yourself," says Uncle Sam. "I hope you'll join the church choir when you're old enough." He places his banjo in its black case. "If you folks will excuse me, I think I'll go across the way for a while."

Aunt Nell continues to play her concertina. No one says a word, but their eyes follow him as he walks down the porch steps and across the road to his bench by Aunt Mabel's burial site. *I feel sad for Uncle Sam.* Threatening tears sting Mabel's eyes, but she makes them go away by looking around.

They go to bed early that first night. Mabel feels rested when she gets up the next morning. Grandma let her sleep in a room all by herself. She happily puts on her new overalls for a day of work on the farm. By the time she gets downstairs, everyone is sitting at the table. They appear to be waiting for Grandma to finish with her last-minute touches. Mabel's eyes quickly find the platter of scrambled eggs, country ham, and buttered biscuits.

"Mabel, please go out to the cellar and get us a pitcher of cream," says Grandma. "You make sure that you close the door. I don't want to meet any strange varmints out there. Be sure too that you put the pin back through the hasp. Here's the cream pitcher."

"Yes, ma'am." Grandma doesn't know it, but she has asked Mabel to do one of her favorite things—fetching the cream. *Grandma lets the cream rise from the cows' milk. It's better than the cream we get in Shoal Crossing.* When Mabel steps off the back steps, she walks across the yard and sees the morning dew sparkling in the sunlight. *I can see my footprints in the grass. They all slide together in lines.* Off in the distance, she sees some of the cows standing at the railings. *They're watching me get their milk. Wonder what they think of that.*

She struggles to open the heavy plank door and carefully walks it over to the ground. Mabel feels her way along the wall, walks down two gray stone steps, and breathes in the coolness inside the cellar. Using the light from outside, she sees vegetable bins, milk cans, the butter churn, canned vegetables in shiny jars, preserves, and finally, the cream. She sets the crystal pitcher down next to the cream on the wooden shelf. Mabel slowly pours the cream into the pitcher from the small bottle.

Mabel pauses just before she walks back up the steps and puts the pitcher to her lips. The long sip of cream causes her to lick her lips and smack its goodness in her mouth. She wipes her mouth on the back of her hand and walks outside, remembering to close the door and replace the pin in the hasp. Hoping no one knows about her sipping the cream, Mabel walks back to the house. She goes inside and places the cream pitcher on the table.

The scrambled eggs, ham, and biscuits taste so good to Mabel that she hardly looks up throughout breakfast. "Who was that fella talking to you on the porch yesterday, Nell? I got distracted when

Mabel and Daddy came home and forgot to ask you about it. Don't tell me you're gonna be a bride. I'd miss your cooking too much," says Uncle Sam in a joking voice.

"You're always trying to get me married off, brother dear," says Aunt Nell. "I'm not going anywhere." Mabel looks up from her plate when she hears Aunt Nell's giggle. "That man came here from back in the woods to ask me to make a shroud for his brother's wife. He said that she wouldn't live much longer. I told him that I'd have it ready by Monday."

"Is he going to pay you for your time and trouble?" asks Uncle Sam.

"Heavens no, Sam. I figure helping someone prepare for their final journey is doing the Lord's work." Aunt Nell is so tall that she has to hunch her shoulders over to get closer to her second helping of eggs. She somehow manages to keep her head bowed and rolls her eyes from Uncle Sam to Grandma. "He brought me a bolt of black cloth," says Aunt Nell. "All I have to do is stitch the edges for them. Reckon they'll help me wrap her. Bless her soul."

"If anybody ever gets to heaven for good works, Nell, you'll be the first in line," says Uncle Sam. They all nod in agreement. Aunt Nell leans back, smiles, and takes in the admiration.

"What's a shroud, Aunt Nell?" says Mabel. "I never heard that word."

"A shroud's just a burial cloth, Mabel," says Aunt Nell. "Some folks choose to bury their dead in a cloth rather than regular clothes. Most of the backwoods people like to use a shroud. We'll take the black cloth and wrap it around her body." Puzzled by wrapping a dead person, Mabel pays close attention to her aunt. "After we get her wrapped, we'll put her in her coffin."

Still curious, Mabel asks, "Is that what she'll be wearing when she gets to heaven?" They all let out a roar of laughter. Mabel feels her face getting hot from the blush crawling up her neck.

"That's a good question, Mabel," says Grandma. "Don't ever be embarrassed about asking a question. That means you're eager to learn." Grandma looks around the table. "Do any of you have the answer for Mabel?" They all just sit there and smile. "You see, Mabel? Grown-ups don't know all the answers. I'm sure I don't know what she'll be wearing or how she'll look when she gets there."

After breakfast, Mabel follows Grandpa and Uncle Sam around the farm as they shuffle things from one place to another. "It's still too wet to plow. The mule and me might sink into the ground," says Uncle Sam. He puts his hands on his hips and surveys the farm. "I guess it's a good day to get the tools and such organized in the barn, Daddy."

"Yep, Son, it's time to try out the new grinding wheel," says Grandpa. The three of them walk over to the barn and open the doors. The grinder, sitting out in the middle of the dirt floor, looks like a bicycle with only the front wheel. Smoke and the mule rest their heads on their stall doors and watch them enter the barn.

"Hop up there, Mabel," says Uncle Sam. "You can peddle and we'll hold the tools to the wheel. They'll be sharpened like new." Uncle Sam pats the seat where Mabel is to sit. With her hands on her knees, she begins to peddle. She watches the sparks fly as they sharpen shovels, axes, picks, and hoes. She only stops when they have to select another implement.

"My legs are tired," says Mabel. "I need to rest." Grandpa says that he wants to try cycling for the few tools they have left. Mabel walks out of the barn and sits down beneath a tree. The shade and gentle breeze feel good to her. She turns and rests her back against the tree trunk. Mabel watches Grandpa peddle slowly as Uncle Sam touches a shovel to the wheel.

Losing interest in the sparks, Mabel looks down at an exposed tree root and sees a caterpillar. Reaching over to pick up a leaf, she puts it in front of the creature's path. *I wonder what kind of butterfly you'll be. Mama says that a caterpillar turning into a butterfly is like the miracle that happens when people change and have a new life. She says it's a new beginning for them. Mama told me that's why people at church are baptized.*

Uncle Sam walks over and sits down beside Mabel. "Shoo wee, I'm about worn out for the day. Daddy's still in there fiddling around." Mabel holds the leaf up for him to see the caterpillar. He quickly puts his hand over his mouth. Uncle Sam's voice sounds muffled as he talks through his fingers. "Mabel, I sure hope you haven't shown that caterpillar your teeth."

"No sir. Why would I show my teeth to a caterpillar?" Not knowing the answer, Mabel covers her mouth with her free hand.

Uncle Sam slides his hand from his mouth just enough to speak. "It's a good thing you didn't. There's a legend that says if a person shows a caterpillar his teeth, those teeth will rot out of his mouth." Mabel clinches her lips over her teeth and takes the caterpillar around to the other side of the tree. "I don't know if it's true, but I make it my practice to never show my teeth around a caterpillar," says Uncle Sam.

"Mama says that you don't need a thermometer as long as the crickets chirp," says Mabel.

"She does, does she? Do you know how that works?" asks Uncle Sam.

"Mama says that you count the chirps and add a number to get the temperature."

"That's good, Mabel. You have to listen and count the number of chirps for fifteen seconds. Once you've done that, you add forty to that number," says Uncle Sam. He stands and rests his hand against the tree. Mabel looks up at him. "They say that it gives you the temperature."

"Crickets don't chirp in the wintertime though," says Mabel.

"Aha, fair maiden, you're right. Therefore, if you don't have a thermometer and the crickets aren't chirping, you'd better trust your weather nose." Uncle Sam reaches down and gently squeezes Mabel's nose. "Your nose knows when it's cold." Uncle Sam throws his head back and laughs. "I'm a foolish sort, aren't I Mabel?"

"No, sir, you aren't foolish—you make me laugh. You're funny. Mama says that you make her laugh too."

"When it comes to laughing, you two are just alike. Your mama and I have known each other a long, long time. Did she ever tell you about the beautiful dragonfly?"

"You mean a snake doctor?"

"Yes, they're sometimes called snake doctors. Folks believe that they can heal a sick snake. Other folks say that they warn snakes when danger is near. Anyway, if I see one, I check around for a snake in case it's true." Uncle Sam reaches down for Mabel's hand and pulls her up. "What I was thinking of is that dragonflies are sometimes called the 'devil's darning needle.' You ever hear of that?"

"No, sir. Mama never told me about that."

"Well, the story goes that the dragonfly comes in the still of the night when you're fast asleep. Guess what it does. It sews up the ears and eyes of those who do evil things."

Aunt Nell steps out on the back porch and rings the dinner bell. "Come on in. The food's on the table, Sam." Grandpa comes out of the barn and the three of them saunter toward the house in silence. Mabel walks between Uncle Sam and Grandpa. Each of them holds one of her hands. *I'm tired from all our hard work. My overalls look just like theirs. I'm a farmer today. I know Mama and Papa will be proud that I'm a hard worker.*

Chapter 7

SUNDAY MORNING BRINGS ANOTHER BUSY DAY to the farmhouse. The entire family gets up early, eats breakfast, and gets dressed for their church service at the crossroad. Grandma says that it's a special day because of the new-fangled arbor.

Aunt Nell surprises Mabel with a new dress. "I was going to mail this to you, but now I don't have to," says Aunt Nell with a proud smile. Mabel thinks it's the prettiest dress she's ever seen. It's made of the palest blue organdy and has a long satin sash. "Put on the matching teddy first, Mabel. I even made you two bows for your hair." Mabel stands back and admires her beautiful dress in Aunt Nell's full-length mirror. She gently runs her hands along the fullness of the skirt of the dress. Aunt Nell smiles at Mabel's approving glances.

"This is the prettiest dress in the whole wide world, Aunt Nell." Mabel twirls around. "Thank you for making it for me. Mama and Sister will think it's beautiful."

Aunt Nell bends down and hugs Mabel. "You're welcome. It looks so pretty with your eyes."

While Aunt Nell powders her face, Mabel walks to the top of the staircase and sits down. *I can't wait to sit under the arbor. Grandpa says it's much cooler in the open air than it is in the church house. I wonder if all the farmers will come to church like they did the last time. All of them are friends with Grandpa and Grandma. They seem friendlier than the people at our church do. Mama says Aunt Nell would rather be in church than anywhere.*

I like church too, but I'd rather just come out to the farm and work with Uncle Sam and Grandpa. I think church is her favorite place because she says "amen" and "praise Jesus" every time she agrees with what the preacher says. Since she likes just about everything he says, she talks almost as much as the preacher does in church. Uncle Sam seems to enjoy church too, but I think he just enjoys the people he sees there. Papa calls it fellowship.

Uncle Sam brings his new wagon around as they all stand beside the house in a line. Mabel watches the slow turns of the big red wheels as Uncle Sam guides Smoke to where they are standing. The wagon is solid black and has four darkly stained wood seats. *Grandpa told Papa that he bought the wagon at Florence Wagon Works.* Aunt Nell gets in first, then Grandma, next Mabel, and Grandpa gets in last. Grandma and Mabel sit behind Uncle Sam and Grandpa, while Aunt Nell sits on the second seat in the back. In order to keep their hats from blowing away, Grandma and Aunt Nell rest their white, cotton-gloved hands on their Sunday dress-up hats. Aunt Nell cinched the bows so tightly in Mabel's hair that they don't move.

When they reach the farm lane, Grandpa steps down and opens the front gate. Uncle Sam eases forward to wait for Grandpa to close the gate. Mabel watches him step up and swing himself beside Uncle Sam. *Grandpa looks handsome in his light-brown suit. His stiff shirt collar looks like it's choking him. He sure is a lot bigger than Uncle Sam.* When they reach the farm lane, Uncle Sam guides Smoke to the right and they begin their short journey to church.

Sitting up so high, riding in a new wagon, and being all dressed up makes Mabel feel like a prissy lady. They all sit quietly and take in the beauty of the farm's acreage. *The birds all seem happy this morning.* Mabel watches them flutter their wings as they follow the wagon along the dirt road. A squirrel ducks for cover as they approach the tree he's sitting beneath. Looking across the fields of weeds, Mabel sees the hint of color coming from the hundreds of wild flowers.

When they arrive at the church, several wagons, mules, horses, and a few automobiles already line the hitching posts. The people stroll around from one cluster of people to the next. Uncle Sam steps down and ties Smoke under the shade of a tree. As Mabel steps down from the wagon, she spots the gristmill where Grandpa takes his corn to be ground. "Never you mind that mill today," says Grandpa. "We'll be back up here Tuesday." *Wonder what Grandpa has to have done at the mill. One of my favorite places to go is out by the waterwheel that turns the grinders.*

As Mabel steps under the arbor, she notices that the deacons used large white canvases to cover the ground. They arranged two sections of wooden chairs in neat rows. While the ladies sit in their chosen folding chairs, in their chosen row, Grandpa and Uncle Sam move about shaking hands and talking in hushed sounds. Though Grandpa speaks more softly than usual, Mabel can still hear his voice above all the others. Mabel takes in the feel of sitting beneath the arbor. *Mama and Papa would like this arbor for church.* Mabel picks up a hand fan and begins fluttering it in front of her face. "Do I get to keep this fan, Grandma?" Grandma nods that Mabel can keep the fan and picks up one for herself. Mabel watches as Grandma flaps her fan up close to her face.

When Aunt Nell's favorite preacherman walks to the front of the arbor and announces that the sermon is about to begin, all of the men hasten to their chairs. Mabel sits between Aunt Nell and Grandma. Uncle Sam sits on the other side of Aunt Nell and Grandpa sits on the aisle seat next to Grandma.

The preacher is a tall, slim man who wears a black suit with a vest. His black handlebar mustache almost reaches his ears. *Wonder why Aunt Nell calls him preacherman.* "Let's begin our day with the children's favorite song, 'Jesus Loves Me,'" says the preacher. He motions for the congregation to rise as they begin to sing. They remain standing as they sing off-key versions of "Bringing in the Sheaves" and finally, "In the Garden."

Before the gathering finishes "In the Garden," four deacons walk to the front and pick up the galvanized pails for the collection. Mabel listens to the clanging of the money dropping into the buckets. When the clanging stops, preacherman stands and begins his sermon. Mabel leans back and readies herself for the shouting and rambling of the preacher. She doesn't have to wait long. He seems to get louder every time he holds his Bible up in the air. Her eyes follow his back-and-forth pacing. *The way he hunches over makes him look like he's chasing a hen for killing.* Mabel smiles to herself as she imagines preacherman trying to catch a hen.

Seeking something else to watch, Mabel's eyes follow the beams of sunlight peeking through the weaves of vines adorning the arbor. She follows a ray of light down to her lap and watches the dust particles scatter from her fanning. As she searches for more light beams, Mabel spots a caterpillar clinging to one of the branches above the congregation. Remembering Uncle Sam's warning, she rolls her lips tightly over her teeth and clinches her mouth shut. *These farmers don't know that caterpillar's up there. Their teeth are gonna rot.* Without another thought, Mabel jumps to her feet and points up toward the caterpillar. "Don't let that caterpillar see your teeth. It'll make your teeth rot out of your mouth!"

Every eye focuses on Mabel and then they seem to look up at the caterpillar in unison. Aunt Nell and Grandma promptly grab Mabel's shoulders, forcing her to sit down. People start laughing. Uncle Sam appears to cover his mouth in order to choke back an outburst.

Preacherman stops the laughter by raising his arms up in the air. "When I was a child, I spoke as a child, and I understood as a child. We thank Mabel for bringing laughter to our hearts," says preacherman. A lady sitting behind Mabel reaches forward and pats her on the back. Mabel scrunches down a little deeper in her chair. She doesn't hear another word the preacher says. Her eyes focus on the back of the chair in front of her.

As soon as the last song finishes, Uncle Sam leans in front of Aunt Nell. "Mabel, come, we'll walk to the wagon together." As they walk through the crowd, several people smile and pat Mabel as if they feel sorry for her. *I'm glad Uncle Sam got me away from Grandma and Aunt Nell. They'll fuss all the way back to the farm.* "There's the wagon, Mabel. Just stay with me."

When they reach the wagon, Uncle Sam pulls Mabel close to him and starts laughing. Mabel looks up and sees his face looking skyward. She watches his red bowtie dance up and down his throat. He laughs so hard that Mabel begins a deep giggle. "You'll always be my special little girl, Mabel. Now, let's get into the wagon." Every time they look at each other, they begin laughing again. *Uncle Sam makes me happy even when I'm scared of what's coming.*

When they all get into the wagon, Smoke slowly pulls them toward the road. Aunt Nell and Grandma busy themselves by talking about preacherman and the new prayer list. Mabel welcomes their chatter about something else; but it doesn't last long. "Mabel, what in the world ever possessed you to shoot up like that in church?" asks Aunt Nell. Mabel meekly shrugs her shoulders as she searches for an answer. While she tries to think of something, Aunt Nell unleashes her outrage. Mabel tunes in and out as her aunt fumes. "Where … world … foolishness … caterpillar? For the life of me, I don't know where you got that. I've never heard of such."

"She got it from me, Nell," Uncle Sam says in her defense. "I told her about the caterpillar yesterday. An Indian in the show told me about it years ago, but I don't know where he got it. I don't know if it's true either. Everybody still got their teeth?"

Mabel watches Grandpa's shoulders start shaking from his silent laughter. Finally, his laughter bursts forth as everyone strains to understand him. "Whew, that sure tickled me, Mabel—you trying to protect everybody's teeth. Looks to me like most of those folks done been smiling at too many caterpillars already," says Grandpa. He lets out a yelp of laughter and slaps his leg. Uncle Sam, Grandma, and Mabel join in the laughter. Aunt Nell keeps a stern expression on her face.

After Sunday dinner, Aunt Nell and Mabel go upstairs to work on the shroud. Mabel's misery at being in close quarters with her angry aunt makes for a gloomy afternoon. *I don't see anything special about that black material. I'd rather be out on the porch with Grandma and Grandpa.*

"I've been thinking," says Aunt Nell, "that it would be nice for you to walk with me into the backwoods to deliver the shroud. I've got to take it to them tomorrow. We can get up, get you dressed in your church dress, and be back by dinnertime. I'd like for you to go with me and pay your respects." She looks over at Mabel sitting on the floor. "Don't you think that'll be fun?"

"No'm," says Mabel. "I don't know those folks and I don't think I should look at someone so sick. I don't even smoosh bugs because I don't want to see them die. I ain't never seen a dead person and don't reckon I want to. Much obliged, but I'll just stay here and help Grandpa."

"I've already checked with Daddy. He said that it'll be fine for you to go with me," says Aunt Nell. "You need to learn to do things to help those in need. Visiting the sick and dying is something we're all supposed to do. We won't stay long. It'll be a blessing for you." *I wish Grandpa would take me back home. That visit don't sound like any fun to me. She's gonna make me go with her—don't matter what I say.* Because she can't think of any more excuses, Mabel smiles back at Aunt Nell, reluctantly accepting her invitation.

Mabel wakes up the next morning with her aunt towering over her bed. She tells Mabel everything she needs to do so that they can leave by ten o'clock. After a breakfast of biscuits and grape jam, Mabel puts on her Sunday dress and Grandma fixes the bows in her hair. Aunt Nell is dressed in black and seems to carry a cloud of gloom over her. So it will be easier to carry, Grandma and Aunt Nell tie some leather belts around the neatly folded shroud. Mabel looks out the front window and longs to be in the fields with Grandpa and Uncle Sam.

Aunt Nell purses her lips and seems proud that Mabel has to mind her. "Come on, Mabel. We'll go out the back door." She wags her finger in Mabel's face. "Remember, this is the Christian thing for us to do. The good Lord will bless you for this." *I don't feel the need for any blessings, but Mama says that I have to mind my elders. Mama says that God loves those who love Him. She says that we shouldn't do things just because we want God to bless us.*

When they get off the cleared farmland and into the woods, the air feels much cooler. The smell of the musky earth drifts through the air. Mabel can feel the ground giving under her weight. She watches as Aunt Nell's heaviness causes mud to ooze up the sides of her church shoes. "How far do we have to walk to get to their house?" asks Mabel.

"I've never been back here. The man told me to walk straight along this path and eventually I'd see the house. I don't think it's too far," says Aunt Nell. She clutches the shroud to her chest and peers over to watch her steps. *Wonder if I should mark our path like Magi did for the soldiers.* Mabel begins to snap twigs with her fingers—just in case Aunt Nell gets lost. "What in the world are you doing, Mabel?"

"I'm just marking our path. Grandpa taught me about that," says Mabel. "How are we gonna get over that big old tree up yonder?" Aunt Nell stops and looks up quickly. "That trunk looks to be taller than me," says Mabel.

"We'll just have to figure that out when we get there," says Aunt Nell. "It's mighty big. That man must've gotten over it or around it to get to our house."

They stop when they reach the massive tree. Aunt Nell places the shroud on the downed tree and hoists her long body up on top of the trunk. She turns her body to rest her legs on the tree. With one more turn, her back is now facing Mabel. "Give me your hand, Mabel, and I'll help you climb up here with me." She extends her left hand out to Mabel. Taking Aunt Nell's hand, Mabel scales up on the fallen tree beside Aunt Nell. "That wasn't so hard, was it? We didn't even get dirty."

Mabel hops down the other side and waits for her aunt to follow. Aunt Nell's black dress hikes up in the back as she slides to the ground. Mabel sees Aunt Nell's petticoat, but holds back her laugh because she knows her aunt's too serious about getting the shroud to the man. Straightening her dress and swiping at her seat, Aunt Nell says, "We won't have to worry about getting dirty on the way home."

Mabel helps her aunt brush off the shroud. They then continue to walk deeper into the woods. After a few more minutes, Mabel sees a wooden house with a rusty tin roof in the distance. As they get closer, Mabel can see that the path leads straight to the front steps. "There's the house, Aunt Nell." Her heart begins to pound for fear of the strangers and the dying woman. *I wish I could just wait here in the woods until Aunt Nell gives him the shroud. Maybe the lady is better and isn't sick anymore.*

Aunt Nell rolls her eyes heavenward and says, "Praise be to Jesus. I was beginning to think that man told me the wrong path."

As they draw closer to the house, Mabel can see that the house rests on heaping mounds of gray stones. The wooden slats on the outer walls look dark and damp from the lack of sunlight. People are standing beside a cot in the breezeway and to the left is the kitchen. To the right are the sleeping rooms. When they step into the clearing, Mabel spots three children sitting in the dirt up under the porch. Two mangy beagles lazily roll their eyes toward Mabel and her aunt. The dogs don't move from their cool hollowed out spot in the dust. The children under the porch stay quiet and watch them as they walk toward the steps.

"Mabel, you sit on this top step and wait for me. This won't take but a few minutes," says Aunt Nell. Mabel sits down and stares back at the beagles. *Those dogs aren't as big as Snooks. I don't like being here. This is worse than the Watson house.*

The murmuring of the men, preacherman, and Aunt Nell from the breezeway silences Mabel's thoughts. She hears Aunt Nell's footsteps moving toward her and hopes they are about to leave. Instead, Aunt Nell sits down beside Mabel. "The gentleman asked that you come hold his wife's hand. She wants to hold the hand of a child while she goes to heaven. Her children are too upset to see their mother. Preacherman says that it would be too hard for them. Can you do that?"

"No'm, I don't want to hold her hand—I want to go be with Grandpa and Uncle Sam. I don't like it here," whispers Mabel.

"We've just wrapped her up to her waist. Mabel, you need to do this. You need to make this woman's final earthly wish come true. You don't have to look at her—she won't even see your face. You can just stand behind her," says Aunt Nell. "I think she's so near death that she'll think you're one of her children. Do this for her; God will bless you."

"I don't need no blessing, Aunt Nell," insists Mabel. "You told me that it would be a blessing to just come here with you." *I wish she'd quit staring at me so hard. Her eyes look mad. She's so close that she's breathing on my neck.* Aunt Nell doesn't move her arm from Mabel's shoulders. She stubbornly waits in silence for Mabel to give her the answer she wants. Mabel's mouth quivers as she answers her aunt. "I reckon I'll do it, but I don't want to. My mama and papa wouldn't make me do this."

Mabel gets up and reluctantly walks beside Aunt Nell to the cot. She stands at the top of the bed, just behind the lady's head. Preacherman takes the lady's lifeless hand, pulls it up over her head, and nods for Mabel to hold on. Mabel's hand trembles in fear as she feels the coldness of the hand. Preacherman begins to pray while her husband spills out his sorrow. Mabel feels tears coming to her eyes as she thinks about the children under the porch. Aunt Nell finally reaches for the lady's hand and bends her arm forward so that it can rest on her chest. They finish wrapping the shroud up her body. Trying to get rid of the feel of the lady's hand, Mabel rubs her own hand against her dress as she walks back to the edge of the porch and sits down.

"Take my hand, Mabel; we can go back home now," says Aunt Nell. After they walk away from the steps, Mabel looks back and sees the children run to their daddy. Mabel and Aunt Nell don't say a word until they get to the other side of the downed tree. "Now, that wasn't so bad, was it Mabel? You handled that very well." Mabel doesn't answer her aunt. "You be certain to wash your hands with soap when we get to the house. We don't know what she died from, do we?"

Not long after they get back to the farm, Grandma calls them to dinner. As they pass the bowls of vegetables around, Grandpa and Uncle Sam talk about what they need to do before they plow the fields. Uncle Sam asks Aunt Nell how she likes the shroud business. She says that she likes being able to help people in need. Mabel keeps her eyes focused on her food. "What was it like for you, Mabel?" says Uncle Sam.

Afraid that she's about to cry, Mabel keeps her eyes down. "I don't like it at all and I'm never gonna help Aunt Nell with her shroud business again." Silence falls over the room as they all look at Mabel. "She made me hold that dying lady's hand. Aunt Nell kept telling me that it would be a blessing, but I told her I didn't need any more blessings," says Mabel in a near-whisper.

Everyone remains silent. "Nell, you mean to tell me that you made this child hold that sick woman's hand?" asks Grandma. Grandma's eyes narrow as she watches Aunt Nell squirming in her chair. "Answer me, Nell. Did you do that?"

"Yessum, I did." Aunt Nell looks from face to face and leans back in her chair. "The woman requested that one of her own children hold her hand, but preacherman said that it would be too hard for them. I volunteered Mabel's service."

Uncle Sam shakes his head in disbelief. "I can't believe you made Mabel do that, Nell. I'm a grown man and I wouldn't have wanted to hold her hand." Uncle Sam scoots his chair away from the table. "You should be ashamed of yourself for putting a child in that position. Evidently, the preacher knew it would be too hard on a child, but you still allowed him to convince you that Mabel could do it. That's horrible."

Aunt Nell hunkers down over her plate with her arms spread wide on the table. She stares at her food and then looks up at Uncle Sam. "Well, dear brother, at least I spend my time helping others. All you know how to do is blacken your face up like a Negro and entertain Yankees." Aunt Nell slides her eyes toward Grandpa to see if he approves of her retort. Grandpa doesn't react.

"I'm going outside," says Uncle Sam. He walks to the door, turns and says, "I'm glad your preacherman didn't suggest that Mabel be the one to wrap her body. You would've made her do that too." He looks over toward Mabel and smiles. "Come take a walk with me, princess."

Mabel feels the tension in the room and looks toward Grandma for her approval to get up from the table. Grandma, peering over her glasses at Mabel, nods her head, giving her permission to be excused.

Trying to go unnoticed, Mabel quietly scoots her chair back and looks over at Grandpa. The silence makes Mabel feel awkward.

With a scowl on his face, Grandpa points his finger at Aunt Nell. "You need to watch what you do in the name of religion, Nell. You're acting like a fanatic when you shame a child into doing something like that. I totally agree with what Sam said."

Grandma gets up from the table. "Nell, don't you ever let me hear of you doing something like that again with a grandchild of mine—or with any child. Tom and Lizbeth provide for their family and their needs. They don't want some busybody like you trying to teach their children right from wrong. In fact, I think you're the one that needs to learn a thing or two about being responsible to your family. You should have told that preacher to go jump in the river," says Grandma. "He's not God."

Aunt Nell stares at the folded napkin in her lap. Mabel stands frozen in place and feels a tinge of pity for Aunt Nell. "Come on, Mabel, let's go walk up our beautiful country lane," says Uncle Sam. Mabel walks toward his outstretched hand and takes hold of it. *Aunt Nell's in bad trouble—I know she's not ever gonna make me another dress.* As Mabel and her uncle walk out the front door and down the steps, a deep sense of relief comes over her.

Walking toward the gate, Uncle Sam and Mabel don't say a word. When they reach the road, the two of them turn to the right and walk up the center of the dusty lane. "There's a place I like to sit on the fence, Mabel. I want us to go there and take in the beauty that surrounds us." Still holding hands, Uncle Sam gently begins swinging her hand and echoes the singing of the birds with his whistle. "Here's my favorite spot. Let me lift you up on this top railing beside me."

"Is this one of your secret places, Uncle Sam?"

"Yes, it is, my princess. I come out to this spot several times a week. I like to survey the land from here—all the flowers and trees. Do you like it?"

"Yessir, it's very pretty." Mabel maneuvers her toes behind the second railing, discovering that she can brace her feet and lean back a bit. "Uncle Sam, do you reckon Aunt Nell's a member of the Klan?"

Uncle Sam lets out a roaring laugh. He hops down from the railing and looks Mabel in the eyes. "That's about the funniest thing I've ever heard, Mabel. I can't imagine Nell riding horseback, all dressed in white, and carrying a torch. My goodness, she can barely stay in a wagon. What in the world ever made you come up with a question like that?"

"Well, she talks like she doesn't like coloreds at all. Josie says that the Klan's like that—she told me about them."

"Josie's telling you the truth, but your Aunt Nell doesn't dislike coloreds—she was just trying to change the subject to me. Nell always brings my vaudeville days up when she's trying to get on your grandpa's good side. I assure you that your Aunt Nell isn't a member of the Klan," says Uncle Sam. He laughs again and hops back up on the railing.

"When you put that black stuff on your face, does it make you feel like you're a colored?"

Uncle Sam rests his elbows on his knees and looks across the road. "That's just makeup, Mabel. It's what we use in show business to change our appearance. It makes me look like I'm a colored man, but it doesn't change who I really am. You see that bird over there in the tree?"

"Yessir, I see it," says Mabel.

"Well, if we went to the barn and made us some wings and put them on, would that make us birds?" Uncle Sam slides down to the ground once again. He holds his arms out like he's spreading his wings and proceeds to pace back and forth like a bird in front of Mabel. She throws her head back and laughs. "You see, Mabel, I'm just an actor playing a role. Putting black on my face doesn't make me colored, just like flapping my arms doesn't make me a bird. Anyone can pretend to be anything they want to be—but it doesn't make it real. It's all make believe."

Uncle Sam places his hands on Mabel's waist and swings her down to the ground. "I'm glad it's just pretend, Uncle Sam. I's afraid you might be in the Klan too," says Mabel.

While laughing, Uncle Sam takes her hand and leads her back toward the house. "You sure know how to make me laugh, Mabel. Yes ma'am, you are one funny girl."

Right after they enter the gate, Uncle Sam looks down at her and smiles. "Don't you worry. No one in our family has ever been a member of the Klan. To my knowledge, I don't even know a member of the Klan. They like to keep who they are a secret, you know. I always figured that they're ashamed of themselves—why else would who they are be such a secret? Daddy raised me to know if you can't say something to a man's face, then it doesn't need to be said."

Mabel feels relieved to know that Aunt Nell and Uncle Sam aren't in the Klan. Satisfied with his explanation, Mabel puts those worries out of her mind.

"When we go inside, Mabel, don't say anything else about the shroud. That's over and done. I'm sure Grandpa and Grandma got it all cleared up," says Uncle Sam. "Besides that, my princess, I believe you and Grandpa will be going to the mill in the morning." They smile at each other and continue toward the house.

Chapter 8

MABEL WAKES UP EXCITED ABOUT HER trip to the gristmill with Grandpa. She looks out the window and sees that the sun is shining brightly. *Grandpa and me are gonna have fun today. I like to go to the gristmill with him. The store's bigger than our stores in Shoal Crossing. I like the way they have the big glass cases with all the things to buy. Grandpa lets me go out by the pond and watch the waterwheel turn. This is my last day on the farm. Grandpa's taking me back tomorrow. He says that we're gonna stop by the Watson farm on the way to Shoal Crossing.*

The fragrance of Grandma's cooking draws Mabel downstairs. Grandpa and Uncle Sam are busily gathering things for the cart. *Grandma says that we're taking some of her butter and eggs to barter at the store.*

"Grab you a ham-and-biscuit, Mabel, because your Grandpa's about ready to go," says Grandma. "He loves to go to the mill more than any soul I've ever seen." Mabel walks over and kisses Grandma on the cheek. "You look to be about as excited as your grandpa, little lady." Mabel takes a bite out of her biscuit. "You'd better go on out there and get in the cart. He might go off and leave you."

"Bye, Grandma. I love you. We'll be back this afternoon," says Mabel. She walks out to the back steps.

"Good morning, princess," says Uncle Sam. "Come here and let me give you a boost up on the cart step." Uncle Sam sneaks a bite of her biscuit as she steps into the cart. "Why, thank you, madam. You're so kind to share your breakfast." They both laugh at his antics. Mabel watches as Uncle Sam places the last box of corn in the wagon. "Looks like you're ready for the road, Daddy."

Grandpa heaves himself into the cart, picks up the reins, and clicks his tongue. Smoke begins to move forward. "Reckon we'll be back directly, Son. Giddy up there, Smoke." Mabel turns and watches Uncle Sam walk up the back steps. "You got ready in a hurry, Mabel. We're sure to beat most of the others to the mill," says Grandpa. Mabel enjoys Smoke's familiar *clip clop* through the gravel. "Skedaddle down and open the gate, please ma'am." Mabel rushes to the gate and swings it open for Grandpa. He pulls just beyond the opening and waits for her. "You've earned the right to take these reins up the country lane," says Grandpa. "Just let me get us turned up the road."

Mabel scoots closer to Grandpa as he passes her the reins. Her heart pounds as she tries to sound like Grandpa. "Giddy up there, Smoke." Grandpa rolls his head back and laughs. "This is fun, Grandpa. I's hoping you'd let me hold the reins. It's scary though." Smoke stays in the middle of the lane and paces herself for Mabel until they reach the main road. Mabel passes the reins over to Grandpa. "This is just about the best place in the whole wide world, Grandpa." Mabel nibbles on her biscuit until she eyes the general store and mill in the distance. The morning's cool breeze gently tousles her hair as she shoves the last bite of biscuit into her mouth.

Several men sit on straight-back chairs on the store's front porch. They've hooked their straw hats on the chair backs, but one man holds his hat by the brim with both hands and turns it as if he's feeling its smoothness. Grandpa guides Smoke up to the hitch. "Whoa. Top of the morning, gentlemen," says Grandpa. Acknowledging his greeting, they nod. "Mabel, you reckon you can carry one of the corn boxes? It's gonna take several trips to get our supplies inside the store."

"Yessir, I can carry it." Mabel stands behind Grandpa as he gets the egg basket from the cart. Two men from the porch come down the steps.

"Let us lend you a hand there, Mr. Hood. Looks like you've got more than you and the little lady can handle."

"Much obliged, gentlemen. She's the best helper around these parts."

With the assistance of the two men, they get the eggs, butter, and corn into the store. The store appears to be much larger than Mabel remembers. Work clothes, boots, shoes, small farm implements, lumber, boxed and bagged staples for cooking, nails, bolts of cloth, and packaged food items sit on shelves that line the gigantic walls.

An aproned clerk stands on a ladder that almost reaches the high ceiling. Mabel is fascinated by the way he rolls himself along the shelves to fill customers' orders. The sparkling clean glass cases contain a menagerie of items including eyeglasses, thimbles, coin purses, folding hand fans, boxes of spooled thread, and a wide variety of candy. "You see anything that catches your eye, Mabel?" asks Grandpa.

"This store has even more things than the stores in Florence." Mabel points to her favorite things as Grandpa watches her hand move about. "I really like that red leather coin purse and the peppermint sticks, Grandpa," says Mabel. She looks up at him. "I haven't had any peppermint candy since Christmas. Mama'd like one of the hand fans. She fans all the time. Do you see anything for Grandma?"

"Oh, your grandma would be happy to get one of those bolts of material up there on the shelf." Mabel looks at the colorful stacks of cloth. "I really like that shiny light blue color to match her pretty eyes," says Grandpa. "Reckon Nell could make her a fine skirt out of that."

"Hello, Mr. Hood," greets the clerk from behind the counter. He seems to be studying Grandpa's face as he peers over his wire-rimmed glasses. His wrinkled face has no expression, but his bright eyes dart about as customers shop. The clerk's hair is oil-slicked to his balding head. Mabel notices the dark stains under his long fingernails as he loops his thumbs through the heavy white straps that hold up his apron bib. "How can we help you today, Mr. Hood?"

"Well, the wife sent this butter and these eggs to barter for some store items. I've got three boxes of corn that need to be ground because we're running short on cornmeal at home. Can't hardly make it without my cornmeal dumplings, you know? I'm hoping that the trade items will offset the cost of the mill," says Grandpa. He pushes the butter toward the clerk, followed by dozens of eggs. "The wife and daughter have been cleaning these eggs for a couple of days; shined them too with a bit of lard. I think they'll sell real well for you."

"Looks to me like you've got enough here to do some business, Mr. Hood," says the clerk. "Folks will buy those eggs and butter, especially when I tell them that they're from y'all's farm. You might even have some credit left over so you can make some additional purchases."

Mabel reaches up and tugs on Grandpa's shirtsleeve. "May I go out to the pond now, Grandpa?"

"Okay, Mabel, but you make certain you don't get too close to the waterwheel."

"Yessir." Mabel pushes her hands into her overall pockets and walks to the screen door. She leans against the door and listens to the slow screech of the spring resisting her weight. Going down the steps, she notices several more wagons loaded for the mill. As she goes around the corner of the store, she can hear the trickling of the water as it falls from the wheel to the pond. She circles the pond and gets as close to the wheel as she can. The morning sun slides through the tree branches and hits the water. The reflections of the store, trees, and wheel in the water captivate her. She stares at all the colors.

"Ain't your name Mabel?"

Mabel whirls around and looks into a familiar face. "Yes, I'm Mabel." She searches the face and recognizes Ruth Watson. Her strawberry-blonde pigtails touch the tops of her shoulders. Ruth pushes both of her hands into her pockets and curls her dusty toes under as she stares back at Mabel.

"Do you remember me? I'm Ruth Watson. You and your grandpa spent the night at our house during the storm last week," she says. Ruth looks down at her feet as a tinge of blush covers her freckled face.

"I never had any idea that you'd be out in these parts because it's so far from your house," says Mabel. "Your hair's in pigtails today. You look different than you looked at your house. Did you come out here with your paw?"

"Nope, Maw and me had to come get some flour," says Ruth. "Maw's scared to drive the wagon into Florence, so we just come out here." Ruth looks at the waterwheel. "I like the sound of the water splashing on that wheel, don't you?"

"I sure do like it. I could hardly wait to come out here by the water. Grandpa's in the store. I hope he sees your maw."

Mabel and Ruth walk over to a tree and sit down under its shade. They both seem hypnotized by the wheel gently churning the water to the pond. "Maw was real embarrassed when Paw brought y'all into the house because her gums have been sore and she can't wear her teeth most days." Mabel shifts her eyes from the pond to Ruth. "She says them teeth hurt her mouth real bad." Ruth tells Mabel that her paw doesn't care about such things, but that her maw does. "Maw says that it's important how a lady looks after herself."

Picking up a stick, Mabel brushes through the dirt. "I have two brothers and a sister," says Mabel. "Brother is a baby, but my older brother and sister go to school." Ruth rests her chin on her bent knee. "How do you like the overalls my uncle gave me?" says Mabel.

"Yep, I like them. I knew they's brand-new because they're still dark," says Ruth. "None of us go to school. The only time we go is when the principal pays us a visit and tells Maw to send us. We go for a few days and then don't go back until he visits again."

Ruth stands up and rubs her toes through the dirt. "Maw says she's tired of being poor. She says that Paw needs to stop his drinking and take care of his family." Mabel sees the sadness in Ruth's face as she talks about her family. "We're always afraid when he goes off for the most part of a week. We ain't got nobody to protect us. Maw cries most every day."

Mabel gets up and the two girls begin walking back around the pond toward the store. Trying to take away some of Ruth's sadness, Mabel changes the subject. "Grandpa and me are gonna bring your family some presents for being so nice to us during the storm. You're gonna get something very special, Ruth. You wait and see," says Mabel. Ruth's shy smile stretches across her face. "Grandpa's taking me to Shoal Crossing tomorrow, so we'll stop by your house then."

"I ain't never had nobody give me a real present," says Ruth. "Maw says that even Santy Claus runs out of toys before he gets to our house. I reckon it's 'cause we live in the country. I did see Santy once in Florence."

Looking across the front of the store, Mabel sees Grandpa and Mrs. Watson talking as he's loading a big sack of flour in the back of her wagon. "There's Grandpa with your mother. Guess it's time to go back to the farm for both of us," says Mabel. "I likc having you for a friend, Ruth." The girls walk over to the wagon.

"Glad to see you two girls had time to play out by the pond," says Grandpa. "Mabel, we're loaded up and ready to go."

"Yessir. Hello, Mrs. Watson. It's nice to see you again." *I hope she can't tell that Ruth told me about her sore mouth and false teeth.*

"Nice to see you, Mabel. I'm glad you and Ruth had some time together. Your grandpa tells me that y'all will be stopping by the house tomorrow. We'll be looking for the two of you," says Mrs. Watson.

Mabel searches Mrs. Watson's face and sees a gentle smile—along with her false teeth. *She's not curling her lips and licking like she did at her farm. Mrs. Watson's really a pretty lady. She's got her hair fixed back and knotted in a bun. Mrs. Watson could fit right into Mama's church group.* "Is there something wrong, Mabel?"

"No'm, Mrs. Watson. I's just looking at your teeth. I mean to say that you look different than you did that night Grandpa and me stopped at your farm." Mrs. Watson puts her hand over her mouth and lets out a cackle. "You look pretty, Mrs. Watson." Ruth moves closer to her mother's side and giggles with her.

"We have to get back, Mrs. Watson," says Grandpa. He tips his hat. "You ladies have a safe trip back to the farm." He tips his hat once more and takes Mabel's hand. She waves good-bye to Ruth as they walk away.

After they sit down in the cart, Grandpa picks up his whip and taps Smoke on her haunches. "Shoo-wee, Mabel, I about started laughing in that lady's face when you got so bumfuzzled about her teeth." Grandpa puts his whip back down and starts laughing. "You got your tongue tied around your eyetooth and couldn't see what you's saying." They both turn red-faced from laughter. "Seriously, Mrs. Watson does look different with those teeth. I think she caught me looking at them in the store," says Grandpa. "I think you and me better leave folks and their teeth alone."

"I think so too, Grandpa." Their laughter wafts through the trees.

"We got us some fine trades for your grandma's butter and eggs," says Grandpa. "He'll sell those eggs before week's end and her butter won't last even that long." Mabel's mind wanders back to Ruth and her sadness about her daddy. Grandpa adds that he got an excellent trade for the blue cloth for Grandma. "Reach under your seat, Mabel; I put some things down there for you."

Mabel reaches underneath the cart seat and pulls out a brown sack with a big peppermint stick peeking out. "There's something else for you." She reaches down again and pulls out another sack. When Mabel looks inside, she can't believe what she sees. She slides her hand into the sack and pulls out the beautiful red leather coin purse with a golden clasp.

"Oh, Grandpa, thank you, thank you, thank you. I've never had a brand-new coin purse of my very own." She kisses him on his cheek. "Plus that's the biggest peppermint stick I've ever seen."

"Well, you've got a coin purse now, Mabel. You've done a lot of work out on the farm. I always say that a job well done deserves a good turn," says Grandpa. "Did you see the penny I put in there? It's bad luck to give someone a coin purse without putting money in it."

"Yessir. Now I have five whole pennies."

"I didn't buy all I could because I gave Mrs. Watson our leftover balance to buy some staples for her family. It wasn't much, but it seems like they're having just as much trouble as I suspected," says Grandpa. "We'll take them a few more supplies when we go that way tomorrow."

Wednesday morning, Mabel feels torn between wanting to stay at the farm and wanting to go home. *I'm gonna miss Grandpa, Grandma, Uncle Sam, and even Aunt Nell; but I can't wait to see Mama, Papa, Bubba, Sister, Brother, Josie, and Drella.* Mabel's dilemma causes her to let out a deep sigh. It'll be fun to take Ruth her new dress. I like Mrs. Watson too. Wonder what all Grandma and Aunt Nell have fixed up for us to take to the Watson farm. After Mabel makes up her bed, she goes downstairs where everyone seems busy.

"What all are we taking to the Watson family, Grandma?" asks Mabel.

"We're sending them some fresh cornmeal, salt, some ham hocks, ham slices, and bacon. We've already got it loaded in the cart for you and your grandpa, Mabel."

When Aunt Nell complains under her breath about going overboard with our gifts, Grandpa says, "Tis far better to bless the living with gifts than the dead." Aunt Nell continues to help, but doesn't say another word.

As Mabel walks to the cart, Grandma bends down for a hug. Aunt Nell kisses Mabel's forehead, and Uncle Sam lifts her up in his arms. "Next time I see you, I bet I won't be able to pick you up. I think you've grown some since you came here last week. It's been swell having you with us, my princess. You come back any time you desire." Tears begin to roll down Mabel's cheeks as she puts her arms around his neck. Reaching for a deep breath, she takes in Uncle Sam's scented aftershave. "No tears, my dear. You just watch out for all the caterpillars in the world." While they all laugh, he stands her up on the floorboard of the cart.

"I'll be back by dinnertime tomorrow. Good Lord willing and the creeks don't rise. Y'all take care of everything and tend to the animals," says Grandpa. He pulls the reins and Smoke slowly turns toward the gate. Mabel twists around and hops up on her knees in the seat; she waves good-bye until they are out of sight.

After opening and closing the gate, Mabel gets back into the cart. Grandpa guides Smoke to the right and holds her to a slow pace toward the crossroad. Sitting in silence, Mabel takes in the beauty of the farm, the trees, and the wildflowers once again. "I sure do love this land, Mabel," says Grandpa. "It's so peaceful out here; I hope you'll always remember what fun we've had on the farm."

"I won't ever forget, Grandpa. I promise, I won't forget," says Mabel.

Turning left onto the main road, they pass the gristmill and the church. "It won't take us long to get to the Watson house. The roads will allow Smoke to keep a good, steady speed." Mabel watches Smoke's tail switch at the flies. "I reckon we'll get to Shoal Crossing just before suppertime. Your mama and papa will be glad to see you," says Grandpa.

Chapter 9

As Grandpa and Mabel sit side by side in the cart, they both search beyond the tree line for the Watson farm. "I think I see the Watson place just a bit ahead, Mabel." Without the pouring rain, everything looks different to them in the light of day. "Yep, this is it. I see their name scribbled on that old mailbox. Everything looks awfully run down." The mailbox appears to be on the brink of teetering over and the fence leans in waves of disrepair. "Early Watson ought to be ashamed of himself for letting this place go like he has," says Grandpa.

Sweeping across the Watson's farm with her eyes, Mabel doesn't see a soul in sight. *I wonder where Ruth and her maw are today. I don't see any of her brothers or her paw.* Grandpa steers Smoke to stand in front of the porch railing. Then he steps down from the cart and walks up on the porch, looking around for a sign of life. "Hello, Watson!" calls out Grandpa as he knocks on the door. He stands back and waits for a response. Mrs. Watson opens the door and peeks out at Grandpa. "Hello, Mrs. Watson. Mabel and I brought some things by for your family."

"Why, my goodness, Mr. Hood, we sure do appreciate that," says Mrs. Watson with a grateful smile. "You gave us some supplies yesterday—that was more than enough." Ruth steps out on the porch behind her mother. Mrs. Watson adds hesitantly, "Early's out to the barn—he's been drunk since late yesterday."

"Well, there isn't any need for us to see him. Let me just hand these goods to you and you can take them into the house," says Grandpa. "Mabel, hand me those things we fixed for the Watsons, please." Mabel gets on her knees and reaches behind the seat so she can pass each package to Grandpa as he holds out his hand for the next one. As he hands each package to Mrs. Watson, he tells her what's inside.

"Grandpa, may I give Ruth her special present?" asks Mabel with a pleading sound in her voice. Grandpa nods his head and turns to hand Mrs. Watson the final package. "Ruth, come over here to the steps so you can open your present." Mrs. Watson takes the family's gifts inside the house. Ruth smiles when Mabel waves a special package in the air toward her.

"I changed my mind," says Grandpa. "I think I'll take the wagon out to the barn to see Mr. Watson for a few minutes. Mabel, you and Ruth stay here on the steps until I get back—won't be gone long."

The two girls, both in overalls, sit down on the top step. Ruth takes the package from Mabel and places it on her lap. "Maw says we're gonna leave the farm if Paw don't straighten up." Mabel, feeling Ruth's sorrow, puts her arm around her friend's shoulder and pats her repeatedly. Tears roll down Ruth's cheeks and dot the butcher paper as she fidgets with the string bow.

"Maybe things will get better and y'all won't have to leave," says Mabel. Ruth turns her red eyes toward Mabel and forces a quivering smile as she wipes her nose on her sleeve.

"Maw wants us to have a nice farm; she wants Paw to work with the boys to clean it up. She says that we've got enough land to plant our own food. There'd be plenty left over to sell at market in Florence. Paw keeps promising her, but he ain't done nothing yet," says Ruth. "Maw says that Paw's gonna drink hisself to death. I'm scared, Mabel."

"Mama and Papa say that all we can do is pray for people like your paw." Mabel gets up and walks down to the bottom step. With her elbows gently resting on her present, Ruth looks down into Mabel's eyes. "I know how to pray for your paw if you want me to," says Mabel. "Mama says that prayers work because God can fix everything."

"Okay, tell me what to do," says Ruth. "I ain't ever prayed much—'cept with Maw ever now 'n then."

Mabel goes back up the steps and sits down beside Ruth. She reaches over and holds Ruth's hand. "First, I gotta hold your hand," says Mabel.

"Why've you gotta hold my hand?" asks Ruth.

"I don't know why, but Mama always holds my hand when she prays—so that's what we'll do. We wanna do this right. We've got to bow our heads and close our eyes real tight, like this." Mabel turns her head toward Ruth and squeezes her eyes shut. Ruth copies Mabel's scrunched-up face. Mabel opens her eyes and looks at Ruth. "That's right."

"I can do all those things, but it don't sound like what Maw does," says Ruth.

"Now, you have to hold my hand, keep your head bowed, and scrunch your eyes shut until I give you the signal that you can open your eyes," says Mabel.

"What's the signal?" asks Ruth.

"As soon as I say 'Amen' you can let go of my hand, raise your head, and open your eyes. It'll be all over then," says Mabel. "When you're praying, 'Amen' means the end."

"Okay," says Ruth. She grasps Mabel's hand, bows her head, and tightly closes her eyes. Mabel does the same.

"I'll say the prayer and you just listen. That's how you're supposed to talk to God. Mama and me pray every night before we go to bed." Since Mabel has never prayed in the company of someone outside of her family, she feels her hand trembling a bit. She takes a deep breath.

"Dear God, please make Mr. Watson mind Mrs. Watson. Amen." They both lift their heads and stare out toward the road. "Mama says that all you have to do is wait and see how God works out your prayer," says Mabel.

"I hope it works on Paw," says Ruth. She pulls the string to untie the bow around her present. After turning the present over, Ruth gently unfolds the triangles that Aunt Nell painstakingly creased to meet in the middle. Ruth's hands shake as she opens the paper. When she sees the dress, she doesn't say a word—her face tells Mabel how beautiful she thinks the dress is. Ruth runs the palm of her hand over the soft material and then she holds it up to her cheek. "Mabel, I ain't never had a dress. Is this one of yours that you're giving me?" says Ruth.

"No, it's made especially for you. It's not a hand-me-down. Aunt Nell made it just like my Easter dress," says Mabel. Ruth stands, holds the dress up, and rests it on her thin body. She kicks out one leg and smiles. "You sure do look pretty with that dress. It makes your eyes look bluer than the sky."

"I'll keep it forever to remind me of you, Mabel."

Mrs. Watson steps out onto the porch. "What is that you have, Ruth?"

"It's a dress just like Mabel's. Her aunt made it specially for me. Ain't it pretty, Maw?"

"Me-oh-my, it sure is a pretty thing. We'll have to save it for you to wear to church one day soon," says Mrs. Watson. "That's such a pretty color for you, Ruth. Your aunt sure can make pretty things."

"Yessum, Mama says that Aunt Nell's a very good seamstress," says Mabel proudly. "She makes shrouds for dead people too."

Mrs. Watson laughs. "Well, I sure don't want her making me one of them no time soon." Mrs. Watson looks over toward the barn. "Here comes Mr. Hood, Mabel. I reckon he's ready for y'all to get back on the road."

Mabel stands up and waves at Grandpa. He nods his head at Mabel, but she senses that he's not in a very good mood. Grandpa pulls the cart up to the steps. "Early Watson sure has been drinking him some moonshine of some sort, Mrs. Watson. I told him the law's gonna get after him," says Grandpa.

"I appreciate you checking on him, Mr. Hood. He goes somewhere up in them woods back yonder and comes back in a fix. Does it about once a week," says Mrs. Watson. "He generally sleeps it off—lessen he brings back a bottle. That's when he stays out to the barn—don't eat or nothing. Oh well, we sure do thank y'all for the food, Mr. Hood. It's a lifesaver for me and the kids. You've answered my prayers to the good Lord."

"Oh, that's the least we can do for your hospitality," says Grandpa. "Y'all saved our lives during that storm. Hop in the cart, Mabel. We've got to get on over to Shoal Crossing."

Mabel walks around to the other side of the cart. She boosts herself up on the step and sits down beside Grandpa. Leaning forward, she peeks around his big body. "Bye, Mrs. Watson. Bye, Ruth," says Mabel. They both smile at Mabel and wave good-bye.

"We'll keep your family in our prayers," says Grandpa.

"Thank you, Mr. Hood. I figure we need all the prayers we can get," says Mrs. Watson.

Grandpa touches the brim of his hat to acknowledge Mrs. Watson's gratitude. He pulls to the right on the reins. Smoke begins trudging toward the road. Mabel looks back at Ruth and they wave until they can no longer see one another. After they cross back over the swale and turn to the right onto the dusty road, Grandpa lets out a sigh and leans back against the seat. Mabel senses the need to remain silent. She sees that Grandpa is in deep thought. In a few minutes, he places his left foot up on the footboard and lets out another sigh.

Tugging at the brim of his hat, Grandpa breaks his silence. "Yessum, I sure found Early Watson sound asleep out there in that barn. I shook him awake, but his eyes were crossed from the moonshine; he didn't make no sense a'tall. Told me he likes to take naps in the barn," says Grandpa. "I never heard such foolishness."

"Papa doesn't ever sleep in the barn," says Mabel.

"No sane man does. Unless, of course, he's got a sick animal," says Grandpa. "I told Watson that he needs to stop his drinking and take care of his family. He told me he's gonna quit because she's gonna take the kids and move over to Florence or Memphis."

"Are you mad, Grandpa?"

"Dogs go mad, Mabel, not people," answers Grandpa almost curtly. "I reckon the right word is angry or maybe disappointed in a grown man. No matter what happens in our lives, there's always something to learn. We can always learn how to be better people—sometimes that includes what *not* to allow into our lives."

"I'm sorry he upset you, Grandpa. You's just trying to help him and his family."

"We're all supposed to help each other, but some folks don't have enough sense to accept it. His wife and children will be better off away from him. Don't you fret over Ruth. Her mother's gonna take care of her kids. Mothers are like that—they'll always protect their young—even if it's from their own daddy."

"I've never seen a drunk man, Grandpa," says Mabel.

"We're in prohibition. It's against the law in the state of Alabama to make, sell, or buy whisky. Watson is either making whisky or buying it from a bootlegger. If he don't watch his step, he'll end up in jail."

Riding along the rutted road, Mabel watches the puffs of red dust coming from Smoke's hooves and wonders why Grandpa allows Early Watson to bother him so much. Without looking, she senses that he is still fuming from finding him drunk in the barn. Knowing not to question him, Mabel thinks about Ruth. *Grandpa's right; Ruth will be better off away from the farm. She's never even had a dress. Maybe she'll start going to school. I hope I never have to move away from Papa. I hope that I'll see Ruth again someday.* When Mabel notices Grandpa's shoulders relax, she feels safe to talk. "Have you ever been drunk like Early Watson, Grandpa?"

"No indeed, I've never done that." Grandpa pushes himself up higher in the seat and looks past Mabel. "How would you like to hear a story about my paw and maw?" Grandpa tells her that it's a story he rarely tells. Mabel turns sideways in the seat to listen.

"My paw, a farmer, was as immoral as they came. He was likeable enough, but most of the time he was self-centered and mean as the dickens. Our family lived up in Tennessee, not far from the Alabama state line. Maw always seemed sickly and had to take to the bed for days on end. When she'd get down, Paw'd leave our farm and carouse all over Bledsoe County. He'd eventually come home, but he'd be staggering drunk from all his shenanigans." Grandpa said that he watched him do that all of his life. "The older I got, the more I knew that I didn't want to be anything like him. Like I said earlier, sometimes we learn how *not* to act from the people in our lives. He use to act just like Mr. Watson. My maw didn't have the strength to leave him, but one day I did."

"Where'd you go?" Mabel asks quickly.

"I told him that I was leaving to join the Confederates. He gave me an old horse and told me not to ever come back. I never saw either of my parents again."

"Do you think they still live in Tennessee?"

"No, they don't. I got word that they're both dead. Maw died not long after I left. Sometime later, Paw ended up dying in or near an old creek—probably drunk. I never have had any desire to go back up there. Everything and everybody I care about is right around these parts."

"That's a good story, Grandpa, but it's sad. I reckon Ruth will be glad to get away from her paw, just like you. Maybe he'll start minding Mrs. Watson." *Wish I could tell Grandpa about me and Ruth's prayer, but Mama says that you never tell your prayers. She says they're a secret between you and God. Mama says that telling your prayers is like bragging.*

Grandpa nods in agreement. "It ain't no way to live for any family. Maybe he'll straighten up. I think he knows his wife isn't gonna take much more." Mabel turns back around in the seat, puts her hands in her pockets, and feels better about Ruth.

After they turn left onto the main road toward Shoal Crossing, Grandpa starts mumbling about having to cross the bridge again. "The only thing I don't like about this trip is that bridge. I don't necessarily trust something made by men—especially when I'm not so sure that they know what they're doing."

"Papa says that the Corps of Engineers is working hard to fix all the flooding problems around here. He says it'll take a long time," says Mabel.

"If anyone can solve it, the government can. Nevertheless, I think folks could just ford the creek like we did when the bridge was out. I don't trust bridges built so high up over water," says Grandpa. "I don't care how tall they build a bridge over Shoal Creek, that water will wear it down sooner or later."

"Papa said that crossing the creek tore up too many wagons. He said that cars sure can't get across without a bridge. When the water's up, he said that nothing can ford it." Grandpa gazes straight ahead. "I don't like the bridge either, Grandpa, but I never heard of it falling with people on it."

"Well, we're about to see if it's gonna hold for us, Mabel." Smoke doesn't seem to know the difference between the road and the bridge. She continues to bob her head as she plods toward Shoal Crossing. Mabel scoots a little closer to Grandpa. Everywhere she looks, she sees water. "Dad-gum-it-all, somebody's wagon broke down up yonder. Not much telling how long we'll be sitting here now. Yep, sitting right here on this death trap," says Grandpa.

Their eyes follow some men gathering around the collapsed wagon. "He probably lost one of his wheels or possibly the axle broke. Maybe they'll be able to pick the wagon up and move it over. I hope there'll be enough room to let the rest of us get by," says Grandpa. Mabel stretches her neck. She watches intently as the men lift the rear of the wagon and move it aside. Several of them maneuver the horse until it's out of the way.

"Good thing that fella has a light load; they'd never been able to move it like that," says Grandpa. One of the men trots forward and starts unhitching the horse from the wagon. "They're finally using their heads. The horse keeps them from moving the wagon far enough to the side." Most of the men walk back to their own wagons. "Now, we'll see if we can get by the breakdown."

Grandpa leans back to wait for their turn. Every time a wagon pulls out and goes around the breakdown, Smoke eases forward. Finally, Mabel and Grandpa reach the front of the line. "After that oncoming wagon moves past us, we'll go around," says Grandpa.

As the cart moves past the broken-down wagon, Mabel watches the men scurrying about to get the wheel fixed. "Why'd they take the wheel off, Grandpa?"

"Looks like a broken axle to me. I've never had that happen, but know from the ones I've helped fix that it's a mess," says Grandpa.

Mabel feels the final jolt of Smoke pulling the cart over the last board of the bridge. *It won't be long now until I see Mama. I like to go to the farm, but I think home's my favorite place of all. Wonder if Mama and Josie fixed us a good dinner. I can't wait to see Brother. Maybe Grandpa will take me to see Ruth the next time I go out to the farm. I wish she'd wear her dress. I sure hope God liked the way I said the prayer. Mama says if God agrees with your prayer, it will be answered. She says God always knows what's best.*

Chapter 10

THE ROAD TO SHOAL CROSSING RUNS past the town cemetery. As they pass it, Mabel turns her head to look away. Despite her attempts to forget the ordeal with the woman in the woods, her thoughts take her back to that day. *Aunt Nell shouldn't have taken me with her to deliver the shroud. She could've let me just sit on the porch and wait with those other children. I still feel sorry for them. It makes me sad every time I think of it.* Mabel rubs her hand on her thigh to try to rid herself of the memory of the woman's hand.

When Grandpa turns onto Mabel's road, she can see Mama, Bubba, and Sister sitting on the front porch. *They're waiting for Papa to come home from work.* Bubba and Sister run for the barn to help with Smoke and the cart. Mama waves and blows kisses to Mabel and her daddy. Mabel notices that Mama has a white porcelain pan balanced against her hip. *Mama's fixing some beans for cooking.*

By the time they reach the barn, Bubba and Sister stand with the doors wide open. Grandpa guides the cart between them and nods in their direction. "Much obliged there, Bubba. Thank you, Sister." Bubba and Sister flash smiles at Grandpa, but pay little attention to Mabel. "Bubba, hold the harness while we climb down. We need to get Smoke into a stall. I know she must be tired from the long trip," says Grandpa.

"Yessir, Grandpa. I know exactly what to do for her," says Bubba.

Sister walks around to where Mabel is stepping down from the cart. "Did you have fun, Mabel?"

"Uh-huh, Grandpa and Uncle Sam sure know some fun things to do. We went to church and even to the mill. They built an arbor for church. Have you ever seen an arbor?" says Mabel.

Mabel watches Sister's face search for an answer. "No, but we've been getting ready for May Day at school. Mama says that y'all are coming to watch the celebration. I'm gonna get to walk around the pole this year. It's next week." Mabel listens intently as Sister shares the latest news. "Mama says that we're gonna make our baskets again this year for our secret friends."

"You girls take what you can into the house. Bubba and I have got to get Smoke settled and the cart straightened up for me to go back tomorrow," says Grandpa. "We'll bring in the rest."

Mabel and Sister tuck things under their arms and hold what they can in their hands. "Where'd you get those ugly old overalls, Mabel?" asks Sister.

"Uncle Sam bought them for me so I could work on the farm. He said that I could bring this pair home and that he'd get me another pair to wear out there," says Mabel. "They're much better than a dress. You can get a lot more work done in these. I even slept in overalls one night."

"I sure don't want any overalls. Boys wear those to school. Mama's not gonna like those things one bit. Just you wait and see. They're not ladylike."

"Uncle Sam says I look pretty in anything I wear. Besides, my new friend, Ruth, lives on a farm and wears them every single day," declares Mabel. "Aunt Nell made Ruth a dress just like the one I wore on Easter."

"Why'd she make her a dress?"

"Grandpa and me had to stay at their house during the storm last week. We wanted to do something nice for them because they helped us," says Mabel. "Aunt Nell liked my idea of giving Ruth her first dress."

Mabel and Sister walk across the yard toward the back porch, each trying to outpace the other. "I don't care who wears overalls in the country, Mama ain't gonna like them," says Sister. Mabel pulls ahead. *I hope Mama likes my overalls. Sister always thinks she knows everything about what Mama's gonna like.*

"Who's been gathering the eggs while I's gone?" says Mabel.

"I reckon Mama's been doing it. Not me and Bubba," says Sister. "She says that we don't need to be worrying about chores when we have so much homework. You like to do that kind of stuff, Mabel, not me."

"I sure do like to help Mama and Josie," says Mabel. "Josie teaches me how to do lots of things when we're out here. That's why she says I'm gonna be a good lady of the house when I grow up. You don't know how to do anything like a lady of a house."

"Do too," snaps Sister.

"Do not," retorts Mabel.

They reach the back steps and Mama opens the screen door. "Put those things down, Mabel," says Mama. "Come here and let me hug my girl. I've missed you so much." Mabel leans into her mama's ankle-length skirt and wraps her arms around her waist. Mama bends down and kisses the top of Mabel's head. "Where in the world did you get those nice overalls?"

"Uncle Sam bought them for me." Remembering her uncle, a smile breaks across Mabel's face. "He wanted me to have them for my work clothes."

"You're not gonna let her wear those in Shoal Crossing, are you, Mama?" asks Sister mockingly.

"Why, I don't see why not. Her uncle was very thoughtful to buy them for her. She can wear them around the house and outside to play. But remember Mabel, ladies must wear dresses to church, school, and social functions," says Mama. Mabel looks up into the depths of Mama's brown eyes. *Sister was wrong about my overalls. Since Uncle Sam got them for me, I knew Mama would like them too.*

"Now, Miss Sister, I want you to make several trips and take all those things into the house. Mabel and I are going out to the front porch to wait for your papa." Mabel turns and smiles at Sister, who promptly sticks out her tongue at Mabel. "I saw that, Sister," says Mama. "You need to learn how to act like a lady, with or without overalls. When you finish that, go out and see if you can do any more to help Daddy. Be prompt about it."

Mama rests her hand across Mabel's shoulder as they walk into the kitchen. Mabel takes a deep breath of Mama and Josie's cooking. "That smells like some of your fried chicken. Is that what it is?" Mama walks her over to the stove top and removes a white dish towel draped over the platter of chicken. "Mmmm, that looks so good, Mama."

"Josie went out and killed it this morning. I've never seen a chicken flop around as long as that one. It just didn't want to die," says Mama. "Did you catch a whiff of those biscuits she made?"

"Yessum, it all smells good," says Mabel. "Grandpa's gonna like our supper."

"Josie and I thought y'all would be coming back either today or tomorrow," says Mama. "We both missed you. Did you feel your ears burning? We talked about you every day; only good things were said."

They walk through the dining room, into the hall, and out to the front porch. When Mama reaches her rocker, she sits down.

"Whew, it's been a long, hot day," says Mama. "Josie says we're going to have a hot summer." Mabel sits down in her favorite spot and leans against the corner post while she listens to her mama. "That means we'll have to be finished in the kitchen before noon each day. That stove will make it unbearable. I don't mind though; I prefer the heat over the cold."

Mabel turns from Mama and looks toward the gate. "I think I hear Papa's whistle. He must be on our road." She gets up and runs along the boardwalk to the front gate. Mabel hops up on the two-by-four that goes across the gate and leans over the top to look for Papa. As soon as he comes into sight, she waves. "Papa, I'm home! I'm home, Papa!"

Papa starts smiling and waving long before he gets to the gate. "Well, my goodness, if it's not Miss Mabel." Papa sets down his lunch pail, picks her up, and lifts her over the gate. "You must have grown two feet." He wraps both of his arms around her and kisses her all over her face. "Yes ma'am, you've been missed around this house," says Papa. He puts her down on the boardwalk.

"Can I carry your lunch pail, Papa?"

"You sure can, but it's light as a feather. I ate everything your mama packed into it." He hands Mabel the black pail. "Well, hello there, Mrs. O'Brien. Are you glad our girl came home?"

"Evening, Mr. O'Brien. I don't think I've ever been happier to see her than I was this afternoon," says Mama. "Seems like she's been gone for forty forevers." Papa reaches his rocking chair and sits down. "I know you got your fill of the heat at the foundry today."

"Those furnaces about burned us up. We've got to find a way to get more air in there," says Papa.

Grandpa, Bubba, and Sister walk around the house to the front porch. Papa stands and extends his hand to Grandpa in greeting. "Hello there, Mr. Hood, it's nice to see you again. Mighty proud you two got home safely." Mabel watches as the two men shake hands. *Papa's always proper when he talks to Grandpa. He says it's the way you act when you respect someone.*

"We tried our hardest to get into trouble, Tom, but we couldn't find anything that could keep us down," says Grandpa. *Wonder if Grandpa's gonna tell Mama and Papa about the storm, the Watsons, and the dying woman.* Grandpa interrupts her thoughts when he begins telling them about the storm on the way to the farm.

Grandpa leans his big frame against the post. Mabel sits at the base of the same post. She looks up at him and listens carefully as he describes the storm as one of the worst he'd ever seen. Grandpa tells them that his greatest concern was for Mabel. "That's why I pulled off the road and went to the first house I saw." Everyone listens intently as he explains what it was like going into a stranger's home. Mabel can see every detail as Grandpa shares descriptions of the Watson family, their farm, the meal, the barn, and his thoughts about the situation. He then gives the details of their return to the Watson farm and their trip home.

"That's disgraceful for a man to behave like that," says Mama. "I don't blame her one bit." Mama pats her foot on the floor. "She has to do what's best for her children, but she's married to that man—for better or worse." Papa leans back in his chair and takes in what Mama's saying. "If the good Lord's willing, that man will change and they'll all stay together. God bless them all," says Mama. "It was awfully nice of them to open their home to two strangers—you know they're basically good people."

Grandpa removes his hat and runs his fingers through his wavy hair. "I sure am tired. I have to make that trip back in the morning. Reckon I'll have to go to bed right after supper and get up with the chickens." He walks down to the boardwalk and rests his foot on the bottom step. "There's a heap of work to be done out on the farm."

That night at supper, Papa tells the family that the government is transferring him to Florence to work at the dam. "With the war and all, we've got to get that dam up and running. I'll start off by going over there a few days a week to get things set up—won't go over there full-time until the fall," says Papa.

"Does that mean we're gonna have to move back to Florence?" asks Bubba.

"No, I think we'll just have to wait and see," says Papa. "I'll have to travel a little longer in the mornings and afternoons." He places his napkin on the table. "Building the dam is going to take years, so we might end up back over there. Not for now though."

"You've been expecting that," says Mama. "That's too good of a job to give up these days. Plus, the only thing left to do would be farming or going to fight in the war." Mama starts stacking the dishes in front of her. "The paper's full of news about the war. We're mighty blessed that you even have a job."

"I don't want y'all to worry about any of this, children. Everything's going to remain like it is for a long time," says Papa. "Your mama and I'll see to it that you're well taken care of."

Grandpa gets up from the table, scoots his chair back to its rightful place, and rests his hands in his pockets. "I'm just thankful that the Great War is being fought on foreign soil. This country can't take another war like I fought in," says Grandpa.

"Everything sure seems to be in a mess these days," says Papa. "President Wilson's draft has our men leaving every day to go into military training—plus I've been reading about the influenza. They say that it's getting bad in the military camps. There's nothing the doctors can do for it—folks just seem to be dropping dead when it hits them. We get newsletters about all that's going on every week—they're calling it the Spanish Flu. Folks up north are already wearing face masks. Reckon we will be too. They're already issuing them to some of the government workers."

"Any time you have a bunch of people living in close quarters, there's gonna be sickness," says Grandpa. "The tent city in Florence is prime breeding ground for sickness. It'll be here sooner or later. It ain't gonna just stay up north." Grandpa puts his hands in the small of his back and stretches. "Building that dam will keep you employed for many a year, Tom." Grandpa tells Bubba, Sister, and Mabel that they should be proud that their daddy is helping America through his work in Florence. "And now, folks, I must go get me some rest. Good night and God bless. I'll see you folks on the morrow."

Mabel and Sister sleep on a pallet in the parlor so Grandpa can get a good night's rest in their bedroom. To make their pallet, Mama uses special quilts. She folds them into double thickness to make the pallet softer.

The next morning, Mabel opens her eyes when Mama comes into the parlor and tells Sister that it's time for her to get ready for school. "Mabel, if you want some sorghum biscuits, you need to get dressed too," says Mama.

"Yes ma'am, I want some," says Mabel. "Is Grandpa still here?"

"He's probably way down the road by now. Daddy left at first light," says Mama. "He told me to thank you girls for the use of your room." As Mama bends over to pick up Mabel's overalls from the floor, Mabel notices that her skirt hikes up in the back. "Get up, Mabel. You need to help me fold the quilts. We can't have the parlor in such a mess all day. Sister, I put your school dress out on the bed."

Mabel gets up from the pallet and drags a quilt with her. Mama picks up the opposite end of the quilt. They meet face-to-face as Mabel walks toward her with her end. On the last fold, Mama kisses Mabel's forehead when she reaches her Mama's hands. "I'll put these away, Mabel. You go get dressed," says Mama. When she gets to her bedroom, Mabel quickly puts on her overalls again and then heads to the kitchen. *I hope Mama don't make me put on a dress.*

Mama gets a small plate and glass of milk for Mabel. Trying to sit down without moving anything, Mabel squeezes herself between the table and chair. She breaks open her hot biscuit and feels its warmth. Watching the biscuit absorb the butter, Mabel reaches for the molasses and pours it over the buttered biscuit. Mabel feels Sister's foot nudging her leg under the table. "Mama, didn't you say that you's gonna bring Mabel to the May Day celebration at school?" says Sister. As they wait for Mama's answer, Mabel presses her foot into Sister's leg.

"I think we'll be able to come, especially since you'll be doing the May Pole dance this year," says Mama. "About the only thing that will keep us away is a downpour." *I can't wait to go watch the May Day dance. Everything they do at school looks exciting to me—Sister likes it too. She showed me the dance. All they do is walk around a pole. I could do that.* "Bubba, you and Sister need to get your books and be on your way," says Mama. "We'll talk about May Day later, Sister. You walk with Sister all the way to school, Bubba."

Like a family of ducks, Mama marches them to the front door. Mabel follows Bubba and Sister out to the road. She watches as Bubba pulls slightly ahead of Sister. *Bubba keeps his head down when he walks. He had to put water on his hair this morning to make it lay down. Sister needs to walk faster if she wants to keep up with him. Her rope curls look pretty.* Sister turns and waves at Mabel. "See you after school, Mabel," says Sister. Mabel mirrors her wave, turns, and goes back into the house with Mama. *I wonder if Grandpa stopped by the Watson farm on his way home.*

Mama sits down at the table with her calendar. "Look, Mabel, the first day of May is next Wednesday. We need to start planning our May baskets. We've got to do most of the work because Bubba and Sister are in school." Mama bows her head downward as she lifts her apron up over her head and hangs it on a nail in the pantry. "Yes indeed, we've got to get busy. I'll be right back," says Mama.

Mama likes special days. We always make May baskets. We fill them with apples, oranges, nuts, and candy. Mama says that it's good to do things for others, especially when it's just to be kind. It's a surprise for someone who doesn't usually get surprises. Each of us has a secret friend that we take the baskets to on May Day. Mama interrupts Mabel's thoughts when she comes into the kitchen carrying three shoeboxes. "We're going to start on our May baskets today, Mabel. Go get the bag of crepe paper I left on my bedroom floor," says Mama. "Be quiet about it—don't want you to wake Brother from his nap."

When Mabel brings the sack into the kitchen, Mama is removing the lids from the boxes at the table. "Do you think I can make my own basket this year, Mama?"

"I think that's the very thing for you to do, Mabel," says Mama. "First, we have to make us some glue. Get a cereal bowl from the cabinet and put on one of my aprons." As Mabel puts on her apron, she longs to look at herself in Mama's mirror. "You look just like a lady ready to cook." Their laughter fills the kitchen as Mabel spins around and mocks her mother's walk. "You're a sight, Mabel Reed O'Brien. Get up on your knees in the chair so you can do some stirring."

Mabel watches as Mama measures some flour, puts it in the bowl, and slowly pours some water into the flour. She directs Mabel to use the wooden spoon to stir the mixture. As she begins to mix the concoction, Mama reminds her to make sure that she gets all the lumps out of the flour. Mama begins placing the rolls of crepe paper out on the table. "Is my secret friend going to be Mrs. Riley again this year?" asks Mabel.

"That's exactly who I was thinking of for you. I think she would be disappointed if she didn't get her basket. But remember, you can't tell," says Mama. "That's why it's called 'secret friend.'" Mama lays the sack on the kitchen counter. "Secrets are nice things to have when you want to give someone a happy surprise." As Mabel continues to stir, Mama begins measuring and cutting the crepe paper. "Looks like you've got that glue mixed just perfectly," says Mama.

They decide to work on Mabel's basket first. Mabel selects red, green, and yellow crepe paper. Mama uses a spatula and spreads the glue around the lower part of the box. Mabel chooses the red strip to go on first. The crepe paper soaks up the glue and clings to the box. They alternate the colors until they reach the top of the box. Because the rows of crepe paper overlap, it takes six rows of strips to get to the top. They put Mabel's basket aside so it can dry and begin working on Bubba and Sister's boxes.

"Now that we've finished all three of them, I can get this bowl washed. The baskets will be good and dry by the time we put the treats in. Take them into y'all's bedroom and put them in the corner so they'll be out of the way," says Mama.

Mabel stacks the three boxes on top of each other and walks to her bedroom. She sets them in the corner and stands back to admire their handiwork. *I sure hope Mrs. Riley will like the bright colors I picked for her basket. Sister's is pink and white; it's pretty too. Bubba's is green and blue—his favorite colors. Mama says that Bubba will make the basket handles out of honeysuckle vines. Mama always makes May Day special for us.*

Chapter 11
Reflections

STARING AT THE STILL PICTURE OF the colorful baskets sitting on the floor, I realize that Mabel has stopped the review. Mabel's thoughts begin flowing into my mind. "We made those May Day baskets every year when I was a little girl," says Mabel. She turns her eyes toward me. "I had forgotten how much I enjoyed making them. Despite the fact that we were poor as we could be, Mama always seemed to have us involved in little projects like the baskets. The baskets are one example of how we learned that we could find joy through giving to others."

"Did you take the baskets to your secret friends that May Day?"

Mabel stands and takes a few steps toward the picture of the baskets. "We delivered them on the first day of May. Bubba and Sister dropped theirs off on the way to school; I took mine to Mrs. Riley later in the day. Though I never saw any of Mrs. Riley's children, she talked to me about them. Mama felt sorry for her because she lived alone."

My thoughts flash back to Mabel. "Giving is an important lesson for a child to learn—it doesn't come naturally to all people. Mama seemed to make it a happy time for the three of you."

Mabel turns and looks at me. "Yes, simple kindnesses coming from the heart pay great rewards to the giver—something I always tried to teach you all," says Mabel. She walks back to her chair and sits down. "Do you see why I loved Grandpa so much?"

"Yes, Mabel, it's easy to understand." As I look at the whiteness of the light in the room, my thoughts continue. "For one thing, he seemed to open up to you. Grandpa was a very positive person—gregarious. He probably never met a stranger."

"He was one happy soul. Grandpa always had a knack for seeing the humorous side of things, as did Uncle Sam. Papa was the same way. Each of their hearts reflected a joyful peace that only comes through loving God. Stopping at the Watsons' farm during that rainstorm is something I'll always remember. Most men would've tried to make it home, but I think Grandpa was concerned about my safety. I'll never forget him cupping his hands around his mouth and yelling out 'hello, the house.' He got the results he wanted though." Mabel smiles at her thoughts.

"The Watson home was really different from what you were accustomed to as a child."

"Yes, it was. God puts those sorts of experiences in our lives so that we can honestly be grateful for what we have. No matter how difficult life seems, there's always someone in worse circumstances. That doesn't make us better—it's meant to make us aware that different people have different crosses to bear."

My thoughts pour out. "You use to tell me, 'There but for the grace of God, go I.' It taught me to understand that anything can happen in a person's life—things that are beyond their control. That really worked on me as a child—especially when I saw the less fortunate. I even recall the first time you said it to me. It was when I was asking you about the little girl that lived on our street who had to wear braces on her legs. After you told me that, I never wondered about her condition again. You told me to play with her just as I played with the other kids. All of this points to what you said earlier about everything happening for a purpose. God put you in circumstances that enabled you to teach us about life."

"That's right," thinks Mabel. "Seeing the Watson home, how it was furnished, what they ate, and their living conditions made me feel a deep compassion for them. As Grandpa said, there's nothing wrong with being poor, but it hurts when you see people suffering. By taking them gifts, we attempted to help them. If anyone ever did for others, it was Grandpa. I learned a lot by watching people like him. Grandpa demonstrated goodness, gentleness, and kindness through the way he lived. Children who are fortunate enough to be exposed to people of high character will grow up with many of those same qualities. Even though we are no longer with them, we always carry a part of their spirits in our hearts. That's why the circle of influence is so important for all of us."

"Now, I want you to tell me about Aunt Nell. Why do you think God put that awful experience into your life at such a young age?"

Mabel looks into the light and her thoughts begin to pour out. "First, I believe it was probably more for Aunt Nell's development than mine—but it did upset me. She wrote Mama a letter of apology for putting me through the whole ordeal. Josie told me about the letter, but Mama never mentioned it. Josie explained that Aunt Nell meant well in what she did." She leans forward in her chair and looks back at me. "I never forgot what Aunt Nell put me through that day. She may have had the right reasons for doing it, but she forced me to participate in something inappropriate."

"As a parent, you encouraged us," I think, "but you never required us to participate in situations that made us uncomfortable. It appears that Aunt Nell used her religion to more or less shame you into doing what she thought was right. A child of your age certainly didn't have the maturity to cope with the situation. You taught us through example—through living your faith and your constant reliance upon the will of God in your life."

Mabel stands and walks toward the picture. She stops and turns. "No one taught me how to raise you all. I just followed the patterns I observed as a child. That's all any parent has—their past. Grandpa pointed out that we often learn what *not* to do from those in our lives. Aunt Nell's treatment of me is an example I always remembered when teaching you children. That's why knowing such a variety of people was so good for me, and ultimately, the three of you."

I follow Mabel's movement in front of me. "Uncle Sam was a unique sort of person. You really admired him, didn't you?"

Mabel smiles and begins to share her thoughts. "He was a wonderful man. I loved to listen to Uncle Sam tell stories. When he talked, it was like he was performing onstage. I suppose that's one of the reasons why I enjoyed telling childhood stories to you all."

"You seemed to be very concerned about the Klan when you were little."

"Yes. Especially after Josie had explained who they were. When I heard Aunt Nell say that about Uncle Sam, I just knew she was one of them. Now I know why that was such a foolish thing for me to think. Uncle Sam explained it all away in no time. We always found something to laugh about in the most serious of circumstances. When he used the example about the bird, I clearly understood that his vaudeville job was simply playing a role. That was merely how he made a living."

I stand and walk toward Mabel. "It was clever of him to use that example to help you understand his vaudeville days, wasn't it?"

"Oh, yes, Uncle Sam was very creative. As you could see, listening to him talk was entertaining because you never knew what he was thinking. Uncle Sam was totally at peace with the world and his love for others could be felt. He seemed so interested in me as a child. I believe he felt a special connection with me because of my name."

We look at one another and I can see the happiness he brought to her. "I'm glad he told me that no member of my family would ever be in the Klan. Children like me often worry about situations that don't really exist. His openness eased all of my concerns. All children need people—especially grown-ups—to talk to them and honestly explain things that come up."

"After seeing you with Grandpa and Uncle Sam, I can understand why those are two people you would enjoy revisiting." I walk back to my chair and sit down. Mabel follows me and sits down too. "I loved it when you prayed with Ruth."

"That was so hard for me to do. I wanted her to believe that I knew how to pray, but all I did was copy Mama as best I could. Ruth was the sweetest girl. She was painfully shy and unsure of herself. If she had lived in Shoal Crossing, I know that we would have been good friends. Did you see the look on her face when she saw the dress? It made me so happy to be able to give it to her."

"I could see the happiness on both of your faces. Did you ever see Ruth again?"

"No, I didn't. I later learned that Mr. Watson finally started working on their farm. He probably still drank, but at least he began cleaning up the farm after the day we visited. Grandpa, Uncle Sam, and Bubba went out there and helped them get their farm back in shape. It took them several visits, but Bubba said that it really looked nice. Bubba enjoyed working with all the Watson boys. Their going out there to work on the farm illustrates Grandpa and Uncle Sam's love for others. They truly lived their faith."

"It's another example of their compassion and generosity. You were blessed to be around such fine people. Did you count that as an answer to your prayer?"

"Yes. It thrilled me as a child to know that God heard my prayer and chose to answer it in the way He did. It's my first memory of one of my prayers being answered. That experience definitely sealed my belief in prayer."

Mabel turns and looks at me. "All of the people you have met through the review had a tremendous impact on who I became as an adult. Now it's time for us to move forward to some of the events I experienced as a child. I want you to see how some events led me to have a deeper appreciation for life and a strong will to overcome obstacles." Mabel turns her head and nods toward the picture.

The baskets sitting on the floor in the picture begin to whirl and blend into many colors. Focusing on the middle of the picture, I see Mabel asleep in her bed in the early morning. The white sheet is pulled up under one arm. She is lying on her side and softly resting her face on the palm of her hand. Gentle rays of sunlight peek through the window and capture the dust particles dancing through the air. When the picture gets completely clear, the storyteller begins talking.

Chapter 12

FAST ASLEEP, MABEL STIRS WHEN SHE feels something crawling on her foot. Now awake, Mabel doesn't want to open her eyes. She moves her foot, but the crawly thing gets back on her foot. Mabel slowly looks down toward her foot and there sits Josie at the end of her bed. "Good morning, Miss Sunshine," says Josie. "You sure was tryin' to get away from that ole bug on your foot." They both laugh.

"I'm glad you're here today," says Mabel. "I reckon I can help you all day long." She sits up in the bed, turns around, and lies back down with her head in Josie's lap. Josie combs Mabel's thick hair with her long fingers.

"You sure can help me. There ain't much for us to do today—'cept change y'all's beds," says Josie. "I brought y'all a set of clean sheets."

"What is that word they call people who wash and iron clothes, Josie?" says Mabel. She sits up, crosses her legs, and faces Josie.

"The word is 'laundress,'" says Josie. "That's what folks call us these days. That's just a fancy word for washerwoman." Josie reaches over and runs her hand along the sheet. "Some ladies do that all day, every day. Not me. I'd rather do all kinds of things—I 'specially like to cook for you folks. The change is a nice thing for me."

"Are you a laundress for any other families?" asks Mabel.

"Oh, I helps out a couple of families, but this is my favorite place to come. Miss Lizbeth is so special to me. This whole family is. I ain't a laundress like them others." Josie gets up and goes over to the door. "You needs to get out of that bed, Mabel. How about me fixing you some hot cornmeal mush? Put on your clothes and come into the kitchen. I've already got the water boiling."

After Mabel gets dressed in her overalls, she walks into the kitchen and sits down at the place Josie has set for her. The hot bowl of cornmeal mush has a dollop of butter melting in its center. Josie gets a teaspoon of sugar and sprinkles it over the mixture. "Ain't you gonna eat some, Josie?"

"You know I am, Mabel. To me, cornmeal mush is good any time, any day." Josie sets her bowl of mush on the table and sits down across from Mabel. "Stir yours for a bit, child. It'll burn your tongue if you don't let it cool a minute," warns Josie.

Mabel watches as Josie lifts a spoonful of mush to her mouth and blows on it. She imitates Josie's attempts to cool their breakfast. "Oh, that's so good, Josie. Your daddy sure taught you how to make good things to eat." Josie smiles at Mabel. "I hope I'll be able to cook like you when I grow up," says Mabel.

"You will, child. If you haven't learned nothing else from me, you've found out how good food taste. When you starts cooking, always taste the food. If it taste good to you, then other folks will like it too." Josie finishes her mush and rests her elbows on the table. She watches Mabel chase down the last bite with her spoon.

Mama walks into the kitchen. "Good morning, ladies," she says. Not waiting for a reply, she continues talking. "Josie, did you stoke the oven this morning?"

Josie gathers the bowls and spoons from the table and takes them over to the dishpan. "No, ma'am, Miss Lizbeth, I didn't think we'd be cooking today. There was just enough heat left for me to heat a small pan of water for some mush. Had to set the pan directly on the coals to get what little heat that was left. Why, is there something you needs to do?"

"I didn't want to cook today, Josie, but I did want to give Brother a bath this afternoon when it gets warmer. You know I like to keep the fires burning when I bathe him. I'm afraid he'll catch a spring cold," says Mama.

"Well, Miss Lizbeth, that ain't no problem at all. Mabel and me can bring in some wood and build you a nice fire," says Josie. She picks up the dishrag and washes out the bowls. After she washes them, she dips each dish into clean water and sets them on the counter to dry. Mabel's eyes move toward Josie as she hears the clinking of the dishes being stacked. Josie dries her hands on the front of her apron.

"Well, there's a catch," says Mama. "I forgot to buy matches last week when I went to the store. We used the last one early this morning. Brother's asleep now and I can't leave him. Do you think you and Mabel can walk to the store and buy some matches?" she asks.

"Sho' is a catch," says Josie. She walks over to the table and wipes it down with the moist dishrag. Josie then painstakingly dries the table with a towel.

"What do you mean, Josie?" says Mama.

Straightening up, she looks at Mama. "Today's Tuesday, ain't it?" says Josie.

Mama looks puzzled at Josie's question. "Why, yes, today is Tuesday, May twenty-first."

"Well, you know coloreds cain't go in either store 'cept on Thursday, Miss Lizbeth," says Josie. She turns and walks to the cabinet, then neatly refolds the towel and hangs it on the nail beside the kitchen window. "Even when I can go in the store on Thursdays, I have to go to the back door."

Mabel looks at Mama to see how she will respond. "Oh, dear me, I'd forgotten about that." *Mama's all flustered and seems embarrassed.* "Well, I'll just write a note telling Mr. Stevens what I want—need to put it on our ticket anyway. I don't have one red cent," says Mama. "Mabel can just hand it to him."

"That'll be fine. I can wait for Mabel outside the store that way," says Josie. "I don't like knocking on the back door for that old codger. Make me feel like I's begging him to take my money. Beats all I've ever seen."

Mama walks over to Josie and hugs her. "I'm so sorry, Josie. I forgot," she says.

Josie pats Mama on the back. "Ain't your fault, Miss Lizbeth. It's how mens like them storeowners lets us know we still ain't free."

"Go put on one of your dresses, Mabel, and comb your hair. I'll write a note," says Mama. "You won't have to talk to Mr. Stevens when you go in. Just hand him the note."

Mabel quickly disappears from the kitchen and goes to her bedroom to change. Feeling the tension Josie feels, she tiptoes back to the kitchen to find Mama folding a small piece of paper. Josie is humming and cleaning out the firebox. "I'm ready, Josie," says Mabel.

"That was quick, child. Get the note from your mama and we'll be on our way," says Josie.

Mama holds out the note for Mabel to take. "If you lose this, you won't be able to get the matches. Hold on to it, Mabel. Since Josie can't go in the store, it's your responsibility."

"Yes, ma'am," responds Mabel. As Josie removes her apron, Mabel walks over to the back door and waits for her. Once the apron is hung on the pantry door, Josie joins Mabel and they go out the door and proceed down the back steps into the welcoming sunshine.

"That sun feel good to me, Mabel," says Josie. "Let's cut across the side yard up to the road. Hold my hand, child, I don't want nothing to happen to you." Mabel reaches over and happily takes Josie's hand. "Your little hand is mighty warm today."

"Yessum, I think it's hot," says Mabel. "I've never been in the store by myself to buy something. I hope Mr. Stevens can read Mama's note."

Josie laughs at Mabel's concern. "Child, Mr. Stevens can sho' read anything—especially when it come to givin' him some money." Josie looks down at Mabel and smiles. "You tickle me, Mabel, when you thinks about those little things to worry about in your head."

"Josie, are you still a slave?" asks Mabel.

"Why, no child, I ain't," says Josie. She stops and looks down at Mabel. "What's going on in your head right now, Mabel?"

Mabel looks up into the Josie's eyes, almost fearful to continue. Then she looks down. "Well, you told Mama that Mr. Stevens doesn't think you're free."

"The last slaves in my family were my grandparents," says Josie. "Look up here at me, child." Mabel looks into the softness of Josie's eyes. "What I was saying is that some peoples still treat us coloreds like slaves. They don't want us to be free—not ever. My daddy taught me that I can always be free as long as I have my mind," says Josie.

"What'd he mean?" says Mabel.

Josie reaches down and picks up a rock from the road. She brushes the red grit from its surface. "Here, hold this rock, Mabel." Mabel feels the smoothness of the rock in her hand. "Now, if that rock had a mind, it could think. Just because you're holding that rock, don't mean that it ain't still a rock. You ain't gonna change it by taking it away from where it wants to be—it's a rock. Put it in a box, throw it into the woods, or toss it into the water—it still a rock and that's what it'll always be. Peoples can be in jail, work for somebody, or be a slave, but as long as they can think about their past, think about their future, and think about the day they'll be in heaven—they's free."

"That's sorta like daydreaming, isn't it, Josie?" asks Mabel. "Sometimes I imagine I'm in school with Sister, but I'm really up in my tree." Mabel looks at the rock and replaces it among its friends.

"That's right, child. Can't nothing or nobody keep you down as long as you have your mind to take you wherever you wants to be." Josie takes Mabel's hand and they begin walking once again. "All the mens can make all the rules they wants to—I's just as free as they is. Funny thing though—they don't know it." Josie looks down at Mabel. *Josie's smart—like Uncle Sam.* They both laugh.

"I sure don't want to go in the store by myself," says Mabel.

"You don't worry about going by yourself. Walk in, hold your head high, be proud of who you is, and hand him your mama's note," says Josie. They cross the road and walk over to the east side of the store. "I'll wait for you right here in the shade of this tree, Mabel. Just hand him the note, get the matches, and come back out here to me. I ain't gonna leave you."

"Yessum." Mabel turns, goes around to the front of the store, and proceeds up the steps. *I hope those men don't notice me. They're the ones who sit out here all the time—telling tales.* She longs to look at them closely so she can remember their faces, but doesn't dare. Mabel grasps the handle to the screen door and opens it. The men look at her when they hear the *screech* of the spring. Mabel quickly scoots inside the store.

"Can I help you, young lady?" inquires Mr. Stevens. Mabel walks to the counter where he is standing and hands him her mama's note. "Oh, so Mrs. O'Brien needs a large box of wooden matches, and she wants me to add the two cents to her ticket. Let me get them, young lady."

Mabel watches Mr. Stevens move from behind the counter and walk to a shelf near the front of the store. *I walked right by the matches. I could've gotten them all by myself. Mr. Stevens has his gray hair slicked down to his head—just like when he comes to church. Mama says he's so hateful that no lady would ever marry him.* He places the matches on the counter and walks around behind it.

"Let me write a ticket for your mama's bill," says Mr. Stevens. Mabel stares into the worn edge of the wooden counter. "There you go, young lady. I'm running short on bags today, so you'll just have to carry them." He slides the box of matches toward Mabel and she takes them from the counter. "Thank you," says Mr. Stevens. "You have a nice day." He tries to force a smile but can't.

As Mabel begins walking toward the door, the box of matches slides open and drops to the floor. Mabel feels the red tinges of embarrassment filling her face. She looks back at Mr. Stevens, but he shows no interest in her predicament.

Mr. Stevens is mean for not helping me. I hope I don't start crying. I wish Josie could come help me pick up the matches—they won't fit back in the box. I'll put some in my dress pocket. Mabel takes a deep breath to stop her tears from flowing and patiently picks up every match. When she finishes, she turns to look at Mr. Stevens, but he is reading the newspaper. *Mama's right about him.* Mabel walks to the door and pushes it open; she rushes by the men on the porch and runs down the steps.

"Child, I's getting ready to go around to the back door and check on you. What's wrong?" asks Josie.

"Mr. Stevens didn't give me a sack. When I's walking out of the store, the box slid open and spilled the matches all over the floor. Old Mr. Stevens didn't help me one bit," says Mabel tearfully.

"Here, Mabel, let me have the matchbox. I'll fix them in no time," says Josie. She slides the inner box out and sees the jumbled matches. "Sho did make a mess, child." Josie softly chuckles.

Mabel reaches into her pocket and hands some more matches to Josie. "I sure wished for you to be in there with me. Mr. Stevens watched me, but he didn't come from behind the counter."

"That old man ain't liked by much of nobody in this town. You ain't no different." Josie continues to restack the matches. "You ought to see how he looks at us colored folks when we goes in there on Thursdays. He act like we's stealin' him blind. That's why I do most of my shopping over in Florence at a colored man's store. I don't go in this store in Shoal Crossing lessin' I have to," says Josie. "Now, they's all fixed. Let's go back to your house. Hold my hand."

"I hope I don't ever have to go to the store for Mama again," says Mabel. Before they cross the main road, she turns to look at the men on the porch. They stare back at her.

"It will be easier the next time you have to go in there. Takes a while to get use to people and they ways," says Josie. "You did a good job. You got the lucifers and now we can build a nice fire for Miss Lizbeth and Brother."

"Are matches called 'lucifers'?" says Mabel.

"That's what Daddy use to call them. You know who Lucifer is, don't you Mabel?" Josie looks down at Mabel.

"No'm, I haven't ever heard of him. Do you know him?" asks Mabel with curiosity in her voice.

"Sho do, child. Lucifer is the devil hisself," declares Josie. "When they first started making matches, they smelt real bad, but they made fire. You know where the devil lives is supposed to be pure fire. So, that's why folks call them matches 'lucifers,'" she says. "I calls them lucifers ever once in a while. That word reminds me of my daddy and that I wants to go to heaven."

"I sure don't want to go live with Lucifer," says Mabel. She looks up at Josie as they enter the side yard. "We ain't going there, are we, Josie?"

"No, child. You and me's going to heaven. We'll be up there with all the angels," says Josie. "Let's take the matches on into the house. We's got a fire to build."

When they walk into the kitchen, Mama's sitting at the table and feeding Brother. "That was a quick trip," says Mama. She reaches over and wipes the applesauce from around Brother's mouth. "He eats like a little horse."

Mabel stands beside the highchair and listens to Brother coo. "He has fun eating, doesn't he, Mama?" She pats his hand.

"All of my children enjoy eating," says Mama. "Did Mr. Stevens add the matches to our ticket, Mabel?" She gently scrapes applesauce from Brother's chin with a spoon and puts it in his mouth.

"Yessum. He put your note with the ticket and said that he added two cents," says Mabel. "I's scared going in there, Mama." Mabel watches Josie take her apron from the pantry door.

"Miss Mabel say she don't have much use for Mr. Stevens," says Josie. "I told her not many folk do." Josie laughs as she puts her apron over her head. "I reckon he don't gee or haw with most peoples. C'mon here, Mabel, let's get some wood and kindling for your mama's fire. You still want me to change the beds today, Miss Lizbeth?"

"Please, Josie, if you have time," says Mama. "Not having any matches really messed up our day, didn't it?" After feeding Brother his last bite of applesauce, Mama takes his bib and cleans his face. "This baby gets food all over everything when he eats."

"Brother just like any other baby," says Josie. "You just forgets, Miss Lizbeth, since Mabel was the las' baby you had." Josie pulls Mabel close. "We gonna go get the wood, light the fire, and then we'll change the beds." Josie opens the door and gently nudges Mabel to go with her.

When Bubba and Sister come home from school that afternoon, Bubba asks Mama if the three of them can walk up to Six Mile creek. "I want to show Sister and Mabel the beaver dam I found the other day," says Bubba.

"You can go, but I don't want these girls trying to wade in any deep water," says Mama. "Since it's drizzling rain, y'all take off your shoes and be careful that you don't slip down on the rocks. You need to get back here around the time your papa gets home from work."

As they walk through the woods toward the creek, Bubba talks about the dam. "Y'all ain't gonna believe the dam I saw. I'll show y'all the trees the beavers cut down with their teeth. They sure have been working hard."

Mabel and Sister trail Bubba. "I don't want to get close to a beaver," says Sister. "If they can cut down a tree, just think what they'd do to us."

"You don't need to worry about them bothering us," says Bubba. "They're scared of people." Bubba's bare feet have bits of grass and mud sticking to them. "They'll hide when they hear us coming."

As they near the creek, Bubba slows down his stride and waves his hand for his sisters to be quiet. Mabel and Sister hold hands as they try to walk in their bare feet without making any noise. Bubba walks to the creek's edge and scratches his head. Mabel and Sister move closer and stand beside Bubba.

"I don't understand this," says Bubba. "The beaver dam was right here." They all crane their necks to see if the dam is under the water. "It was too big to be under the water or to get washed away." Bubba's eyes begin searching. "Look over yonder. That pile of sticks looks to be what the beavers used. Somebody's done tore up their dam. Wonder why they'd do that?" muses Bubba.

Disappointed, the three of them walk over to the neatly stacked pile of sticks, limbs, and leaves. Mabel picks up a small limb and looks at its pointed end. "Look where the beaver's teeth gnawed on that limb," says Sister.

"They've really got some sharp teeth," agrees Bubba. The drizzle turns into a heavier rain. Mabel watches Bubba swipe away the water dripping from his red hair. "Somebody doesn't want this dam here and tore it all apart, but I've got an idea. We can help the beavers." Bubba explains that he thinks they should rebuild the dam. He says that they can use the sticks the beavers cut.

"We can't build no beaver dam, Bubba," insists Mabel.

Bubba tells them if they will hand him the sticks and limbs, he can do it. Mabel and Sister agree to his plan and start gathering as many sticks as they can carry. Bubba helps the girls make a nice pile beside the creek. Then he selects the biggest branches and pushes them into the mud across the narrowest width of the creek. Bubba carefully piles the sticks across the first line of branches. He keeps stacking until all the limbs the beavers had cut are used.

By the time they finish, Mabel and Sister are able to add some sticks on the edge of the dam. "Is that how the dam looked, Bubba?" says Mabel. "I hope the beavers like it."

"It looks just like it, Mabel; I even packed mud around the sticks. That's how they do it," says Bubba. *Bubba looks pleased with our hard work.* "I just hope they ain't moved to a different place. Y'all can't tell nobody that we did this. It's gotta be kept a secret."

"Why's it got to be a secret?" asks Sister with a puzzled look on her face.

"Because the beavers didn't take the dam apart and stack the limbs. Some person did it," responds Bubba.

"Okay," says Sister. "We promise not to tell—don't we, Mabel?" Mabel nods in agreement. "Hope we don't get into trouble," adds Sister.

The rain turns into a downpour. "We'd better get back home," says Bubba. "Remember, not a word about this to Mama and Papa." The three of them take off running toward the house. When they hurry up the back steps, they find the pile of towels that Mama left for them on the back porch. As they are drying off, Mama comes to the back door.

"Y'all dry your hair real good and then go change into some dry clothes," says Mama. "Bring your wet clothes back out here. Just hang them on your pegs." Mama takes a few steps back into the kitchen. She raises her voice and says, "Your papa's home and got drenched too. As soon as you get finished, come to the table for supper."

When Bubba, Sister, and Mabel are dressed, they take their wet clothes out to hang on their pegs and go into the kitchen. Papa's sitting at the table talking to Mama. "Well, don't we all look like a bunch of wet hens with our hair all slicked down," says Papa. "Your mama's the only dry hen in this house." Giggling, they all look at each other. *Papa's hair looks the funniest. His ears look a lot bigger.* "Let's all bow our heads for the blessing," says Papa.

After he finishes the prayer, Papa begins passing bowls of food to the right. When the last bowl makes it around the table, they all end up back in front of Papa. "Did you show the girls the beaver dam, Son?" says Mama.

Mabel and Sister keep their eyes on their plates as they listen for Bubba's answer. *I can feel Mama and Papa looking at Bubba. Wonder what he's gonna say.* "Yessum, they sorta got to see it," says Bubba. He stuffs some green beans into his mouth and starts chewing. *I ain't ever seen Bubba eat so many beans at once—he don't even like them. Bubba sure doesn't want to talk about the dam.*

"Couldn't you find it?" asks Mama. She has a confused look on her face.

Bubba points at his reddened face as if he can't talk with food in his mouth. *He's stalling. Bubba's gonna get in trouble. I can feel it in my bones.* "No'm. I took them to where the dam was, but somebody tore it all to pieces. They stacked the sticks and stuff up on the creek bank." Bubba takes a huge bite of mashed potatoes and innocently looks at Mama. *I hope Mama doesn't ask me any questions. Bubba's trying to keep our secret from Mama and Papa. I sure don't want to be the one talking. Sister's staying busy too.*

They all turn their heads as someone knocks on the back door. Papa gets up from the table and goes over to open the door. "Hello, Jim. We're just eating our supper," says Papa. "What can I do for you?" Mabel's ears listen only for the sounds from the back porch.

"Yessir, Mr. Tom. I's sorry to bother you in this downpour and all, but somebody done built a beaver dam back across the creek. The beavers had one built and I took it down, but I reckon your three children put it back across there. My wife see'd them this afternoon," says Jim. Mabel feels the red creeping up her neck. She doesn't move, afraid she might miss something Jim says. In silence, Mama glares from one face to the next. "I'm afraid with this rain that the creek's gonna get backed up so much that it'll drown some more of my pigs like it did last time we had a big rain." Mabel hears Papa mumble something to Jim. "I sure would appreciate that, Mr. Tom."

As Papa walks back into the kitchen and sits down, Mabel takes a huge bite of potatoes. "Is Jim right about his wife seeing the three of you building a dam back across the creek this afternoon?" Papa asks with a serious look on his face. In unison, two answer, "Yessir, Papa." Mabel can't talk, but she nods in agreement.

"I'm going to finish my nice supper, but you three aren't going to eat another bite. First, I want you to change back into those wet clothes you just took off." Papa keeps eating and talking as they stare at him. "When you get your clothes changed, I want the three of you to go back to the creek and tear down whatever you built across it." They scoot away from the table without a word. "I'll be up there in a little bit to make sure you do a good job. Those pigs are Jim's livelihood," says Papa. "If one of them dies from your messing around, you're gonna buy that pig. Not me."

Bubba, Sister, and Mabel get their soggy clothes from the pegs and go to their bedrooms to change. When they are ready, the three go out the back door and huddle miserably on the porch. Mabel can't believe how cold the wet clothes feel against her skin. "We shouldn't have listened to your dumb idea, Bubba," she says. "I told you we couldn't build no dam." Sister nods her head in agreement. "This wet dress gives me the shivers."

Bubba takes on a threatening look. He draws his lips tight to his teeth. "You two just shut up," snaps Bubba. "You did every bit as much as I did to build the dam." The three of them lock their eyes in a defiant stare. "You two whiny girls need to shut up and take the blame just like I am—like a man. If either of you says another word, you're gonna be sorry when we get outside," says Bubba. "You'll be crying when I get through with you."

"Bubba O'Brien." Papa's stern voice startles them. "If I have to get up from this table, *you're* the one that's gonna be sorry—*before* you go outside." Bubba seems frozen in place—his face turns pale. Bubba's hateful look melts from his face. He lowers his eyes and turns away from his sisters' stare.

"If you so much as lay a hand on either one of those girls," warns Papa, "I'll have your hide out in the barn. Now, stop arguing and go do what I told you to do. Remember, if one of those pigs dies, you're gonna have to make it up to old Jim. I have a sneaking suspicion that all of this was your idea, Son."

"Yessir, Papa," says Bubba meekly. "We'll get it all fixed back." Without another word, Bubba turns and walks down the steps. Sister and Mabel follow him out into the backyard. Already cold from their wet clothes, the three of them can't talk for their teeth chattering. They walk as fast as they can toward the creek. "When we get up there, I'll get in the water again and y'all can stack the limbs back by the tree," says Bubba.

Just before they finish their job, Mabel looks up and sees Papa standing with Jim. *I hope old Jim knows we didn't mean any harm to his pigs.* When Bubba sloshes his way out of the creek, Papa walks toward the three of them. Jim turns and goes back toward his house. "The next time you want to rebuild a dam, Son, I hope you do it for the government. Otherwise, leave the dam building to beavers and engineers," says Papa. "Jim said y'all did a good job of rebuilding it—his land was beginning to flood." Papa motions for them to follow him home.

After they get back home, they all put on dry clothes. Papa calls them into the kitchen and directs them to sit down at the table. "Son, don't you ever let me catch you lying to me again. You know that's something we don't tolerate in this family."

Bubba places his arms on the table. "I didn't tell you a story, Papa. I did take them to where I had seen the dam."

"No, you didn't actually tell a lie—you knowingly left out the truth. Do you three know what that's called?" Staring into Papa's face, the three of them shake their heads, showing him they don't know the answer. "You omitted the truth when you knew it. That's called the sin of omission—which means it's still a lie."

"Yessir," says Bubba as he sadly looks into Papa's eyes. "I won't do it again."

"If you know the truth, you tell it," says Papa. His eyes move to Mabel and Sister. "You two girls kept your mouths shut while Bubba evaded the truth. You're just as guilty as he is."

"Yessir," answer Mabel and Sister in unison.

"I know y'all are still hungry, but you're gonna have to go to bed right now without your supper. Don't any one of you ever leave out the truth when you know it—not ever again."

When Mabel and Sister crawl into bed, they both stare up at the ceiling. "It's not even dark outside. I don't think I can go to sleep," says Mabel.

"Well, you'd better be quiet and pretend," says Sister. "I don't think Papa's in a very good mood."

"No, he sure ain't," says Mabel. "Bubba sure got us in a mess. I'm hungry." She closes her eyes and eventually drifts off to sleep in the warmth of the clean sheets that she and Josie put on the bed earlier in the day.

Chapter 13

THURSDAY EVENING AFTER SUPPER, THE O'BRIENS gather in the parlor as usual. Sitting on the floor with the paper spread in front of him, Bubba interrupts the silence. "Papa, today was the last day of school. We've got to go get our report cards tomorrow before noon; then we'll be out for the year. I sure am glad."

"Me too," chimes in Sister.

"Well, I hope your report cards are good ones," says Papa. He stands up, reaches for his hat, and puts it on his head. "Your grades are like a paycheck—the harder you work—the higher the pay."

"What are you doing, Tom?" asks Mama. She looks up at him and smiles.

"I thought it'd be nice to go out and sit on the porch for a while," says Papa. Before he finishes his sentence, Bubba, Sister, and Mabel start putting away their things.

"It is a little cooler outside," says Mama. "Let me go check on Brother and I'll join y'all."

When Papa gets out on the porch, he takes a deep breath. "This is perfect weather out here tonight," says Papa. He walks over to his rocking chair and sits down. Mabel settles into her usual place—

leaning against the post on the top step, while Sister and Bubba sit on lower steps.

"Look who's wide awake," says Mama as she steps out onto the porch. "I went in there and Brother was having a good time kicking his feet up in the air. Thought I'd bring him out here and see if I can rock him to sleep."

"He must have heard us stirring around in the house," says Papa. "A fella like him needs to keep up with everybody else, you know."

"He's a bundle of energy, for sure," says Mama. Mabel watches as the tips of Mama's toes tap the porch floor and send her rocker back and forth. Then she turns her eyes to look down at Sister resting her head on her knees. Bubba's staring at the road. The light from the lamp in the living room gives the house a soft glow in the darkness.

"We've got a wonderful night to go walking, kiddoes," says Papa. "The moon is lighting the road just enough for us to see."

"Where you want to walk, Papa?" says Bubba. He stands and faces the porch, resting his foot on the bottom step. "Since school's out, we don't have to get up as early in the morning."

"I'm not going with y'all," says Mama. "I've got to get Brother back to bed here in a few minutes. Y'all go on and enjoy yourselves."

"We'd sure like to have you come with us, Mrs. O'Brien," says Papa. He stands and pulls his hat on a bit tighter. "I think we'll walk up across the main road—toward the schoolhouse." Papa leans over and kisses Brother on his forehead. "Won't be long before he'll be going with us."

By the time Papa goes down the steps, Mabel, Sister, and Bubba are waiting at the front gate. Bubba opens the gate; they all step out onto the road. "Y'all be careful. I'll see you when you get back," says Mama. Papa tips his hat.

"Let's get out in the middle of the road, kids," says Papa. "Looks like most folks have already turned out their lights for the night."

Papa and Bubba lead the way, with Mabel and Sister walking close behind. "This moonlight's perfect," says Papa.

I wouldn't walk out here in the dark without Papa. The shadows of the trees look spooky to me. Mabel reaches over to hold Sister's hand. "This is a little fun, but I think I'd rather be at home with Mama," whispers Sister.

"Let's walk with Papa," says Mabel. The two girls quicken their strides and soon catch up with Papa and Bubba. "We want to walk with you, Papa," says Mabel. As they begin crossing the main road in front of the store, Papa reaches down and takes Mabel's hand in his.

"The store looks strange at night," observes Bubba. "Nobody's hanging around it."

"Things do look different at night," remarks Papa. "This is the way y'all walk to school every day, isn't it?"

"Yessir. Sometimes we cut across that yard up yonder, but it's just as quick on the road. Mr. Williams doesn't seem to care when we cut across his yard but, like I said, it's just as fast out here."

"The grass is usually too wet in the mornings," says Sister. "Gets my socks soggy."

"I'll be glad when I get to walk to school with Bubba and Sister," says Mabel.

"It won't be much longer, Mabel. Not long at all," says Papa. He takes off his hat and wipes his forehead on the shoulder of his shirt. "I'm working up a sweat from pulling this little hill."

"Do you reckon you'll ever buy an automobile, Papa?" says Bubba. "I hear tell that lots of people are driving them in Florence. You could get to work a lot faster."

"I could die a lot faster too, Son," says Papa with laughter in his voice. "In the first place, I can't afford one—they cost about four hundred dollars. In the second place, they scare me to death. I see them off in ditches almost every day. We'll stick to walking and our wagon for the time being."

"When I go to work, I want to buy one for us," says Bubba. "I can drive Mama to Florence to shop and things like that. Sure would make things easier. I can even drive you to work." Bubba gets in front of Papa and walks backwards. "I wish we could buy one."

"If wishes were horses....." Papa surveys their surroundings and then looks at Bubba. "We'd have to save money for a long time. I'm not one bit interested in having you drive me around in an automobile. Shoo wee, it makes my hands sweat just thinking about it."

"If Grandpa pays me to work on the farm this summer, I might be able to buy one," says Bubba.

"I'm gonna be making some money too," says Sister. "I can help him."

Papa throws his head back and laughs. "You kids think your Grandpa's gonna pay you four hundred dollars for working on the farm? You've got another think coming," says Papa. "You'd have to work out there all year—and then you still wouldn't have enough money. Four hundred dollars is a heap of cash."

"Can I start saving to buy one, Papa?" asks Bubba. He turns around and drops back beside Papa.

"Why sure, Son," says Papa. "That's the only way to ever get one. I sho' ain't interested in buying or driving one."

Sister points up ahead. "There's the school, Papa. Is that where we're gonna turn around?" Papa responds by nodding his head.

"I reckon I might be able to save enough money by the time I get to high school," says Bubba.

"If that's what you want to do, Son, you'll do it," says Papa. "Let's walk up there to the steps and sit down in the moonlight before we head back home."

They each sit down on a step, but Mabel chooses to stand in front of Papa. "You like to walk, don't you, Papa?" says Mabel. "Why do you like to walk so much?"

Papa leans back and rests his elbows on the step above him. "I started taking long walks when I was about your age, Mabel. My daddy, brothers, and me use to walk all over Florence. Daddy couldn't even afford to have a horse and buggy. All of us walked wherever we went. Now that I'm older, I still love to walk. I reckon it's what you get used to," he says.

"Mama says that she can't walk as far as you do every single day," adds Sister.

Papa laughs as he takes off his hat and runs his fingers through his hair. "I've gotten use to it, that's all." Papa stands up. "Reckon it's time to head back home. It's probably close to ten o'clock; I've got to go to work in the morning," he says. Papa replaces his hat on his head and says, "It seems like the temperature's dropped a bit. That means the house will stay cool through the night."

"I'm excited about working on the farm this summer," says Bubba. "When do you think Grandpa will want us to come out there?"

"Oh, I don't know, Son," says Papa. "Seems to me that it'll be sooner rather than later. They have to plow, plant, and harvest their crops. There will be plenty of work to do. Your grandma and aunt will be busy canning." Papa starts a low whistle and then interrupts himself. "There'll be more work than you and Sister ever bargained for."

"Papa, look at the bottom of the hill. It's a parade," says Mabel. *I've never seen anything that pretty.*

They stop and look toward the bright lights in the distance. "What is that, Papa?" asks Bubba.

"If my eyes aren't failing me, it looks like the Klan visiting someone in Shoal Crossing. They appear to be out in front of old

Mrs. Goodin's house." Papa sounds troubled. "Let's stop here so I can try to figure out what they're doing. I've never seen the Klan out riding, but from the descriptions I've heard, that's who it is. They're smack dab in between us and our house." Standing in silence, all four of them watch the movement of the men on horseback.

Bubba looks worried as he asks, "How're we gonna get home, Papa? We're gonna have to walk right by them."

"I'm afraid you're right, Son. We can't stand out here all night. I certainly don't want to watch them kill somebody—then they'd have to make sure we didn't talk. Maybe they're lost. I wouldn't think that they have any cause to get after Mrs. Goodin. Maybe it's her son, Flint, they want."

They resume walking down the road—slowly. *Those torches make pretty light. The Klan looks like ghosts sitting up on horses. This is what Josie meant when she said that people are scared of them. I know I am.* While Mabel and Sister hold hands, they struggle to keep up with Papa and Bubba. Papa steps over to the side of the road—in the shadows—and they all follow.

"Okay, kids, here's what we're gonna do," says Papa in a hushed tone. "We're gonna walk right down this road. There's no way to go around them. I'm going to ask them if they need anything. They're probably at the wrong house."

"What if they don't want us to talk to them, Papa?" says Bubba.

"Then we'll be on our way back to the house. Those men don't have any cause to be angry with us because we're out walking. All of you be quiet and stand over to the side of the road while I'm talking to them," says Papa. "Don't draw attention to yourselves. If anything gets out of hand, Bubba, you take the girls and hightail it as fast as you can to the house. Run in the shadows so they can't see where you're going—although they'll probably know."

I'm scared I'm gonna start crying. I wish I'd stayed home with Mama and Brother. Josie said that she'd never seen them in Shoal Crossing, but here they are between us and our house. Sister pulls Mabel closer to her when they start walking. Nobody utters a word. Papa starts a low, nervous-sounding whistle and adjusts his hat several times before they reach the men on horseback.

Papa leaves Bubba, Sister, and Mabel standing in the shadows on the side of the road. He walks over to the group of men. "Evening, gentlemen," says Papa. "Are you sure you're at the right house? This is where Mrs. Goodin lives. She's almost eighty years old." Papa appears small as he looks up at the men on horseback.

"Evening, Mr. O'Brien," says one of the men. "We're at the right house all right. We're looking for the driver of that truck parked over yonder in front of the Goodin house."

"That's Flint Goodin's truck," says Papa. "The Goodins are nice folks. I know they don't want any trouble. Mrs. Goodin is too old to get upset. Y'all might literally scare her to death. I know you don't want anything to happen to her."

"We ain't looking to bother Mrs. Goodin, O'Brien. We want to talk to Flint Goodin," says a Klansman.

"Do I know any of you fellas?" asks Papa.

"Let's just say that we know you. No need for you to know us, O'Brien. In fact, it's best that you don't even try to figure out who we are."

One of the Klan walks his horse forward. "Flint Goodin's been driving the darkies to and from Florence in the evenings. We ain't gonna allow that. A white man's got no cause to be driving niggras around," says the Klan member.

"Well, Sir, I don't know anything about Flint Goodin's business, but why don't y'all let me go in and get him," suggests Papa. "I'm worried about what the sight of y'all might do to Mrs. Goodin—she's not in good health. We need to keep this as peaceful as possible."

"Okay, Mr. O'Brien," says a Klan member. "We ain't looking for no trouble neither. We just want to caution that Flint fella to stop accommodating them niggers again. He knows why we're here. He's been warned several times. Some people don't listen until you put the fear into them."

Papa pulls his hat tighter to his head. Walking around the men on horseback, he ambles up to the front door of the Goodin house. "Flint Goodin?" Papa calls out. "It's Tom O'Brien here. I need to talk to you for a minute." Papa waits and then repeats himself. "It's Tom O'Brien, Flint. I'm coming in to give you a message." Papa opens the front door and disappears inside the dimly lit house.

In the shadows of the trees, Bubba, Sister, and Mabel stand frozen in place. Bubba holds his arms back, tightly blocking his sisters. *I ain't ever been this scared. Wish I could take off and run home, but I've gotta stand here like Papa said. Sister's shaking so hard, I can feel it. We's in a mess.* Mabel peeks around Bubba's arm. *Them men look big sitting up on those horses. Wonder why the torches don't catch their sheets on fire.*

After a few minutes, the Klansmen seem to get impatient. "O'Brien!" shouts one of the men. "You need to hurry up and bring Flint Goodin out here. We ain't waitin' all night. Bring that nigger lover out here to us. Now, O'Brien!"

Pushing his back against Sister and Mabel, Bubba moves them more deeply into the shadows. He whispers, "Y'all get ready to run. Sounds like they're gonna cause some trouble. Wish Papa'd come out of the house."

Sister starts whimpering in soft tones. "We need to run home, Bubba."

"Hold on. There's Papa on the porch," murmurs Bubba. He pushes them back one more step. Mabel stumbles and lands on the ground. For the first time, the men turn and look at them. Bubba and Sister quickly and quietly pull Mabel to her feet. The three of them resume their big-eyed stares into the flames of the torches. Several of the men snicker at the sight of them.

Papa, seeming smaller than ever, walks back out to the middle of the road. He has to lay his head almost back to his shoulders as he looks up at the men. "I talked to Flint and told him what y'all said about him running a taxi service for the coloreds."

"Yeah? What'd he have to say for hisself?" asks one of the Klan in a hateful tone of voice.

"He said he won't do it anymore," says Papa. "He said that he promises you that that's the truth."

"Thought you's gonna bring him out here, O'Brien. Why didn't you let him come speak for hisself?" asks another man with ridicule in his voice.

Papa looks up at the man. "He's not gonna budge out of the house," says Papa. "I found him up under his mother's bed. That man's got a death grip on her bedposts. Poor Mrs. Goodin's in bed and has the covers pulled plumb up over her head."

"He'd better straighten hisself up or we're gonna have a death grip on his damn neck. If you see him again, O'Brien, you'd best tell him to leave them damn niggras alone," says a Klansman. "We ain't gonna tolerate his kind in this town, Florence, or anywhere else around these parts. He's gotta change his damn ways."

"Gentlemen," says Papa, "Flint's just trying to make a living—like all of us these days. I really don't appreciate your using cusswords in front of my three children. We don't use that sort of language in our home." Papa nods his head in the direction of Bubba, Sister, and Mabel. "Seems to me you fellas should be home with your families instead of out trying to tend to someone else's business. I don't see a thing in the world wrong with Flint driving the colored folks to Florence. He's trying to make money so's he and his mother can eat."

Seeming a bit angry, Papa continues in a firm voice, "I don't blame him for not coming out here in front of a mob. Now, Flint said he's not gonna do it anymore. He'll keep his word. I think it's best for you men to get out of Shoal Crossing and go back to wherever you came from. We don't want any trouble in this town. It's a peaceful place and we all get along just fine without your kind. You got what you came here for. I've helped you all I can."

"Well, we'll be watching him, Mr. O'Brien," says a Klansman.

"You needn't get so riled up, O'Brien," says a different man. "We ain't got no bones to pick with you or your children. We know you're a good Christian man and a hard worker. We'll be leaving now. If you see Flint Goodin again, you make sure he understands that we're not gonna put up with it no more."

The men begin turning their horses around and leave in a slow gallop. All of the O'Briens watch them ride away. When the Klansmen reach Mr. Stevens's store, they turn to the right and ride out of sight. Bubba, Sister, and Mabel walk out to the road where Papa's standing in the dust the horses raised.

"Shoo, Papa," says Bubba, "that about scared the liver out of me."

"They're nothing to mess with, Son. Did y'all see those guns? I'm sorry you children had to hear them cussing," says Papa. "Let's all hold hands and start walking back to the house. No telling where the Klansmen went or what they're doing. I'm just proud of how the three of you stood there without flinching."

"I's scared to death, Papa," says Sister. "I's shaking so hard, I was scared they'd hear my bones rattling."

"Me too, Papa," says Mabel. "I've never been that scared in my whole life. Where do you think they're going?"

"I have no idea, Mabel," answers Papa. "I'm just glad they're gone. I know Mrs. Goodin and Flint are glad too. He probably won't let go of his mama's bedposts before sunup."

In a short time, the four of them reach their front gate. "Now, y'all be quiet when we get into the house. Let's go in the kitchen and get a glass of water," says Papa. "We don't need to wake up Brother this late. Your mama's probably awake. I see the lamp's still on in the parlor."

The screen door screeches as Papa pulls it open. The four of them tiptoe through the dining room and into the kitchen. "Bubba, get a match and light the lantern," says Papa. "Be quiet about it."

"Yessir," says Bubba. "It's hard for me to see." He bumps into a chair on his way to the matchbox. It makes a racket scooting on the floor.

"Shhh," says Papa. Mabel and Sister don't move.

"What's all the ruckus about in here?" says Mama. She steps inside the kitchen door off of the hall as Bubba puts a match to the lantern. Mama waits in silence until the lantern is lit and Bubba slides it to the middle of the kitchen table. "Did y'all have a pleasant walk? What's wrong with all of y'all—you look like you've seen a ghost."

"Everybody sit down at the table," says Papa. "I'll fix us a glass of water."

No one says a word. The only sound in the room is Papa pouring water into the glasses from the pitcher. After he gets the water poured up, Papa sets the glasses on the table. He looks at Mama and asks, "Would you like a glass of water, Lizbeth?"

"That'll be nice. My mouth's kind of parched," says Mama.

"Mama, you ain't gonna believe what happened to us tonight," says Bubba.

"Well, I can tell by the looks on your faces that something happened. Who's going to tell me about it?" says Mama with a look of confusion on her face. Bubba, Sister, and Mabel glance over at Papa.

"We had a lovely walk, Lizbeth. We went to the schoolhouse, sat on the steps for a few minutes, and then headed for home," says Papa. He takes a gulp of water. "When we were coming back down the hill, we saw a group of Klansmen out in the road on horseback."

"Did they have on the sheets and were they carrying torches?" asks Mama. They all take a drink of water and nod their heads yes. "You mean to tell me that y'all saw the Klan in Shoal Crossing?"

"We certainly did, Lizbeth," says Papa. "There was no way for us to avoid them. They were blocking the road out in front of the Goodin's house. I decided to talk to them because I thought they were at the wrong house. The kids stood across the road and in the shadows."

Mama looks at each of their faces. "Bless my babies' hearts. Were they at the wrong house?" she asks.

"Nope," says Papa. "They were looking for Flint Goodin. Seems he's been driving the coloreds into town to make some extra money for himself. The Klan doesn't want him doing it anymore."

"Oh, dear," says Mama. "Josie has used his services several times to go to Florence. I never thought anything of it. She rides with him when she goes over there to shop and when she goes to visit the colored church. Josie's never mentioned any trouble about it."

"She won't be using his services again. I went inside the Goodin place to tell him what they wanted. That poor fella had a death grip on his mama's bedposts—up under her bed. Mrs. Goodin was in the bed with the covers pulled up over her head. She didn't say a thing. He was stretched out spread-eagle. Didn't move a muscle. Old Flint couldn't hardly talk for his teeth chattering. If I hadn't been so scared myself, it would have been funny," says Papa.

"Well, I reckon y'all won't be taking any more late-night walks, will you?" says Mama.

"No'm. Not me," says Mabel. "I's wishing I's here with you and Brother."

"Me either," says Sister. "That was scarier than anything I've ever seen."

Mama scoots her chair away from the table and gets up. She replaces the chair under the table and rests her hands on the back of it. *Mama's not one bit happy about what we got into. Uh-oh, she's gonna fuss at Papa. I hope she don't fuss at us. We's just walking with Papa.*

"Tom," begins Mama, "it seems to me that you could've avoided this entire mess by waiting for the Klan to leave. Why didn't you wait up by the school until they left?" Mama stares at Papa, waiting for his explanation.

Papa looks up at Mama. "I thought that they were probably at the wrong house, Lizbeth. Plus, if there was any fighting, I didn't want them to see us. We were caught between a rock and a hard place. It never crossed my mind about Flint Goodin doing anything," says Papa. "I was concerned about Mrs. Goodin too."

"You should've been more worried about our three children," says Mama. The light of the lantern dances in the darkness of her piercing brown eyes. "What if those men had turned on you because you were sticking your nose into their business? What could Bubba, Sister, and Mabel have done?"

"I know, I know," says Papa. "Now that I think about it, it wasn't very smart." Papa gets up from his chair. "Kids, we should've held back and waited. Your mama's right. That was the most dangerous thing I could've done."

"The best policy," says Mama, "is not to trouble trouble unless it troubles you." She pats Bubba on the shoulder. "Don't ever put yourselves into a situation that endangers your physical safety. Your papa's lucky that they knew him and didn't turn on him."

"She's right, kids," says Papa. "You really don't need to get in the way of someone else's problems, unless you know for a fact that you have the solution. I really believed that they were at the wrong house. Then when I found out they weren't—it was too late. Adults make mistakes too, don't they Lizbeth?"

"We sure do."

"There's another important lesson in this experience though, Lizbeth," says Papa.

She smiles at Papa and asks, "What might that be?"

"Well, those men were up to no good. They are evil critters out looking for trouble. My daddy always taught us boys that if you don't stand up against evil, then you believe as the evildoers do." Papa smiles at Mama. "Saying nothing is not in my blood."

"I agree with that too, Tom," says Mama. "I hate it that the children had to see that wickedness in action."

"It's okay, y'all," says Bubba. "Now, at least, we know for sure the Klan's in Shoal Crossing and to stay away from them. I could tell they were dangerous."

"They cussed a lot," says Sister. "That's what scared me."

"Me too," says Mabel. "They's saying things that made me know that they're mean."

"Well, you're all home and safe now," says Mama. "I'm sorry you had to see the ugliness in some people. All we can do is pray for them; maybe one day we'll witness a change. Those people are filled with hatred. God was watching over you, for sure. Your papa's right about evil and trying to correct it. We need to go to bed now. Bubba, after we leave the kitchen, blow out the lantern. You and Sister have to walk to school tomorrow to get your report cards. We all need to get some sleep—it's late."

"Yessum," says Bubba.

Mabel and Sister make their way into the bedroom, undress in the dark, and put on their nightgowns. "I never wanted to be home with Mama so bad in my whole life," says Sister.

"Me neither," says Mabel. "I reckon we're just gonna say our own prayers tonight. Mama must have forgotten. She's too mad...I mean angry, to pray tonight."

"I reckon," says Sister. "Night, Mabel. I'm glad we're home."

Chapter 14

On the weekends, especially on Saturday afternoons, the O'Brien family typically prepares for church services on Sunday. On the first day of June, they are excited because all of the church members are to bring home-cooked food for their first dinner on the grounds after church the next day. While Mama and Papa are sitting in their rocking chairs, Bubba, Sister, and Mabel are within earshot of their parents: Mabel's in the sandbox, Sister's tapping a stick on the boardwalk, and Bubba's leaning against the corner post with his legs stretched out. Snooks is sound asleep in the flowerbed—lying on his back with his paws up in the air.

"You children know that your heads need to be washed before church tomorrow," says Papa. "Since we've had so much rain, I was thinking we might go up to Six Mile Creek and get your heads scrubbed." Papa looks at each one of them. "Anybody object to that?"

"Do I have to go, Papa?" asks Bubba. "I'm old enough to wash my own hair here at the house."

Mabel stands up and walks over to the bottom step. "I think it'd be fun, Papa."

"I do too," adds Sister.

"Well, that's two yeses and one no," says Mama.

"How do you plan to wash your hair, Son?" asks Papa.

"I'll just draw me a bucket of water up from the well, heat it, wash my hair, and then get all the soap out," says Bubba. "That water's cold at the creek. The girls take too long."

Mabel and Sister look at Bubba. Mabel turns her head and looks at Papa. *He's gonna get in some bad trouble, telling Papa how grown-up he is. Papa doesn't like that.* Mabel's eyes switch over to Mama's face. *Mama doesn't like it either. She's thinking that Bubba's getting too big for his britches. Papa says that it's fine for us to grow up, but we need to act the size of our own britches.*

"I'll make a deal with you, Bubba," says Papa. "We've got to kill a chicken for your mama and Josie to fry up for dinner on the church grounds. If you can wring the chicken's neck, pluck it clean, and get it ready to cook, you can wash your hair at home."

"Aw, Papa, I don't want to kill no chicken," says Bubba.

"Do you think your papa enjoys killing a chicken? Surely you don't think that Josie or me enjoy killing a chicken," says Mama. "It's just what grown-ups have to do to feed their families, Bubba." Mama's toes are touching the porch faster and faster to make her rock. "Boys out in the country do it every day. They even help kill pigs and calves for their meat. That's what men have to do to feed their families." Mama stops rocking and stares at Bubba. "If you want to be a big man, we'll show you how."

"All right, Papa, you've got a deal," says Bubba with a sigh. He stands up, stretches, and touches the porch ceiling by standing on his tiptoes. "I don't want to do it, but I will."

"Can I watch, Papa?" says Mabel. "I've never seen Bubba wring a chicken's neck."

Sister says, "I don't want to watch. I'll stay in the house with Mama, I reckon."

"You can watch, Mabel," says Papa. "You have to sit on the back steps and be quiet. You can't get in the way."

Papa stands up from his chair. "Let's go, Bubba. We have to get the buckets as well as build a good fire for boiling the water and singeing the chicken feathers. When you dip the chicken in the hot water, it makes for cleaner and easier plucking." Papa walks over to the steps and Bubba follows him out into the front yard. "Lizbeth, you'll need to pick the one you want us to get."

Papa walks around the corner of the house with Bubba lagging behind him. Bubba stops, picks a leaf from a bush, and stares at it in his hand as he walks. Mabel's eyes follow Papa and then Bubba. *I know Bubba's sorry he ever said he's too big to go to Six Mile Creek for a hair washing.*

"After I pick out the hen, I'll get y'all some shampoo for your hair. You'll need some towels too," says Mama. Both girls watch their mama as she starts rocking again. "We've got some biscuits to take for the picnic tomorrow. Is there anything else you want?"

"I'd like some deviled eggs, Mama," says Mabel. "They always taste good when the chicken's cold."

"What about some potato salad?" chimes in Sister. "That's my favorite thing you make."

"Both of those sound really good, girls. Guess we'll need to gather us some eggs," says Mama. "Sister, you get the egg basket from the pantry in the kitchen."

To get outside, Mabel, Mama, and Sister walk through the house. After stopping to get the egg basket, Sister catches up with them on the back steps. When they reach the backyard, they walk over to the chicken coop. Papa and Bubba are busy gathering everything they'll need to dress the chicken.

"We're just out here gathering some eggs, Papa," says Sister. While Sister waits at the gate, Mabel and Mama walk into the coop.

They find fifteen eggs and take them to the basket—one by one. "You gonna make all of them into deviled eggs?" Sister calls out.

"I sure am, Sister," says Mama. "We like them—most other folks do too. I expect we'll have a big crowd tomorrow. Deviled eggs are a good idea, Mabel." Mama walks around looking at each of the hens. They tend not to be too concerned about either Mama or Mabel. They're more interested in the laying mash Mama sprinkled all over the ground. Their deep-red feathers glisten in the sun. "You can help me peel the potatoes, Sister." Mama reaches down and pets one hen's back. "Here's the one I want for our picnic, Tom," calls out Mama. *That poor chicken don't know what's coming her way. Bubba's not as scared as she's gonna be.*

"See which one it is, Bubba?" says Papa. He stands up beside the roaring fire he has burning on the ground. "Go over there and look at it real good. Pick out a marking or something that you can recognize."

Bubba pours the last bucket of water into the galvanized tub. "Yessir, I see which one it is. She has that black stripe running through her wing."

"Okay, Sister, you get to carry the basket of eggs in the house. We need to wash them off real good," says Mama. "Tom, we're going back in the house. Mabel's just gonna stay out here with you two."

Mabel saunters with Mama and Sister over to the steps. As they go into the house, Mabel takes a seat on the second step.

Papa takes a small bucket and sets it under the clothesline. "We'll hang her up here and let the blood drain into this bucket," says Papa. "It looks like we've got everything ready, Son. Let's go over to the coop so's you can bring the hen out."

Mabel watches as Bubba attempts to open the gate. *Bubba's trying to stall, just like he did when Mama asked him about the beaver dam. I'd be changing my mind about going to the creek to wash my hair if I's him. Papa's opening the gate—now he's gotta go in the coop.*

When Bubba walks into the pen, the hens seem to know that he's there for no good reason. Their clucking sounds become more numerous and they scatter away from him. Bubba surveys the group for the hen Mama chose. When Bubba starts moving toward her, she takes the opposite corner. They continue this ritual for a few minutes.

"Bubba, you have to hem her in and pick her up by the feet. She's gonna flop around on you. She'll flap her wings, but you can't let go."

Bubba makes a dive for her feet, but she gets away. Filthy from his chase with the hen, Bubba gets up and begins the ritual again. After several more misses, he finally works the hen around until she's in a corner with no place to go. Bubba bends down and wraps his hands around her feet. *That hen sure don't want any part of Bubba. She's flapping her wings like she could fly to Memphis and back.* Bubba holds the hen away from his body and exits the coop. "Just give her a few minutes to calm down, Son," says Papa.

"Shoo wee, this hen's heavy when she's fighting," says Bubba. "Tell me again about how I do my wrist, Papa."

"She'll be still in just a minute, Son. As soon as she gets still, just softly run your hand down to her neck and let go of her feet. When you get your hand around her neck, make a few quick circles. On your last spin, kinda speed up and then snap your wrist back around like you need to go the other way," says Papa.

"Yessir, I've got it. That's how Josie does it," says Bubba.

To get a little closer to the house, Mabel slides up one step. She places her elbows on her thighs and splays her fingers across her eyes. *This way I can open and shut my fingers and won't have to watch something if I don't want to.* Mabel practices looking through her fingers and then closing out the scene. *Bubba looks plumb scared to death. I don't know if he's scareder of the hen or killing it. Wonder if he's proud of being a grown-up now.*

"Okay, Son, you've got her calm. Now's the time to slide your hand down to her neck. When you whirl her around, do it firmly and quickly. We don't want her to suffer. Remember to get back when she flops around on the ground," instructs Papa. "You sure you want to do this?"

"Yessir, I want to try, but I sure don't want to hurt her. I'm gonna spin her as hard as I throw a baseball," says Bubba.

Mabel feels the sweat between her hands and face. She quickly wipes her hands on the sides of her dress and puts them back up over her eyes. Peeking through her fingers, she watches as Bubba slides his hand down the chicken's feathers to her neck. He stands there for what seems like a long time to Mabel. Now, holding only the hen's neck, Bubba looks up at Papa and bends his arm like he's getting ready to throw a ball. Feeling sorry for the hen, Mabel closes her eyes and sucks in some fresh air between her teeth.

Opening her eyes, she watches as Bubba whirls the chicken around once, twice, three times. Mabel closes her fingers over her eyes and opens them just in time to see the chicken pop up in the air. She looks at Bubba as he stands there—almost stationary—with the hen's head in his right hand. Speechless, they all watch as the chicken lands on the ground with a muffled *plop*.

Mabel can't believe what she sees next. The chicken, now with no head, gets up and tries to run. Unable to maintain its balance, the hen falls to one side and flops around in a big circle. The chicken eventually stops flopping. Papa tells Bubba to throw the head in the trash and to pick up the hen. Lifeless, the chicken offers no resistance this time when he picks her up by her legs.

"You stay put, Mabel," says Papa. "There's no need for you to get your dress messed up from the hen. You can stay there and watch." Papa walks over to the clothesline by Bubba. "Just loop a knot around her legs; and then we'll tie her to the wire, Son. You did a good job. I was afraid you weren't gonna whirl her around hard enough, but you did it the right way," says Papa. "Very good job, Son—your mama will be proud of you too."

"That's a lot harder to do than it looks. I never realized how heavy a hen is," says Bubba. Bubba's hands are still trembling. "I never had so much trouble tying a knot."

Mabel leans back with her elbows on the step above where she sits. *Now I know what Mama and Papa mean when they tell us that we're running around like chickens with our heads cut off. Poor little hen. She was walking around the coop eating laying mash—then Mama picked her out of all the rest. Now she's hanging over that bucket and her head's in the trash. Bubba's bigger and stronger than I thought. He was scared though. I could tell by the look in his eyes. I think Papa's proud of him.*

Several hours elapse after Bubba has successfully dressed the hen. Mabel joins Mama, Bubba, and Sister on the front porch. The screen door opens and Papa walks onto the front porch with the rest of the family. Papa says, "Okay girls, it's time for us to go get your beautiful hair washed. Here's a towel for each of you. I'll carry the shampoo. Here, Sister, you be in charge of the comb. Bubba, you're welcome to walk with us, if you'd like to."

"No thank you, Papa," says Bubba. "If it's okay with you and Mama, I'd like to walk up to Shoal Creek to see if I can catch a fish or two." *Bubba's face always turns red when he talks.* Reaching down to pick up a rock, he chunks it over the fence and looks up at Papa.

"I think that sounds like a good idea, Son," says Papa. "Don't be messing around too close to that deep water down there. It's dangerous." Bubba nods his head in agreement with Papa's warning and starts walking around to the backyard. "You be back home in an hour or so. We've got to go help set up everything for the church picnic."

"Yessir," says Bubba. "I'm just gonna fish from the bank. I ain't going out in the water."

"That's good," says Papa. He turns and looks at Mama. "Do you want to walk with us, Lizbeth? We'd be happy to have you."

"No, Brother and I will stay here. I've got too much cooking to do. Josie's coming in an hour or less to fry up the chicken. We're going to make the potato salad together. I have the potatoes ready, but now I've got a mess of eggs to boil." Mama gets up from her rocker and walks toward the door. "You girls don't give your papa too much trouble."

Mabel and Sister wait on the other side of the open gate. Papa walks along the boardwalk toward them. "Girls, I'm ready to scrub your pretty little heads." He locks the gate behind him and begins his happy whistle as the three of them walk up to the main road. "Look at them fellas at the store, girls. The one that's flinging his arms the most is the one telling the tallest tale," says Papa. "It sure is a beautiful day to be walking with you two lovely ladies."

Papa's always happy to be doing whatever he's doing. Mama says that she's never seen anyone like him. She says he worries sometimes, but he never talks about it much. That's the way I want to be. "Papa, do you think we'll move to Florence?" asks Mabel. "I hope we can stay here." Mabel looks up at his face, as he seems to think about what he's hearing. "I want to go to school at Shoal Crossing like Bubba and Sister."

"Well, Mabel, it's awfully hard for me to get over there every day to work; I don't think we'll be moving until sometime in the fall—if we move at all."

"What about school, Papa?" says Sister. "I like my school."

"Girls, you're worrying way too far ahead of time. You're also worrying about something that hasn't even happened yet. If we move, you'll be in a school you'll love just as much as Shoal Crossing, I promise," says Papa. "I'm more concerned about the war and influenza than I am about us moving. The right thing for all of us to do is to turn all of our worries over to God. He will take care of us."

"Mama says that the influenza is awful because so many people are dying from it," says Sister.

"Between our men dying in the war and our people dying from the influenza, our country's in a bad way. That flu isn't down here yet, but I'm afraid it's gonna come. As I said, we have to have faith that God will protect us, girls." Papa stops walking and announces, "Here's the creek. It's time to get down to business."

They walk from the road, down a slight embankment, and stand beside the creek. The clear water is trickling over the stones as each of them reaches down and touches the water. *That feels cold to me. The last time we washed our hair here, it was a lot warmer. I hope Papa can wash our hair in a hurry.*

"The water's cold," says Sister. *"Brrrr."* She takes a step back and wipes her hand dry on the towel. "It's gonna feel really cold on our heads."

"We'll work as fast as we can, Sister," says Papa. "Let's take one of the towels for you to kneel down right here." Papa reaches for the towel in Sister's hand and spreads it out neatly in a dry spot beside the creek. He unbuttons his shirtsleeves and rolls them up past his elbows. Mabel recognizes his shirt as one he wears to church with a starched collar attached. "Okay, Sister, I reckon you'll go first. Kneel down here on the towel."

Mabel is relieved that Sister's going first. She moves over to the side so she can get a better view of the washing. Papa gets down on his knees next to her, sloshes his hand in the water, and pours some shampoo into his hand. Leaning close to the water, Sister dips her hand down and cups the water onto her hair. She makes shivering sounds as she gets her hair soaked. Papa laughs and encourages her to do a good job. "Hand me your towel, Mabel," says Papa. He places it over Sister's shoulders. "Maybe that'll keep the water off of your dress." When she straightens up, Papa stays on his knees and douses the shampoo on top of her head. Sister helps him lather the soap all over her head.

"This is really cold, Papa," says Sister, "but it sure does feel good to my head." She looks around at Mabel. "You're next, Mabel, so you'd better not laugh."

Mabel remains silent and watches to see how they're going to get the soap out of Sister's hair. "Lean back over the water, Sister," says Papa. "It's time to rinse your hair now." Papa stands and takes a collapsible tin cup out of his back pocket, unfolds it, and dips it into the water. He pours the water over Sister's hair until the water finally runs clear. "I think we've got enough squeak in it to say it's clean, Sister." Sister stands and pulls the towel over her head. "Rub it as dry as you can, Sister, and then we'll need the towel for Mabel's shoulders."

Filled with dread, Mabel walks over and kneels down on the white towel beside the creek. She fears the feel of the cold water on her head, but doesn't want anyone to know. *Now I'm glad that I don't have long hair like Sister. Mine won't take as long.* Mabel stretches and leans as far over the water as she can. She cups some water in her hand and quickly splashes it onto her hair. The water feels like she's pouring ice on her head. "Are you ready to soap it now, Papa?" says Mabel. She and Papa lather the shampoo all over her head. "You scrub it better than Mama. Her fingernails are too sharp." Papa uses the cup and rinses her hair repeatedly. Mabel's hair is sticking out in all directions as she stands up.

"Okay, Sister, give us your towel," says Papa. "Since your hair's so long, you might want to use this other towel a little bit more." He folds his tin cup and puts it back into his hip pocket. "Let's go over there and sit down on that log, girls. The sun will help dry your hair."

The three of them walk over to the log and sit down. The warmth of the sun feels good to Mabel. She senses the cool dampness of the water on her dress collar and reaches up to touch it. *This is almost as pretty as Grandpa's farm. The sound of the water reminds me of the gristmill. I like the way the sun shoots down between the tree limbs. This is where we built the dam for the beavers. The sticks are still stacked over by the tree from when we had to tear it down. Bubba got us into some bad trouble and we almost killed Joe's hogs.*

"Here, Mabel, I'm finished with the comb. I got all my tangles out," says Sister.

Mabel rubs her hair a little longer and then starts combing it. *Papa did a good job washing my hair. I can feel that it's clean.* "Thank you for bringing us to the creek, Papa," says Mabel. "I like the way you make my hair squeak. Mama says that's a sign it's good and clean."

"You're welcome, Mabel." They all remain on the log and continue taking in their surroundings. "Girls, do you realize how blessed our family is?" says Papa. "We may have to move to Florence, but you need to understand that I don't have to leave y'all and go fight in the war. There's plenty of children all over the United States who don't have their daddy at home." He reaches down and picks up a twig. "No matter what happens, we can always find something to be thankful for in our lives. Our family doesn't have one thing to complain about, does it?"

"No sir," agrees Mabel. "Why don't you have to fight like the other daddies?"

"It's because I work for the government. I reckon they figure all of us at the dam are worth more here than overseas," says Papa. "We need to be thankful too that the flu hasn't hit our little town. People are dying from it every day. It's worse than the war."

"I don't think it'd be bad to live in Florence," says Sister.

"It doesn't matter where we have to live, just as long as we're together and have our health," says Papa. "You have to always consider what's most important in your life and then try to keep everything in the right order." Papa stands up and walks back over to the creek;

he starts walking toward the road. "After God, the most important thing in my life is my family. That's why I work so hard." Mabel and Sister walk over and each takes one of his hands. "I reckon it's time for us to get back home," says Papa.

When they get to the house, Bubba's sitting on the front porch. "I didn't get a single bite," says Bubba. "Nobody around me had any fish either." He stands and pulls his brown knickers down to the top of his socks. "Are we ready to go to the church now, Papa?"

"Yeah Son, I just want to step inside to let your mama know I'm back from the creek and going to the church," says Papa. "You girls come on in here so she can see your hair. I think you need to dry it a little more with a fresh towel."

Bubba follows them into the house and down the hall to the kitchen. Mama and Josie are sitting at the table putting the potato salad together. "Did you enjoy your hair washing, girls?" says Mama. Mabel and Sister nod in agreement. Josie looks up at Mabel and smiles. "Mr. O'Brien, are you and Bubba off to the church now?" asks Mama.

"We're gonna have to be there for several hours, Lizbeth," answers Papa. "I guess it'll depend on how many people come to help us set it up. How are you, Josie?"

"I'm doing real well, Mr. Tom." Josie keeps turning the potatoes and mayonnaise. "Sounds like y'all's gonna have a nice picnic at church. We gonna have some baptizing tomorrow," she adds—never looking up from her stirring.

"Y'all gonna baptize in the creek?" asks Papa. "If you are, there's gonna be some whooping and hollering because that water is still mighty cold." They all laugh as Papa jumps around.

"That's right where we'll be," says Josie. "It won't be until the afternoon after the service, so maybe it'll be a little warmer." Josie dips her spoon into the cooked potatoes and then adds them to the bowl. She dips a teaspoon into the mustard and puts it into her mixture. "You know we's gonna do some shoutin' when they come up out of the water—don't matter if that creek's cold or hot. We'll be singing too."

"That's right, Josie," says Papa. "That's a happy time—when the preacher shows everybody that their sins can be washed away. There's nothing like being saved to totally turn your life around." Josie nods her head in agreement with Papa. "Well, I suppose Bubba and me will go on to the church, Lizbeth. You need anything from the store?"

"No, Josie and I have everything all set. We've got to fry the chicken. You two stay away as long as you want to," says Mama. She looks up and smiles at Papa. He and Bubba walk back up the hall to the front door.

"There's somebody sitting out on the back steps waiting for you two," says Josie. She rolls her eyes toward the back door.

"Do we need to dry our hair some more, Mama?" asks Sister.

"I don't think so. It'll dry just fine in the sunshine," answers Mama. Mabel and Sister go outside and find Drella sitting on the steps.

"Hey, Mabel. Hey, Sister. I've been waiting for y'all to come home. Did y'all get your hair all clean for church?" says Drella.

"Hi, Drella," says Sister. "Papa about scrubbed my hair off my head, but it sure is clean." She walks down and sits beside Drella. Drella's wearing a dress made of flour sack material. "Did Josie make that dress for you?"

"She sure did," says Drella. "It's about my most favorite." She rubs her hand along the material on her leg. Drella stops at one of the pink rosebuds in the design and traces it with her finger.

"It sure is pretty," says Mabel. She sits down on the step just above Sister and Drella, who turns and smiles up at her. *Drella has the prettiest eyes I've ever seen. I like it when she smiles.* "Your hair looks nice the way Josie fixed it with the little ribbons to match the roses."

Drella reaches up and feels of one of her pigtails. "I told her that she's making too many pigtails in my hair," says Drella. "What y'all been cooking in the fire out there, ash cakes?" Mabel and Sister look at her.

"What are ash cakes?" asks Sister. "Those ashes are left over from Bubba having to singe the chicken feathers."

Mabel leans forward to listen more closely to Drella. "Ash cakes are little cakes you cook in the ashes. Mama Josie told me that her daddy use to make them before they went out in the fields to work." Drella looks over her shoulder at Mabel. "She told me that her daddy's daddy was a slave—they about lived on them."

"What do they taste like?" asks Mabel. She gets up and steps between the two girls to get to the ground. Drella reaches out for Mabel's hand and Mabel pulls her up. They both face Sister.

"They's good. Tastes kinda like cornbread and a pancake mixed because we put syrup on ours," says Drella.

"Do you think Josie would make us some today?" says Sister.

"I ain't asking her, but if Mabel asks, she'll do it," says Drella. They both look at Mabel. "You gonna ask her, Mabel?" Mabel looks down at the ground and feels the flutter in her stomach. "You're the only one she'd do it for, lessen it's your mama," says Drella.

"Tell me what to say," says Mabel.

"You tell her that we's sitting out here talking. Then you tell her about the fire," says Drella. "Next, you tell her that you want her to make all of us some ash cakes." Drella smiles at Mabel and Sister puts her hands in the praying posture. "Go do it, Mabel. Them ashes ain't gonna last all afternoon," says Drella.

Without a word, Mabel walks up the steps, opens the screen door, and walks across the porch. *Ash cakes—I've got to remember it. Ash cakes, ash cakes, ash cakes.* Mabel tries to keep the words in her head so she can tell Josie what they want. She opens the back door and steps into the kitchen. *Ash cakes, ash cakes, ash cakes, ash cakes.*

Mabel stands beside Josie at the stove. *Ash cakes, ash cakes, ash cakes.* Josie looks down at Mabel and puts her arm around her shoulder. She looks back at the skillet and turns some of the chicken pieces over.

"What is it, Mabel?" says Josie. "Don't let none of this grease get on your pretty face. Why you looking at me like that?"

"Ash cakes," says Mabel. Josie rolls her eyes away from the sizzling chicken and down at Mabel. "Can you please make us some ash cakes like you and your daddy use to make when you were a little girl?" Mabel surprises herself by getting all of the words out in one breath. "We's talking about the ashes in the back yard, so Drella told us about the cakes. Can we make some?"

Josie puts her hand on her hip and laughs. "You girls is always looking for something to get into," she says with laughter lingering in her voice. She gingerly picks up a piece of the chicken with the tongs and places it on a white platter. "If it's all right with Miss Lizbeth and the ashes are still hot. Let me ask your mama. I'll be out there directly to check them ashes. You go on back outside." Mabel walks over to the back door. "Hey, Mabel, you tell them other two not to be sending you back in here again."

"Yessum, Josie. Are you mad at me? I mean angry with me?" says Mabel. Josie laughs again as Mabel feels a touch of sadness that she did something wrong.

"No, Mabel," says Josie. "I ain't mad and I ain't angry neither. I just know them two put you up to coming in here while I's cooking. That's all. Now, come here and give Josie a hug." She stretches her arm out toward Mabel. Mabel walks over and puts her arms around Josie. She buries her face into her apron. "Don't you ever worry about old Josie being upset with you. That day ain't never gonna come, child."

"Yessum."

Mabel walks outside to the back steps and sits down. Sister and Drella stare at her. "What did she say, Mabel?" says Sister. "Is she gonna make us some?"

"She said that she'll be out here in a few minutes and for you two not to send me back in the house again," says Mabel. She gets up and walks into the yard with Sister and Drella. "Josie sounded like she's gonna do it though." They all hold hands and dance around in a circle. "I sure hope Mama says it's okay."

"Let's look for some four-leaf clovers," says Drella. "Whoever finds one is gonna be good luck for us to have some ash cakes." They all get down on their knees and run their hands over the clover. "Most of them is three-leaf clovers."

"I found one," says Sister. Sister stands up and walks over to Mabel and Drella. They look at it and turn their attention back to finding one for themselves. "I found the good luck for us to have some ash cakes."

"I found one," says Drella. "Now, we've gotta help Mabel find one." They all stay down on the ground and look until Drella finds another one. "Here, Mabel. Now you've got some good luck."

"Okay, girls, come help me carry these things out to the fire," Josie calls out. They run up the steps and into the screened porch. "I've already mixed our batter. Sister, you carry this can of sorghum. Mabel, you carry this pancake turner. Drella, you get to carry this knife for spreading the sorghum." They all walk down the back steps and out to the dying embers.

"Does it take long for them to cook?" asks Sister. "Ever since Drella told us about them, I've been hungry."

"No, it ain't gonna take long," says Josie. "I'm gonna give each of you enough of this dough to make your own—special for the size of your hand."

Josie gets down on her knees by the ashes. "There's still enough heat in there to cook. Now, y'all watch how I make my patty and then you do the very same thing." Josie hands each of them a firm ball of ash cake dough. The dough fits perfectly in Mabel's hand. They all watch Josie as she rolls her dough around in her hand and forms a ball. The girls copy her. Josie then starts pressing the dough out flat between her hands "Now, you wants to pat it out until it's about as thin as mine. If it's too thick, it ain't gonna cook through." Mabel pats her ball of dough until it spreads out over the palm of her hand and appears to be the right thickness.

As each girl finishes, she holds her ash cake dough up to Josie. "Did you really do this with your daddy, Josie?" asks Mabel. Josie places her ash cake in the whitest ashes. Drella, Sister, and Mabel do the same. They all stare at the ash cakes resting in the ashes.

"I sure did, child," says Josie. "My daddy and me did this just about every morning—specially when we'd work in the fields all day. We'd cook them just like we're doing and put them in a sack. Then we'd eat them 'long 'bout the middle of the day." Josie takes the turner and lifts up the edge of each cake. "Looks like they're ready to flip over right now." Josie skillfully turns each of the cakes over and each girl stretches over to see what the cakes look like.

"Y'all don't worry about the ashes. We don't have to eat those," says Drella. "When Mama Josie takes them out, we have to let them cool; then we can blow most of the ashes off." Drella smiles over at her mama. "Then we pour some syrup on them and eat."

Josie removes each of the ash cakes from the coals. She gently brushes the ashes from each of the cakes with her fingers. *This is more fun than I've ever had. I wish I could know all the things Josie and her daddy did. They lived like the pioneers that Mama reads to us about in books. Mama says that Josie's smart. I think she's just about smarter than anybody I know.*

"Y'all check for ashes before we spread the molasses on the cakes," says Josie. "If there's too many ashes, just blow them off. You can dust them away with your fingers." Josie watches as each of the girls checks their cake. "When you think it's clean enough, I'll put the syrup on it for you and you're ready to take a bite."

"Mmmm, this is so good, Josie," says Sister. "Now I know why you liked them when you were a little girl."

"I like mine too," says Mabel. "They aren't crispy like your corncakes, but they taste good." Mabel takes another bite and smiles at Josie.

"My daddy wasn't a slave, but his daddy was," says Josie. "Peoples back in those times just about lived off of these." Josie stares down at the cake. "If the slaves didn't have a good master or a good crop, or anything went wrong, they ate whatever they could to stay alive." Josie looks into the faces of the girls as they enjoy their cakes. "You think about it. If this was all you had to eat, you'd near 'bout starve to death. That's why you best be thankful for what you have to eat every day."

After Mabel puts her last bite into her mouth, she gets up and goes over to Josie. She bends down and puts her cheek next to Josie's cheek. "Thank you for making these for us, Josie," says Mabel. "They sure are good." Mabel stands back up. "I like hearing your stories about your daddy."

"You welcome, Mabel," says Josie. "The good Lord watched over peoples back in the slave days and is still watching over us until this day." Josie unfolds herself and gets to her feet. "Don't you girls ever let nobody tell you that you can't make it. There's always hope for a better day as long as you have air to breathe and God in your heart. That's why all of us just have to keep on keeping on."

"Did it make you sad to make these, Mama Josie?" asks Drella.

"No child, I ain't sad. I's just thinking about how good our God is to His children. I'm thankful that we can find our way through this life on earth. All we've got to do is listen and watch," says Josie. "My daddy showed me that—the Lord has taught me that too. It don't matter how hard times gets; we can always find hope comin' 'round the corner. Just like those ash cakes filled peoples and gave them hope for a better tomorrow."

"That makes you happy, doesn't it Josie?" says Mabel. "That's what makes Papa happy too."

"That's right, Mabel." Josie stoops down to pick up the knife and pancake turner. She puts them into the bowl and hands it to Mabel. "Sister, pick up that sorghum, please ma'am. Drella and me's gotta get on home to get ready for church tomorrow." She hands the bowl to Mabel. "Tell your mama about the ash cakes. Tell her that Drella and me's gone on home. Y'all enjoy your picnic tomorrow. You got some good food to take to the church."

Mabel walks over to Josie, sets the bowl on the ground, and wraps her arms around Josie's waist. Josie bends down and hugs Mabel. "I love you, Josie," says Mabel.

"I love you too, Mabel," says Josie. "I'll see your pretty face on Monday."

"Bye, Josie," says Sister. "Bye, Drella."

Drella and Josie walk across the back yard holding hands. They pass the barn and move out of sight. Mabel and Sister walk back to the house in silence.

Chapter 15

After supper Saturday evening, the O'Brien family gathers in the parlor. Rather than talking on this particular night, they use their time to read by the light of the kerosene lamp. Mama and Papa sit in their chairs reading their Bibles, and Bubba, sprawled out on the floor, looks at the Florence newspaper. Mabel and Sister have one of Mama's old catalogs and quietly turn the pages to find clothes and toys they like. They fold down the corners on the pages they find particularly enticing. They'll soon find an opportunity to show them to Mama. When Mama gets a new catalog, Mabel and Sister will make paper dolls from the pictures they select tonight.

"Mabel, you need to tell your papa about the ash cakes you girls cooked this afternoon," says Mama.

Mabel gets up and walks over to Papa. She stands in front of him and waits for him to close his Bible. He looks up at her and smiles. Mabel notices that his shirtsleeves are still rolled up from earlier in the day. "Josie taught us how to make ash cakes today, Papa. It was fun and they tasted real good," says Mabel. "She cooked them in those ashes you and Bubba left out there. We had to rub off the ashes before we could put sorghum on them."

"My goodness, I've never heard of such a thing," says Papa.

"Josie says that the slaves use to make them. Her grandpa was a slave and taught Josie's daddy how to make them."

"Did you eat the ashes?" asks Mama.

"Yessum, we ate some. Josie showed us how to get most of them off though," says Mabel. "She taught us that some people had to eat that every day."

"What are they made of, Lizbeth?" says Papa.

"Josie said that she just mixed some cornmeal, a tad of sugar, and a little water. The batter is a lot thicker than what she uses for cornbread," says Mama. "The girls seemed to really like them."

"Sister and me can make you some, Papa," says Mabel.

"I'd like to try them," says Papa. He stands up, places his hands at the back of his waist, and arches his back. "Me-oh-my, I'm tireder than I am when I put in a full day's work at the foundry." He and Mama laugh at his exhaustion. "Let's see. We killed a hen, dressed it, had a hair washing, worked at the church, cooked, and now we've gotta get our clothes ready for church." He walks over to the door and steps outside. *Papa says he likes to take a deep breath of fresh air before he goes to bed.*

"Okay, children, it's time to lay out your church clothes. Make sure your shoes are clean, brush your teeth, and get in bed," says Mama. "We've got a big day tomorrow."

"Mama, I don't feel good," says Mabel. "My throat feels raw when I swallow."

"Come over here to the light, Mabel," says Mama. "Now, open your mouth real wide so I can see your throat." Mabel kneels down and waits to hear about what Mama sees. "It's as red as fire. Let's go to the kitchen. I'll fix you some warm saltwater with vinegar so you can gargle."

Mabel follows Mama to the kitchen. "This will make it feel better in no time. Don't swallow it, Mabel. Just spit it in this empty glass," says Mama. Mabel throws her head back and makes a gurgling sound as she holds the gargle in her mouth. "You need to do this whole glass." Mabel repeats the gargling two more times. "Now, does that feel better?" says Mama.

"A little, but it still hurts, Mama," says Mabel. She rubs her hands up and down her neck. "Will you put some warm rags on it?"

"I sure will," says Mama. "You go on to bed. I'll be in there in a few minutes. I think I'll let Sister sleep in the parlor. I don't want her catching that sore throat."

"Yessum." Mabel goes into the bedroom, puts on her nightgown, and crawls into bed. *My throat hurts bad. I don't have an earache, so maybe it'll go away after Mama puts those warm rags on it. We've got to go to church in the morning—it'll be better by then.* Mabel closes her eyes and drifts in and out of sleep.

Mama walks into the bedroom. "I've got to get Sister's nightie, then I'll be back to put the cloths on your throat," says Mama. *Mama always tiptoes when she thinks somebody's sick or asleep.* Mabel's eyes follow Mama as she moves about the room. "I'll be right back, Mabel," whispers Mama.

"Yessum." *It hurts to talk.* Mabel closes her eyes once again. In a few minutes, she hears the door open. Mama walks quickly across the floor to the bed.

"Here you go, Mabel," says Mama. "That should make your throat feel a lot better. Has your throat been hurting all day?"

Barely moving her lips, Mabel whispers, "No'm."

"That's odd. I'll let you rest, but I'll be back in here to check on you." Mama pats Mabel's hand. "You'll be better in the morning. We'll probably be able to go to the dinner on the grounds. If you're not better, Brother and I will stay home with you. Don't worry about it." Mama stands up, walks toward the door, and stops. "I'll be back in a few minutes."

"Yessum. Thank you, Mama," says Mabel. She closes her eyes once again and falls asleep with the soothing warmth of the cloths around her neck.

Sunday morning, Mabel opens her eyes and looks up into Papa's face. "How's my girl feeling this beautiful morning?"

Mabel swallows and her throat feels raw. "My throat hurts, Papa." Mabel closes her eyes in disappointment.

"Well, it'll get better when it gets warmer up in the day. Your mama and Brother are gonna stay here with you while Bubba, Sister, and I go to church. I'm sorry you're going to miss the dinner on the grounds," says Papa. He leans down and kisses her forehead. "I've got to go early so I can ring the bell this morning. Then I've got to walk people to their seats."

Mabel looks up at him. She moves her lips and whispers, "Okay."

"I'll see you when we get back home. We'll say a prayer for you at church. You'll be better in no time," says Papa. He leans over and kisses her forehead once again. "You feel like you've got a little bit of a temperature." He turns and walks toward the door. "I love you, Mabel."

"I love you, Papa," says Mabel. She turns over with her back to the door. As she listens to his footsteps walk up the hall, a solitary tear rolls down her cheek.

Mabel stays in bed all day with her sore throat. Mama makes a series of visits—alternating each trip with warm tea, warm saltwater gargle, and warm cloths for her throat. Mabel sleeps most of the day.

Papa comes in to see her several times and assures her that the dinner on the church grounds was no fun without her. Bubba and Sister are not allowed in the bedroom. When one of her children is sick, Mama always requires total separation from the rest of the family. She even separates the sick one's dishes and eating utensils.

Before everyone goes to bed Sunday evening, Mama warms some cloths for Mabel's throat. When she enters the bedroom, Mabel is sitting up in bed. "Can Sister come in here and sleep tonight?" says Mabel. "I like to have her to talk to."

"No indeed, Mabel," says Mama. "You've still got a fever and your throat's red as fire. She can come back in here when your fever breaks. You don't want her to get sick, do you?"

"No'm," says Mabel. "I's just feeling a little better and thought it'd be all right."

"We'll see how you do tomorrow. You know Josie's coming in the morning, don't you?" says Mama. "She's going to be upset if you're sick. You're her favorite helper." Looking to find a dress for Sister to wear on Monday, Mama moves about the room as she continues to talk. "I'm going to get your papa to go to the commissary and get you some aspirin for your fever. I think that'll make you feel a whole lot better."

"Yessum," says Mabel. She scoots down in the bed. "Does it taste bad?"

"Not at all," says Mama. "You swallow it with a glass of water. It's a tiny pill." Mama clutches Sister's clothes in her arms. "I'll check on you in a little while. I'm happy you feel better. I won't wake you up when I come back. I love you, Mabel."

"Night, Mama," says Mabel. "I love you too."

Mabel sleeps through the night, but still has a sore throat when she swallows on Monday morning. Disappointed, Mabel lies in bed and listens for movement in the house. She hears Mama stirring in the kitchen. She falls back to sleep and awakens when Josie opens the bedroom door.

"Child, what's this I hear about you being sick?" asks Josie with concern in her voice. She walks over to Mabel's bed and sits down beside her. "Your mama told me that you have a sore throat." Josie feels Mabel's forehead and begins combing through Mabel's hair with her fingers. "Your hair's still nice and clean. I'm gonna fix you some nice hot mush and a cup of lemon tea." Josie stands up and looks down at Mabel. "I don't like for my baby to be sick. You know old Josie loves you, don't you?"

Mabel's blue eyes look into Josie's. "Yessum, I know that," says Mabel. "You don't reckon those ash cakes made my throat sore, do you?"

"Lawd child, your head's still worrying about things," says Josie with a chuckle. "No one else got the sore throat from the ash cakes. I suspect it's from the creek, don't you? That water's mighty cold."

"Yessum," says Mabel. "It was really cold."

"I'll be back with you a breakfast tray, Miss Mabel O'Brien."

By that afternoon, Mabel feels much better, but Mama requires her to stay in the bedroom. Before Josie leaves for the day, she walks into the bedroom. She sits down on the bed beside Mabel. "What's that you've got, Josie?" says Mabel.

"This here's some alcohol for me to put on this cloth and rub on you. It'll cool your fever down," says Josie. "My daddy use to do this for us girls."

Mabel rolls her eyes toward Josie. "Did you ever have a sore throat?"

"Child, ain't a soul walking that ain't had a sore throat. They generally don't stay with you too long. Best thing is to keep that sore throat in bed until it goes away," says Josie. "Now this is gonna feel real cool." Josie stands and begins rubbing the alcohol behind Mabel's neck, down her arms, and finally on her legs. "Let me feel of your earlobes. Uh huh, just what I thought. That alcohol's cooled you already."

"That felt good, Josie," says Mabel. "Do you reckon Mama will let me put on my overalls so I can go sit in the sunshine on the front porch and wait for Papa?"

"I don't see why that would cause any problem. She ain't gonna let you be 'round none of the other children though," says Josie. "Your mama is a real stickler about her rules, you know. Let me go ask her. Be right back."

Josie re-enters the bedroom with a smile on her face. Mabel immediately scoots up into a sitting position and smiles back at Josie. "I's getting almost as good as you, Mabel, with being able to talk peoples into things like you do me." Josie goes over and gets Mabel's overalls, a blouse, and her shoes and socks. "Now, I promised her that you'd just sit out there and wait for your papa."

"Yessum," says Mabel. "That's all I want to do."

"He'll be coming down that road any time now," says Josie. "I'm gonna walk you out to the porch—then I've got to be on my way."

The two of them walk hand in hand up the hall to the front door and out onto the porch. Mabel takes a deep breath. "It feels good out here, Josie. Smells good too. I'm glad you begged Mama into letting me come out here," says Mabel.

Josie laughs as she walks Mabel to the post she likes to lean against. "Child, we's bad, the two of us, the way we beg, ain't we?" Josie walks down the steps and turns to look at Mabel. "Now, don't you go gettin' me in no trouble. You sit right there in that sunshine till your papa gets here. Bubba and Sister are out back. Your mama's finishing up supper in the kitchen. I gotta go now, baby. I'll see you in the morning."

"Bye, Josie," says Mabel. "I love you. I'll stay right here." Josie turns and strolls over to the side of the house, around the corner, and out of sight.

The sunshine feels good, but I'm still cold. Mabel leans her head back, resting it on the post. *My throat still hurts and I feel tired. I'm gonna try to play like my throat's not sore so Mama will let me play with Sister tonight.* Mabel closes her eyes and soaks in the warmth of the sun. Mama comes to the door and steps outside.

"There's my girl enjoying the evening sun," says Mama. She walks over and sits down in her rocking chair. "Your papa's going to be surprised to see you out here. Your face looks flushed, Mabel. Are you certain you feel better?"

"Yessum," says Mabel. "I feel a little better. It feels cold out here though."

"Come over here and let me feel your head. You look feverish to me," says Mama. Mabel uses all of her strength to get up and walk across the porch. Mama puts her hand on Mabel's forehead and then feels both of her ears. "Sit down on Papa's chair. I'll let you stay out here until he gets home, but then you need to go back and get into bed. You're still running a fever."

They both look up as they hear Papa say, "Well, good afternoon, ladies." He reaches over and unlatches the gate; he walks up the boardwalk with a big smile. "I'm glad to see you up and about, Mabel. I brought you some aspirin for your fever."

Mabel stands up so Papa can sit down in his rocker. "Can I sit on your lap, Papa?"

"Why sure you can." Mabel crawls up in his lap and rests her head on his chest. "The druggist at the commissary said that this aspirin will break her fever, Lizbeth. I don't understand why it's not going back to normal. Mabel's usually the healthiest one in the family," says Papa.

"When you come in for supper, she needs to go back to bed. I'll give her some aspirin after she eats," says Mama. "It'll probably take a few more days. That throat of hers is really red." Mama stands up from her chair. "I'll go finish up supper and call you in a few minutes."

After Mama goes into the house, Papa starts rocking Mabel. "I sure do hate it when you kids feel bad," says Papa. Mabel closes her eyes and listens to the deep sounds of Papa's voice in his chest. "We had a good day at work, but I was anxious to get home and bring you the aspirin. Nothing much matters when someone in the family's sick. We'll get you better soon." Papa kisses Mabel's forehead. "The aspirin will make you feel better."

Mama comes to the door and talks through the screen. "Time for supper, Tom. Take Mabel to her bedroom, please. We're eating in the kitchen. Mabel, I'll bring your tray into your room in just a minute," says Mama. "Josie made you some of her good broth."

"You heard your Mama, Mabel. Hop down so we can go inside," says Papa. Mabel doesn't move, so Papa straightens his legs and makes a slide for her, just as he has done so many times in the past. Mabel slides down his legs and lands on the floor with a *thud*.

Papa stands and steps over her. "Come on, Mabel, we've got to go eat supper." Attempting to mind Papa, Mabel gets up on her knees and starts crawling toward him.

"I can't walk, Papa," says Mabel. "My legs won't hold me up—my legs hurt." While he's standing there, holding the door open, Mabel looks up at him and tears begin streaming down her face.

"Mabel, you get up this minute. I mean it, young lady. We don't have time to play. Crawling is for babies. Get up this minute," says Papa sternly.

She collapses on the porch—sobbing. "Papa, Papa, Papa," cries Mabel. "Help me get up, Papa."

"What's all the commotion about, Tom?" says Mama. She rushes out on the porch and stoops down beside Mabel. "Mabel, what's wrong?"

"I … I … I can't walk, Mama," says Mabel. "My legs have knots in them." Heaving with sobs, she puts her head down on her folded arms. "Papa won't help me." The hurt from Papa's refusal to help her is far worse than the pain in her legs.

"Tom, you've got to carry her to her bed. Mabel wouldn't act this way unless there was something wrong," says Mama.

Papa gets down on his knees, turns Mabel over, and maneuvers his hands underneath her body. He lifts her up into his arms and kisses her forehead. Now with tears rolling down his face, he whispers, "God love my baby. I thought you were playing, Mabel. Papa's gonna take care of you." He looks up at Mama. "Hold the door wide open, Lizbeth. I don't want to bump into anything with her."

Mabel puts her arm around Papa's neck. As they pass Mama on the way inside, Mabel sees the fear in Mama's eyes. Papa rushes into the house and carries Mabel to her bed, talking to her constantly. "Papa's going to take care of you. You'll be all right. I love you too much to let anything happen to you."

Mama follows them. "Tom, you go tell Bubba and Sister to eat while I change Mabel's clothes," says Mama. "She's burning hot. Come back in here as soon as you can." Papa quickly disappears from the room. "Now, now. Everything's all right, Mabel. You just got too tired out there. Mama and Papa are going to take care of you. You know that, don't you?"

Through the blurriness of her tears, Mabel looks at Mama and whispers, "Yessum." After Mama changes Mabel into a nightgown, she lies on her back and drifts in and out of sleep. She sporadically sees her parents coming into her room—never leaving her alone.

Mama brings her some hot tea, but Mabel only sips a few teaspoons down. When Mama bathes her in alcohol, like Josie did earlier, it makes Mabel feel better. *I'm too tired to talk and my throat still hurts. In the morning, I'll tell Mama how much my head hurts. My legs hurt too and my neck feels stiff. I'll be better tomorrow when Josie comes.* Mabel barely opens her eyes when Papa brings a lantern into the room and leaves again. She rolls her eyes over and sees Mama sitting in a chair beside the bed and reading her Bible.

She hears Papa come back into the room. He gently touches Mabel's leg. "Lizbeth, I'm going to make me a pallet and sleep in here tonight. I want you to go on to bed because you're going to have a hard day tomorrow."

"I'm fine, Tom," says Mama. "I don't know if I can go to sleep. It worries me because this is so unlike Mabel. She never complains about anything."

"I know—it worries me too. I've been thinking about something; here's my plan," says Papa. "I want to leave at sunup and go look for Dr. Reed so he can come check her. After I find him, I'll go on to work."

"I think the doctor does need to see her. This isn't acting like an ordinary sore throat, cold, allergy, or flu," says Mama. "That'll make everything a lot better for us to know for sure what we're dealing with." Mama stands up and kisses Mabel on her forehead. "I love you, Mabel."

Mabel peeps through her eyelids into Mama's face. "Papa's going to sleep in here tonight," says Mama in a soft tone of voice.

"Lizbeth, will you please get me some quilts, a sheet, and a pillow?" says Papa. "I'll put the pallet right here beside her bed."

"I'll be right back, Tom," answers Mama. "I've got to check on Bubba, Sister, and Brother. They're being so good—Sister and Bubba washed the dishes and put them away for me."

When Mama comes back with the quilts, she and Papa start spreading them on the floor. Mabel feels the gentle breeze the quilts create when they fan them in the air. "This will do just fine, Lizbeth. I won't have any trouble sleeping here at all."

"Now that we have that all fixed, I want to go get the aspirin so I can give Mabel another one," says Mama. "Be right back."

When Mama comes back, Papa is sitting in the chair and reading the Bible. "That was a fast trip," says Papa. "Do you want me to give her the aspirin?"

"No, I can do it," says Mama. She sits down on the edge of the bed. "Mabel, honey, I need to give you an aspirin. This will make you feel better." Mabel opens her eyes and pushes up on her elbows so she can swallow the pill and water. "Papa can give you another one later."

"My legs hurt, Mama. Will they be better tomorrow? I can't move them," says Mabel.

"I sure hope they will, honey. Now, you try to go back to sleep. Sister and Bubba said to tell you that they hope you feel better. They miss you," says Mama. A weak smile passes over Mabel's lips.

"Lizbeth, before you leave, I think we need to say our prayer in here with Mabel tonight."

"That's a good idea, Tom," says Mama. Mabel opens her eyes and looks up at her parents.

"Let's kneel down here by Mabel's bed," says Papa. Mama kneels and slips her right hand under the nape of Mabel's neck. Papa kneels beside Mama and places Mabel's left hand between both of his hands. "Let's bow our heads and pray. Lord, our heavenly Father, we come to You tonight as two troubled parents. We pray, Lord, that You will wrap Your loving arms around Mabel's body and restore her health from the soles of her tiny feet to the top of her beautiful head. We thank You, Lord, for blessing us with her as our child on earth. We pray that we shall never fail her as her parents. Lead, guide, and direct us in our care of her. Lord, we thank You for the blessing of her healing that we know will come in Your time. We pray for Your patience and guidance in all matters. Amen."

Mama leans over and kisses Mabel's cheek. "Good night, Mabel, I love you."

Papa stands and reaches down to help Mama to her feet. "The Lord will heal her. We've got to keep our faith," says Papa. He kisses Mama on her forehead. "Now, young lady, you need to go get some rest. Mabel and I need some rest too. We'll see you in the morning."

Mama turns and tiptoes out of the room. Papa reaches in his pocket, pulls out a handkerchief, and wipes the tears from his eyes. He blows out the lantern and lies down on the pallet. Mabel stretches out her hand. Papa reaches up and holds it. "Goodnight, precious Mabel. I love you."

Mabel's lips move, but no words come out. She finally murmurs, "Good night, Papa. I love you." She falls asleep.

Chapter 16

TUESDAY MORNING, IN THE EARLY LIGHT of day, Mabel hears Papa softly whistling as he folds up his pallet. *Papa's always happy. I'm glad he spent the night by my bed. I think he gave me an aspirin when it was dark.* She watches as he makes his way to the door. He turns, looks back at her, and smiles when he sees her looking at him. After Papa blows her a kiss, he quietly closes the door. Mabel hears his footsteps trailing toward the kitchen. *It's too early for breakfast. I still don't feel good.* Disappointed, she goes back to sleep.

Mabel reawakens when she feels Mama rubbing her arm. "I have you some hot tea and a small bowl of oatmeal fixed, Mabel. You're going to like the oatmeal. I fixed it just the way you like it—lots of butter and sugar. I cooked it extra special, so it won't hurt your throat." Mabel looks at Mama and sees that she's already dressed for the day. "Let me help you sit up."

Mama places her arms under each of Mabel's arms, helps to pull her into a sitting position, and places extra pillows behind Mabel's back against the mahogany headboard. "It feels good to sit up," says Mabel weakly. She attempts to pull her legs to her chest. "I still can't make my legs work. What's wrong with my legs, Mama?"

"If I knew the answer to that question, you'd be walking into the kitchen," says Mama. "Your papa left early because he's sending Dr. Reed to the house. We'll find out what's wrong when he comes."

Mama turns and picks the tray up from the seat of the chair so she can sit down. "Now we need to get some food in you for some strength." She scoops up the almost-liquid oatmeal in a spoon and puts it to Mabel's lips.

"I can feed myself, Mama," says Mabel. Reluctantly, she opens her mouth and holds the oatmeal there to take in its sweetness. "Mmmm ... that tastes good." Mama places the tray on Mabel's lap and watches every bite Mabel takes. "You made this the way Josie makes it, Mama. It doesn't hurt my throat."

"Dip your spoon in the tea and take a drink of it," says Mama. "You know tea heals our bodies. That's what they say, at least. It always gives me extra pep in the mornings."

Mabel gets a teaspoon of tea and sucks it into her mouth. Rolling her eyes toward Mama, Mabel checks to see if she's going to get in trouble for slurping. *Mama doesn't even care if I don't show my manners.*

"Did Papa give me an aspirin in the night?" asks Mabel. "It makes me feel better."

"Yes, as a matter of fact, he did. He said that you were moaning a little bit, so he gave you one. I knew they'd help. After you finish eating, I want you to take another one. If we can keep your fever down, you'll be feeling better."

Mabel continues to alternate teaspoons of oatmeal and hot tea until she feels full. "That's all I can eat, Mama. It sure did taste good," she says.

Mama stands up beside the bed and lifts the tray from Mabel's lap. "I'll take these dishes and wash them. I'm keeping your dishes extra clean with bleach," says Mama. "I don't want anybody giving you their germs and vice versa." As she walks toward the door, Mama continues talking. "I'll be right back." Mabel scoots down in her bed and pulls the sheet up over her head to shut out the sunlight. She falls back to sleep.

"Miss Lizbeth? I don't see Mabel in here," says Josie. "I reckon she must be outside playing."

Hoping Josie doesn't see her under the sheet, Mabel keeps very still. Mama steps inside the bedroom. "My goodness, I guess she's feeling better. I'll go look out the kitchen window to see if I can find her." Mabel can feel her stomach shaking from her noiseless giggles.

"Okay," says Josie. "Reckon I'll change her bed sheets while she's playing." Josie walks over to the bed, takes hold of the top of the sheet, and pulls it back. Josie jumps back from the bed with a look of shock on her face. "Lawd child, you 'bout gave old Josie heart failure." She and Mabel laugh together. Josie reaches down and picks up her hand. "Let me touch you so's I can see how you gonna feel today." Josie flashes a big smile at Mabel. "Yessum, you feels good, Miss Mabel O'Brien."

"Did you really think I's outside, Josie?" says Mabel. "That made me get tickled." Mabel holds up her arms for Josie to hug her. "Are you gonna be here all day?"

"Yes, ma'am, far as I'm concerned, I'll be here as long as Miss Lizbeth want me to stay," says Josie. She sits down on the side of the bed. "She told me that the doctor's gonna come see you today. I need to rub you down with some alcohol and get you a fresh nightgown. We don't want you having no fever when he come."

"I can tell when my fever goes up—it makes me feel bad," says Mabel. "When I don't feel very good, I just sleep." Josie runs her fingers through Mabel's hair. "That feels good," says Mabel with a soft smile on her lips.

"I'm gonna get the cloths and come back to clean you up," says Josie. "I needs to comb your hair too. It still feel clean though." Josie gets up and walks to the door. "Be back in a minute."

Mabel stares at the ceiling and drifts in and out of sleep. She opens her eyes when Josie comes back into the room. "Is it afternoon yet?"

"No child, it's round about 9 o'clock," says Josie.

"I'm tired, Josie. I feel like I've been awake for a long time," says Mabel. "My legs hurt so bad. There's pains in my feet and legs." Mabel closes her eyes. "Is it time for me to take another aspirin yet?"

"I imagine we can get you one after I get you cleant up. I'll rub your legs real good and that will help them not hurt." She pours some alcohol on a cloth and puts it behind Mabel's neck, pressing gently as she moves to Mabel's shoulders. "I know that feels good, don't it?"

"Yessum," says Mabel. "It feels cold though." Josie lifts each of Mabel's arms and rubs the alcohol from her shoulders down to her fingers. She turns Mabel on her side and makes circular motions down her spine. "That gives me chill bumps."

"It's because you still feverish," says Josie. "My daddy use to do this to me and my sister when we'd get sick. He always say that it'd break our fever." Josie stands, pulls the sheet back over Mabel, and lifts the sheet from her legs. "Now this gonna help them strong legs to come back. Your mama told me about how you can't walk."

Mabel falls to sleep with Josie's gentle deep massaging of her feet and legs. Josie hums as she looks at Mabel's limp feet. She gets down on her knees and rubs the bottoms of Mabel's feet with her strong hands. Josie continues her humming as she gets up, straightens the sheet, and pulls the quilt back over Mabel. "God gonna take care of this child; I know He will. God, she got a whole lot more livin' to do—let me help her have the healin' she needs. Let me have my daddy's healin' touch. God, you knows I love this child." Leaving Mabel alone, Josie returns the cloths and alcohol to the kitchen.

A little later, Mama walks into the bedroom and stands beside Mabel's bed. "Mabel, you need to wake up so Dr. Reed can talk to you." With her eyes half open, Mabel sees Dr. Reed standing at the foot of her bed. The oil in his black hair shines in the morning light and holds it close to his head. A tall man, wearing a black suit and tie, he nods at Mabel and smiles. Without saying a word, he walks around and takes Mama's place beside her bed. Mama moves to the end of the bed.

"I hear you aren't feeling well, Mabel," says Dr. Reed.

"No sir, I don't," says Mabel. She stares into his brown eyes and then wonders why he's reaching for something from his bag. He pulls out a stethoscope and puts it around his neck.

"I want to listen to your heartbeat," says Dr. Reed. He places the listening device in each of his ears and then holds the other end on Mabel's chest; he listens in silence. "That sounds good. Now, I want you to roll over on your side so I can listen to your lungs." Mabel twists her body over and feels the stethoscope touching her back. "Now, take a deep breath for me." He moves the stethoscope to another spot. "One more deep breath for me," says Dr. Reed. Mabel follows his instructions and rolls onto her back as soon as she feels him move away. "Your heart and lungs sound strong. That's very good news, Mabel."

"I just don't understand her feeling so awful for so many days," says Mama. "Her temperature shoots up, she can't stand, she sleeps almost constantly, and her throat hurts. Everything seems to come and go." Mama looks into Mabel's face. "This is not like her at all."

"I understand," says Dr. Reed. "Now, Mabel, I need to look at your throat." He takes out a tongue depressor. "Open your mouth and stick out your tongue. I need to see way back there." Mabel follows his instructions once again. "It is a little mottled, Mrs. O'Brien. Looks like it's beginning to clear up in patches. What have you been doing for it?"

"She's been gargling with warm saltwater and vinegar several times a day," says Mama. "I've been giving her an aspirin about every four hours; plus, she's had alcohol baths for her fever."

"That's good," says Dr. Reed. "Now, Mabel, can you lift your head off of the pillow for me?" Mabel lifts her head. "Can you lift your arms?" She lifts her arms. "That's good." Dr. Reed removes the covers from Mabel. "Can you wiggle your toes?" Mabel tries, but it makes the calves of her legs hurt too much. She winces with her attempts. "Bend your knees for me, Mabel." Again, Mabel tries, but her legs don't move.

"It makes it worse when I try to move," says Mabel. "My legs hurt, Mama."

"I know they do, honey. Dr. Reed is here to make you better," says Mama.

"Has your head been hurting, Mabel?" asks Dr. Reed. Mabel nods yes. "Okay, now I want you to show me how you can scoot up in the bed and sit against your pillows." Mabel sits up, pushes her hands deeply into the bed, and heaves her body into a comfortable position. "That's good, Mabel, but I can see that you're very tired. You had a hard time moving." He begins feeling of the calves of her legs. Mabel cringes every time he moves his hand.

Josie comes to the door and Mabel looks over at her. Mama turns and looks too. "Come in here with us, Josie; I want you to hear what the doctor has to say," says Mama. "I'm afraid I won't remember everything." She tiptoes to the end of the bed and stands beside Mama. Josie reaches over and takes hold of Mama's hand. Mabel feels better with Josie in the room too.

Dr. Reed puts his instruments back into his bag on the chair seat. Then he places the bag on the floor and sits down. "Generally speaking, Mabel is doing much better than I expected from Tom's description. I believe that she has a very mild case of infantile paralysis, Mrs. O'Brien," says Dr. Reed.

"What in the world is that?" asks Mama anxiously. "Will her legs get better? Will she be able to walk?"

Dr. Reed looks up at Mama and Josie. "We don't know the exact cause of it, but it has been around for many years. In 1916, there was an epidemic in New York. It's highly contagious in the initial stages—especially to the very young," says Dr. Reed. "During the New York epidemic, there were about thirty thousand cases; less than ten thousand were serious enough to cause death or permanent paralysis. Those, of course, were the most severe cases."

Dr. Reed looks back at Mabel. "Fortunately, Mabel's case does not appear to be one of the serious ones. Of course, she has the muscle pain and spasms, fever, sore throat, and general malaise, but it appears to have limited itself to her lower legs. In the cases that cause death or lasting paralysis, it spreads up into the back, arms, and sometimes the lungs. It devastates the body rapidly—that's why I believe her case is mild."

"What can we do for her to get her well?" asks Mama.

"Exactly what you're doing," says Dr. Reed. "There's no cure for it. It simply has to run its course. She needs plenty of bed rest and doesn't need to be around any other children. Again, Mabel seems to have a very, very mild case. Of course, the time required for recuperation is different for each person. Have any of your other children been around her? Do any of them have a sore throat or headache? It's very contagious."

"When one of my children gets sick, I keep them totally away from everyone else," says Mama. "I even separate the sick one's dishes. Bubba, Sister, and Brother have not been near her since Saturday evening. They all seem fine—healthy as they can be."

"As I said, infantile paralysis just has to run its course. I'm going to ask the nurse to stop by here next week to give me a follow-up report. Mabel, you're gonna be fine." He pats Mabel on the arm and smiles warmly at her. "Now, remind me, how old is your baby, Mrs. O'Brien? I recall I delivered him back in the late fall."

"That's right, Dr. Reed. Brother will be seven months old this month," says Mama. "You know that Bubba and Sister are older than Mabel."

"Can we go into the kitchen?" says Dr. Reed. "I need to wash my hands. I'm certain Mabel wants to lie back down for some more rest." Josie, Mama, and Dr. Reed leave the bedroom. Mabel scoots back down in her bed—exhausted.

In the early afternoon, Mabel awakens to the sound of different people walking out in the hall. Mama comes into her room. "Why's everybody walking so much, Mama? Why are you so dressed up? It's not Sunday, is it?"

Mama crosses the room and sits down in the chair. "Dr. Reed says that you're going to be fine, Mabel, but he wants me to take Brother, Sister, and Bubba to Florence for a few days. He says that it's very dangerous for Brother to be in the same house with you so sick."

Mabel feels tears welling up in her eyes. "Mama, who's gonna be here with me?" She pulls the sheet up and wipes away her tears.

Mama attempts to soften the situation for Mabel. "Your favorite person in the whole wide world is going to take care of you." Mama smiles and tries to relieve Mabel's fears. "Josie's going to be here with you all day, every day, until we come back. She's the best nurse I know and she loves you so much. Josie is the one person I would allow to take my place caring for you."

"Who'll be here at night?" says Mabel.

"Your papa will be right here with you. I don't want to leave you, but I have to be sure Brother doesn't get sick. He's not as big and strong as you are, Mabel. His little body might not be able to take it," says Mama. "I know you don't want anything to happen to Brother. Can you be brave for me and get well?"

"Yessum," says Mabel. "How are you gonna get to Florence?" Mabel looks over at Mama and waits for her answer.

"Dr. Reed's going to let us ride with him in his wagon," says Mama. "He's going to take us to your Aunt India's house. They have plenty of extra rooms for all of us." Mama stands, leans over, and kisses Mabel's forehead. "Josie's gone home to get her things and to take Drella over to Aunt Apple's house. Drella's going to stay there while her mama's with you. So, you see, you'll be taken care of all day, every day."

"I wish I could go to Aunt India's." Mabel hesitates for a moment and says, "No, I don't reckon I feel like it just yet."

"The thing for you to do, Mabel, is get well. That's all that matters to your whole family. When I come back next week, you'll be fine," says Mama. "I love you."

"I love you too, Mama," says Mabel. Tears come back to her eyes. "I'm gonna get well so I can go outside." Again, she wipes away her tears.

"We'll be leaving as soon as Josie gets back," says Mama. "Now, I want you to try to get some rest." Mama kisses her once more. "Josie's happy to be taking care of you." Mabel closes her eyes as Mama walks to the door. *I've got to get well so Mama can come home. Josie and Papa will help me. I'm gonna miss Mama.* She hears the door close and silence falls over her room.

Mabel doesn't wake up until Josie comes back into the bedroom with a glass of water and an aspirin. "Your mama didn't want to wake you up to tell you good-bye, Mabel," says Josie. "She told me to give you this aspirin for your fever. Dr. Reed say they helping with your fever, aching legs, and sleep." Josie hands Mabel the glass and puts the aspirin into her mouth. Mabel gulps the aspirin down. "We gonna get you well, child. I gonna see to that. I done made you some good potato soup for supper. It'll feel good to your throat—your papa likes it too."

"Is Papa home from work?" says Mabel.

"No, child. He'll be here in a little while," says Josie. "Is there anything else you want before I go stir your soup?"

"No'm." Mabel turns her head toward the sunlight. "Can you open the window for me? I might be able to hear Papa's whistle," says Mabel.

"I sure can, child," says Josie. "Dr. Reed said to open the window in the afternoon. He say that the fresh air will help you—glad you reminded me." After Josie lifts the sash, she tiptoes out of the room. Mabel listens to the faint sounds drifting through her window. *There's a dog barking way up by the store. I can hear different kinds of birds singing and every once in a while I can hear the leaves moving on the trees. I like hearing those sounds—wish I's up in my tree.*

Mabel's ritual of trying to get well begins that evening with Papa staying in her room all night. On Wednesday morning, and for many days to come, Josie cooks Mabel's breakfast, lunch, and dinner. In between meals, Josie gives her aspirin, bathes her in alcohol, keeps her supplied with clean nightgowns—and in any way she can, she encourages Mabel to feel better.

Thursday morning, June 6, Josie comes into Mabel's room after returning her breakfast dishes to the kitchen. Mabel watches her walk across the floor. Josie takes the chair and pulls it close to the bed. She looks into Mabel's eyes and firmly asks, "Mabel, do you wants to get well?"

"Yessum," says Mabel. "I don't like having to stay in bed. I don't want to be sick."

"I wants to help you as best I can, child. My daddy knew a lot of cures for peoples when they'd get down sick. I remember one he used on folks he sometimes took care of," says Josie.

"What'd he do?" asks Mabel.

"He'd sweat the sickness out of them peoples," says Josie. "I see'd my daddy take a blanket and boil it in water, wrang it out, and wrap them folks in the hot blanket; they'd get well after a few of his visits.

I think we can do that to you by putting the heat to your legs. I been thinkin' real hard on it."

Josie stands up and goes to the window. Looking outside, Josie seems to be gathering her thoughts. "I've got some tree roots all ready to boil for you; I have to ask your papa if he thinks it'll be all right. If he say I can, we'll start doing it tomorrow morning. Have to do it 'bout three times a day, I figure."

"Does it hurt?" Mabel asks tentatively.

"Aw, you'll be plenty hot. It might hurt a little at first, but then you'll get use to it," says Josie. "I wants to do them wraps and start you moving your legs against my hands. It'll make your legs strong again. That's a promise to you, my baby." Josie walks back to the chair and sits down. "I'll ask your papa when he get home from work this evening."

As soon as Papa comes home, he walks into Mabel's bedroom where Josie is straightening the bedcovers for the last time before she leaves. Josie tells Papa about what her daddy use to do to help people get well. Papa seems delighted that she knows something to do for Mabel and they agree that she will begin the heat wraps Friday morning. "Anything you can do for my girl will be greatly appreciated," says Papa. "If it works, it'll be a miracle. If it doesn't, then there will be no harm done. At least you've tried."

Friday morning, after breakfast, Josie tells Mabel to rest until she comes back. "When I comes back in here, I'll have your first hot wrap ready for your legs. It gonna make you feel better, child." As promised, Josie returns to the bedroom in a short time. She begins by lifting Mabel's legs and spreading an oilcloth over the mattress. "I put that down to keep your bed dry." She leaves and comes back with the damp blanket. "I wrang out almost all of the water, so's we won't have no mess. Gotta work fast before it cool too much," says Josie.

Mabel feels the heat from the blanket as Josie weaves it around and on top of her feet and legs. "That feels good, Josie," says Mabel.

She watches as Josie quickly covers the hot blanket with another oilcloth and spreads her bedcovers back over her legs. Josie walks up along the bed, gently tucking the covers under Mabel. Finally, she tucks the covers under Mabel's chin and under her shoulders. "Got to get that heat built up, child. You gonna be sweatin', so I've got a cool cloth to wipe your face." Josie sits down in the chair and watches Mabel's face.

"Whew, it's hot, Josie," says Mabel. Josie wipes her face. "This is the first time my legs haven't hurt. They don't hurt at all." Mabel's face reddens as the heat continues to build. Josie almost constantly wipes her face and neck with the cool cloth.

"After the blanket cools, I'll take it away, but you got to stay under the covers 'til your body cools down on its own," says Josie. As she wipes Mabel's face, she begins humming. "You a brave girl, Miss Mabel O'Brien. You and me's gonna get you up from this bed in no time."

When Josie finishes removing the blanket and oilcloths, Mabel continues to sweat beneath the bedcovers. "I feel tired, Josie," says Mabel. "Is it okay for me to sleep now?"

"Yes, child, but I's gonna be back in here to change you out of that nightgown in a little while. Be sure to keep that cover over you real tight—don't want you to get a chill."

Josie constantly works on Mabel throughout the day. By the third wrapping session, Mabel is totally relaxed. "Josie?" says Mabel. "When you gonna exercise my legs? Will it be today?"

"We might try that a few times tomorrow, child." A happy smile fills Josie's face. "I's so happy—we gonna get you well."

Friday afternoon, when Papa comes home, he immediately sees a change in Mabel. For the first time in almost a week, Mabel sleeps soundly through the night. Josie returns on Saturday and begins her loving care of Mabel for another day. "I sure am happy she's feeling better, Josie," says Papa. "Last night is the first full night's sleep we've gotten. Your daddy's cure must be the right one."

"Yessir, Mr. O'Brien," says Josie with a tone of satisfaction in her voice. She smiles broadly before her next words come out. "When it come to caring for folk, my daddy sho' knew what he's doing." Mabel looks up at Josie's face from her bed and sees how proud Josie is of her daddy. "My daddy didn't have a bad bone in his body, Mr. Tom."

"I'm sure he didn't, Josie," says Papa. "Wish there were more like him in this world. It'd be a better place, wouldn't it?"

"Yessir," says Josie. "Now, if you don't mind, I needs to get busy with Miss Mabel and her legs."

Josie stays with Mabel all day, every day, for another week. She feeds her, bathes her, sings to her, tells her stories, puts hot wraps on her legs, exercises her legs, and encourages her faithfully. By Wednesday, June 12, Mabel can move her legs without them cramping. "I don't want you jumping out of bed too fast, child," warns Josie. "I's gonna let you be sitting up on the side of the bed when your papa come home today. I wants you to be sure and wiggle them strong legs for him."

When they hear Papa close the front door that afternoon, Mabel is sitting on the edge of her mattress—legs dangling and feet moving. Josie sits in the chair that she's moved close to Mabel. Papa walks straight to the bedroom and opens the door. Josie and Mabel can't hold back their laughter when they see Papa's face. He rushes across the room, picks Mabel up in his arms, and dances around the room with delight. Josie stands up and claps to the rhythm of his dance steps. "Thank You, Lord, and thank you, Josie," says Papa when he stops dancing. "Thank you for making my baby well again." Their laughter fills the room.

Chapter 17
Reflections

THE PICTURE STOPS MOVING AND THE window in Mabel's bedroom comes into focus. With only a moment's pause, Mabel begins sending me her thoughts—they enter my mind rapidly. "All of the events you've just watched really made me change in many ways—in a relatively short time." She stands, her white hair glistening in the light, and looks down at me sitting in the chair. "Let's walk over there. I want us to move closer to the picture. There are several things I want to talk about with you."

I stand and follow her. "I can't believe all of the things your family had to overcome—especially you."

With a gentle smile on her face, she looks back at me and keeps moving toward the picture. "I always told you kids that I had a wonderful life, but it was truly different from anything you experienced. I learned from it all. No person lives life on earth without pain and hardship. Some suffer for what they have done while others suffer because of what is done to them. Many suffer simply because they become victims of circumstances they can't control."

"I've seen each of those, Mabel."

"The key to getting through all of our troubles is to look to God. Believe it or not, you should be grateful for your suffering. You must wait and watch for God's higher purpose in your life on earth."

She now stands in front of the picture and smiles. "Always look for God's teaching in all things. That's when believers can turn their minds to a higher place and become better for having experienced the suffering. God doesn't make any mistakes. He hones us through what He allows in our lives." Mabel raises her hand and magically returns the picture to an earlier scene.

"That's you and Josie standing outside the store—the day you went to buy matches. It was interesting to watch. Things were so different back then, weren't they?"

She continues to look at the picture and appears to think through her choice of words. "A child doesn't necessarily see or experience the rules adults make until they get away from home. All of the rules for different groups of people, like Josie only being able to shop on Thursdays, totally confused me as a child. It hurt me because I truly didn't think Josie was any different than me."

I nod in agreement as I take in Mabel's thoughts.

"When you consider the rock and the example she used, Josie clearly had things figured out. She had the ability to remove herself from the limits others set for her. She went to that higher place. The storeowner had his rules and she followed them, but he really didn't have any control over her. Josie simply allowed it and went along with it. She used the rock to show me that no one can change who or what you are."

"Josie seemed to have a deep sense of self," I think. "The example she used about the rock not changing was a wonderful way for her to describe her mindset. She made it understandable."

Mabel nods in agreement. Her thoughts continue. "I used Josie's thinking in many situations throughout my life. We don't have to suffer from our circumstances. Josie never seemed to let her situation get her down. She had an inner peace about her that I never saw broken. Nothing could get her off course. I believe it came from her abiding love for God and her devotion to Him. All of us must stay true to ourselves and to our faith. It gives us a strong sense of hope and, as she put it, a strong sense of freedom. What a blessing for me to be so close to her."

"That's a wonderful lesson she gave you. You encouraged us to use our minds in creative ways and you let us know that we could accomplish anything. What we didn't have wasn't what was important. We weren't allowed to wallow in self pity. It was how hard we were willing to work to get what we wanted—what we dreamed of becoming."

"The key is to use positive thoughts—negativity keeps you from making progress. Now, let's look at another episode that I think was important." Mabel moves to the next picture. "I'll never forget the whole ordeal with the beaver dam and Papa's discussion with us at the kitchen table that night. Early in our lives, Papa and Mama made us believers in the importance of honesty."

As I look at the picture of them sitting at the table, I recall many such discussions with Mabel when I was a child. "You always insisted on honesty too, Mabel. If my memory serves me correctly, I recall that you never accepted partial truths either."

"Now you know where I learned about honesty. I simply passed it on to you all. No relationship can survive without honesty—especially a family. It must be taught from an early age. I believe that honesty is the foundation of a strong moral character."

My thoughts go to my childhood. "I never told you, but I always thought that you knew the truth before I even uttered the first word of an explanation. You made me honest." We smile at each other and, once again, I see that knowing look in her face.

Turning her attention back to the pictures, Mabel moves to the scene where Papa, Bubba, Sister, and she are standing in the middle of the road, watching the Klan ride away.

"This night truly brought the Klan to life for me. I had heard bits and pieces about them, but it seemed like a myth until the night we went for a walk. Never did I think that I would see them in Shoal Crossing. At first, the beauty of the torches, the flowing white sheets, and stately horses fascinated me, but when we had to stand near them, it frightened me. They were not kind to Papa."

"When I saw you go through this, it frightened me too." I watch her face as she remains absorbed in the picture. "The language they used and their general attitude toward Papa was threatening. Do you know if Flint Goodin continued his taxi service?"

"Yes, he did," thinks Mabel, "but he never allowed the coloreds to ride with him again as far as I know. Papa told that story for years. He said that the Klan would have had to drag that bed outside in order to talk to Flint that night."

Mabel smiles at her thoughts. "Papa always managed to see the humorous side of even the most serious situations. Those men were as mean as they could be and scared us to death."

"Your mama wasn't happy with his decision during your walk."

"Mama and Papa always taught us not to get involved with situations that might bring us harm. Papa broke that rule the night we went for a walk. Mabel looks in my direction. "If you can help someone—do it. On the other hand, don't do it at the risk of bringing harm to yourself or anyone else. Children must learn to think through things before they act—adults do too. My parents tried to teach us to leave well enough alone."

Mabel looks back at the picture. "Experiencing the presence of the Klan made me understand how serious some people were about limiting colored people and what they could do. It frightened me because I'd never seen or heard so much hatred. I knew then what people like Josie were up against. It probably was my first experience with actually seeing discrimination against colored people and anyone who attempted to help them improve their lives."

"I know you were proud when your papa stood toe-to-toe with the Klan and their evil ways."

"Yes," thinks Mabel. "That was the first time I witnessed someone standing up for what they believed was right. Papa was right when he said that if you ignore evil, you approve of it."

"Did it change your feelings for Josie?"

"No indeed, but like everyone else, I learned to keep my mouth shut," thinks Mabel. "Nothing could sever the ties I had with Josie. It made me even more considerate of her and her feelings. After this incident, I knew that people outside of my family could never understand my deep devotion to her."

Mabel turns to the picture once again. "Adults forget how much a child can grasp from the innuendos of daily life around them—somehow it becomes a knowing within a child's being. All of this points to the fact that we must use caution with who and what we allow into our lives. Children are not born with prejudicial opinions—they learn them from their environment and experiences."

"Maybe that's why Mama and Papa kept so many adult issues from their children. You did that too until we got older."

"I believe it's important for children to be allowed to live their childhoods. Some parents try to push children too hard, too fast. God created the parent-child relationship for a purpose. I believe that purpose is to act as God's surrogate in guiding the child through daily life. To me, that guidance includes setting an example, directing the child through daily living, and keeping the child safe. Too many parents tend to ignore their responsibilities and the world ends up with those children becoming troubled adults."

Mabel lifts her hand and changes to the scene where she is sitting on the back steps watching Bubba prepare to wring the chicken's neck.

"That was really difficult to watch. Why do you consider that one of the most important events?" I look at Mabel and her thoughts flow into my mind.

"This illustrates that children also seem too anxious to grow up. It's a constant struggle to get the right balance. Just because children want to do adult-like things, doesn't make them ready for it. A child longs to do all the things that adults do. Children should be encouraged to develop interests—not necessarily adult activities—but to learn how to do things that will make them independent lifelong learners. I longed to be as old as Sister, but I never longed to be grown—until much later. My childhood was the happiest time of my life. I loved the people, the things I learned, and the joy of discovery in each day. Children should enjoy their childhoods rather than trying to find ways to grow up too soon. It should be a normal flow of events—a natural development."

"You learned a lot from watching Bubba move away from the childish things you and Sister enjoyed."

"Yes I did," thinks Mabel. "I also learned that all children cannot be treated the same way. They each grow and mature at different rates. Each child has a different set of interests and abilities. Parents must appreciate those differences in their children."

She turns and looks at me. "When I was raising you all, I saw the differences and allowed you to mature accordingly. Each of you eventually pursued totally different paths; and I have always been equally proud of you as individuals."

Mabel turns her attention back to the picture. She changes it to Papa holding her in his arms while dancing around the bedroom. Josie is clapping her hands with a big smile on her face. "This was a happy day for me." She smiles.

I look at the picture and the happiness of that moment is rekindled. "It's amazing that you overcame such a horrible disease. When Dr. Reed visited, it was evident that he could identify the disease, but there was no treatment he could provide. I know it was frightening for your parents."

"My condition only serves to show you how difficult it was to survive back then. I know that it was a hard decision for Mama to leave. She did it to protect Brother—and that was the right decision. If he had come in contact with my germs, it probably would have killed him. At the time, I was very sad, but I had to fight the illness instead of feeling sorry for myself. In those days, we simply had to accept things the way they were. The conditions, though difficult, made us survivors. We learned to live, eat, and play with what we had. We appreciated it all—no matter how insignificant it seemed. Parents didn't spend much money on their children in 1918—they plainly couldn't."

"As a family, you all really had to support each other through the different trials you experienced," I think. "It would be hard for any child to grasp why a parent would have to leave under those conditions. It was a very sad situation, but also a risky one for Brother."

"Back then, survival was merely a challenge we met daily. Everyone had hardships. Our family was no different. I've often wondered what my parents would have done without Josie. It's truly wonderful the way she stepped in, took me under her care, and worked with me until I got well. I now know that it was all God's will for her to be there. Without her, my life probably would have been very different—or nonexistent."

"When did Mama and the other children come back to the house?"

"Mama and Brother came back the Saturday following Papa's dance with me. She was only away from home ten or so days. Bubba and Sister went to Grandpa's farm for the summer. They worked out there until early September," thinks Mabel. "Once I got up and started walking that week, I never had any more difficulty with my legs. I got well and stayed well. Dr. Reed would've been smart to have asked Josie about what she did for me. I've often wondered if he ever used Josie's cure."

"Josie was like a miracle worker, wasn't she?"

"Yes, she was. I believed that she could make me well and she did. After she'd put those hot blankets on my legs, it seemed like every muscle in my body completely relaxed. Mama and Papa were always grateful to her for what she did for me. She literally, and singlehandedly, saved my life," thinks Mabel. "I will never forget her love. She certainly did not have to do what she did. If an angel ever walked on earth, it was Josie."

"Believe it or not, Mabel, I remember your using some of Josie's treatments on us when we'd get sick or hurt. I remember too how you used to put the dry heated cloths on our throats. As I watched all the things Josie and Mama did, I thought of you."

"That's precisely where I learned them all—the hot tea, the broth, the dry heat and moist heat, the saltwater gargle, the cool cloths, and the oatmeal or porridge. As I said earlier, God allows things in our lives for a reason. Without my experiences as a child, I would have never known those things. I watched and listened very closely as a child—especially to Mama and Josie."

"God taught you in a very real way," I think, "and from an early age."

"Yes, that's true. God teaches all of us as we grow and mature. The secret is to listen and watch for God's messages. He purposely puts people and situations into our lives that serve to mold us into what we need to be for the future. The secret to happiness and success is heeding those messages."

My mind recalls Mabel using those thoughts with me as I matured. "Over the years you told me to watch and wait to discover what God wanted me to do. No matter what happens, there's a reason and there is something to be gained from it."

"That's right. I learned early in life to wait and watch for what God's plans were for me. The problem with us on earth is that we become too anxious and want things to happen in our own time frame. That's just not the way God works His will for our lives."

Mabel turns and starts moving toward her chair. "Now, let's go back and sit down." As soon as we're seated, she looks at me. "It isn't long before you've got to go back. I hope that you're seeing how God prepares us. When you leave here, if you carry nothing else with you, remember that everything happens for a reason. Even though I have been studying this for some time now, I am amazed by the works of God in every individual's life. Remember it and watch for those messages in the time you have remaining on earth."

I nod in acknowledgment of her instructions. She turns and looks back at the picture. "We're going to review a few more events I think were important to my childhood. Some pretty unusual things happened in that summer of 1918. Things I had never faced in my short time on earth. Mama and Papa hadn't experienced them either." I look at the picture of Mabel's childhood bedroom window—my curiosity piqued. The picture blurs, swirls into a mass of colors, and refocuses on Mabel lying in her bed. The storyteller begins talking once again.

Chapter 18

ON MONDAY, JULY 15, JOSIE AND Mama busy themselves getting the O'Brien house ready for the Ladies Aid Society meeting on Tuesday. The Society meets at a different member's home each month. The ladies support the soldiers and their families by writing letters and knitting socks, mittens, and caps. They send boxes filled with soap, razors, newspapers, and snacks to the soldiers at least once a month. When they hear of a family having a particularly difficult time, they cook meals for them.

Mabel awakens and listens to Josie and Mama's distant chatter in the kitchen. As she lies there, she remembers that today and tomorrow will be all about the ladies coming to the O'Brien house.

Mama opens the bedroom door and Mabel pretends to be asleep. "Good morning, sleepy girl, you need to get up and get dressed. We've got a busy day ahead of us," says Mama. Mabel slowly opens her eyes and sees that Mama's selecting a dress for her. "I want you to look nice today and tomorrow. There will be a lot of company coming and going both days."

Mabel sits up in the bed. "I've put your dress out for today. Be sure you put on your nice shoes and socks." Mama walks over to the door to leave. "Josie has already been here for two hours. Get up and get dressed, Mabel."

Mabel stretches for the ceiling as she stands beside the bed in her blue nightgown. *Come on, Mabel, you heard Mama. She'll be coming back in here in a minute. I've got to get the bed made up and put on my dress. I wish I didn't have to put on shoes and socks today. It's too hot.*

Stretching her back once again, Mabel yawns as she relaxes. She walks over to the blue and white gingham dress Mama chose for her. *At least this dress isn't hot.* Mabel walks back to her side of the bed and begins to smooth out the sheets; then she fluffs her pillow. *I wish Sister was here to help me do this.* She pulls the top sheet up, places the pillows on the sheet, and walks the off-white chenille bedspread up to cover the pillows. *Gotta make this bed smooth or else Mama'll make me do it again.* She swipes her hands over the bedspread to chase away the wrinkles. *That's a good job. Mama will like the way it looks.*

Mabel hears a soft knock on her door. "Come in." The door opens and Drella smiles at Mabel. Mabel smiles back and says, "I didn't know you were here. I've got to put on my dress. Go over there and look out the window so I can change."

"Why've I gotta look out the window?" asks Drella.

"'Cause Mama says that it's not polite to get dressed in front of people that aren't in the family," says Mabel.

"I get dressed in a dark corner at our house," says Drella. "I don't even want Mama Josie looking at me." Drella stares out the bedroom window.

"I can't go barefoot today," says Mabel. "We sure can't get in Mama's and Josie's way when they're so busy." She unbuttons the three white buttons at the neck of the dress and slips it over her head. "Drella, will you button my dress for me?" She backs up toward Drella.

"Can I turn 'round yet?" says Drella. She turns and Mabel is standing in front of her. "These sure are some tiny buttons." Drella struggles until she gets finished. "Mama Josie sent me in here. She knew you'd need some help." Mabel listens to Drella while she brushes her short hair. "I don't think they'll be wanting us to bother them today either. I'm gonna be watching Brother as soon as he wakes up from his morning nap."

"Let's go to the kitchen, Drella," says Mabel. "I hope they've got something for me to eat."

"You go on in there," says Drella. "I'm gonna start watching Brother. Mama Josie said that I have to watch him so they can get their work done."

Mabel opens the door and walks toward the kitchen while Drella walks toward Mama's room. Mabel quietly enters the kitchen and sits down at the table. "Well, there's Miss Mabel," says Josie. She walks over to the hot oven and pulls out a sheet of her fresh butter cookies. "Now, don't you be eyeing these cookies, Mabel. They's for the ladies coming tomorrow to your mama's meeting." Josie puts another sheet of cookies into the oven. "I figure the ladies will eat about three cookies each, don't you, Miss Lizbeth?"

"I think that's a good estimate, Josie," says Mama. "Their appetites should be satisfied with the ham-and-biscuits you've made, the cookies, and the two pies you'll make in the morning. I just want to get to a place where we can let the oven cool down before it gets too hot outside."

"What are y'all gonna serve for the ladies to drink?" asks Mabel.

"We'll have some sweet tea with lemon, coffee in the urn, and lemonade for those who want that," says Mama. She walks over to the back window and stares outward as though she is thinking. "Josie, you'll have to wait to chip up the ice right when they get here. It should be about eleven or so."

"We'll have it all done, Miss Lizbeth," says Josie. "Those ladies will be mightily impressed when I get the dining room all fixed up for them." Josie walks over to the oven and opens the door to look at her last batch of cookies. "The cookies need about five more minutes."

"Mabel, you can have one of the ham-and-biscuits for breakfast; then I want you to go out on the front porch," says Mama. Mabel searches Mama's face to try to figure out why she has to go to the front porch. "I have a special package coming through the mail and need for you to be out there when the postman comes."

"Is it something you ordered from Montgomery Ward?" asks Mabel excitedly.

"You just can't ever tell what the postman will bring," says Mama with a smile. "It's something for our whole family. While you're waiting, I want you to straighten up the front porch and sweep it off real good. Be sure you do the steps and boardwalk too."

Mabel pushes the last bite of biscuit into her mouth and walks out to the back porch to get the red-handled broom. *Mama knows I don't like to sweep the porch. That's usually Sister's job. Wish I's out at the farm with her. The work out there's more fun.*

Mabel walks back into the kitchen with the broom and says, "I'll call you, Mama, when the postman delivers your package." *I wish Drella could be out there with me. Maybe it won't be long before the postman comes.*

When Mabel gets out on the front porch, she starts sweeping the floorboards. She becomes fascinated with the dust as she scoots it over the edge. *I reckon Mama's got something coming for the house. I'da never thought there'd be this much dust on the porch. I sound like an old lady thinking about the dust.* Mabel giggles at the thought of her being old.

She continues down the steps and slowly works her way to the front gate. *I think I hear the* clippity-clop *of the postman's horse pulling his cart.* Mabel moves closer to the gate and hops up on it. She leans over to see if it's the postman she hears. *It's him. He's turning onto our road. He'll be here in a minute.*

Mabel quickly walks back to the steps so she can watch him pull up in front of the house. She sets the broom up against the porch. *This is gonna be fun to see what Mama ordered.* She stares intently at the enclosed postal cart pulled by a single black horse. The mail carrier stops at their front gate, gives Mabel a wave, and goes around to the other side of the cart. *It must be a big package. He usually just opens the back door and takes out what he's delivering.* She walks out to the gate.

"You O'Brien ladies expecting a package today?" says Mr. Hertz, the postman. He peeks over the horse's haunches to see her face. "This is a mighty nice package, young lady. Come on out here and help me with it."

Mabel opens the gate and walks around the back of the mail cart. She stands beside Mr. Hertz as he opens the door. "This is about the nicest package I've ever delivered."

Mabel's eyes seem to freeze when she looks up into her Grandma's distinctive blue eyes. "It's Grandma!" exclaims Mabel. "Grandma is the special package Mama wanted me to get."

"Hello, Mabel," says Grandma. She reaches out and takes Mr. Hertz's hand as he helps her step down from the mail cart. "Thank you so much, Mr. Hertz. I do appreciate the ride from the country. These two pennies are all I have to give you for your trouble," says Grandma.

Mr. Hertz tips his hat at Grandma. "It's my pleasure to help you or Mr. Hood out at any time. I'll be back around to pick you up about this time on Wednesday. Now, let me get your valise from the back of the cart. I don't think it's too heavy for you to carry, Mabel."

Mabel and Grandma walk around to the back of the cart. She takes the suitcase from Mr. Hertz. "No sir, it's not heavy at all," she assures him. Grandma gives Mabel a kiss on her forehead.

Grandma smells like the sweetest flower I've ever smelled. Her white hair pulled up in that bun makes it look like she's not even hot. I like the way she lifts her black skirt when she walks. She really is a prissy lady—just like Mama says she is.

"Thanks again, Mr. Hertz, for the ride. I'll be out here waiting for you on Wednesday—good Lord willing," says Grandma.

Mabel opens the front gate and reaches for Grandma's hand as they walk toward the front porch. When they get up on the porch, Grandma sits down on a rocking chair and Mabel sets the suitcase down. She goes to the screen door and tells her mama that her package is here. "That was a long, hard ride this morning," says Grandma. "It wouldn't have taken so long if he didn't have to stop at every nook and cranny along the way." She leans back and smiles at Mabel. "It's nice to be here."

"Well, aren't you a sight for sore eyes, Mrs. Hood," announces Mama as she comes out of the house. She wipes her hands on her long white apron as she walks over to Grandma. Leaning down, she kisses her mother on the forehead. "I told Mabel to wait out here for a package. She had no idea that it would be you, Mother."

"It sure was a surprise, Mama," says Mabel. "It's the best package we've ever gotten."

"We like nice surprises, don't we, Mother? Mabel, you take the suitcase into y'all's bedroom while your grandma and I go to the kitchen for a nice cold glass of tea," says Mama. "I know you're worn out from that long ride, Mother. Let's go inside and relax." Grandma stands up and pats Mabel on the top of her head. "Mabel, Josie wants you to come around to the well. She needs your help after you set the suitcase down," says Mama.

"Yessum," says Mabel. She quickly takes the suitcase to the bedroom and sets it down. *Wonder what Josie wants me to do at the well.*

Mabel rushes back out the front door, stopping briefly to pick up the broom. Then she runs down the steps and scampers toward the backyard. *She probably wants me to help her do something for the meeting tomorrow.* When Mabel arrives at Josie's side, she rolls her deep-brown eyes over at Mabel and lowers the water bucket into the well. A glimmer of a smile rests on Josie's face.

"Mabel, I needs for you to get those two vases off the back steps for me," says Josie. "Be careful with them. They're your mama's favorites. Rest the broom against the house."

"Yessum," says Mabel. She walks over to the steps and puts down the broom before picking up a vase in each hand. "What are you gonna do with the vases, Josie?"

"I's gonna fill them with water. You're going to carry one and I'll carry the other. We's going around to the front rose bed," says Josie. "We needs to have some fresh-cut flowers for the parlor and the dining room."

Josie tugs at the rope and lifts the galvanized water bucket to the side of the well. She reaches over and picks up the dipper. "Put that vase up here on the ledge so's I can pour this water. Hold tight 'cause it's gonna get heavy." After Josie finishes dipping out the water for both of the vases, she hangs the dipper on its hook and lowers the bucket back to the water. "Let's go 'round front now, Mabel."

Mabel firmly holds her vase as she struggles to keep up with Josie's long stride. "I'm glad you let me help you, Josie," says Mabel. She looks up and Josie smiles down at her.

"You knows I's gonna always have you as my helper if I thinks it's something you can do," says Josie. "Let's start over there on the far side of the fence. I noticed those flowers look hardiest. They gets the morning sun." Josie kneels down on the ground and her eyes search over the red roses.

"Mama likes bouquets for special things like her meeting, but I don't like to watch the roses die," says Mabel. "I like for them to stay on the bushes, don't you, Josie?"

"Oh, I thinks the good Lord intends for us to enjoy them wherever we sees them."

"Won't it kill them when you cut them?" asks Mabel.

"Child, everything that lives is gonna die. Look at these little rosebuds," says Josie.

Leaning closer, Mabel watches as Josie cradles a cluster of buds in her dark-brown hand. "These buds are like a newborn child. That hint of red you see is the promise of things to come." Josie moves her hand to a newly opened bloom. "Then, you see this one here? It's just been open for a few hours. That's like you, still young and still growing."

Bending forward, Mabel lightly touches the rose that is like herself. "Now, look at this one; it's in full bloom. It's standing proud and tall. It's all grown-up like your mama and me, but look at this wilted one—it's about to die. It's old." Josie pulls the scissors from her apron pocket.

Josie begins snipping the roses she wants. "God has a plan for all living things, Mabel. Every living thing comes from some sort of seed; we's born, grow, become adults, and then we wither in our old age."

"That's a good story, Josie," says Mabel. "I'm gonna always remember it, but I's wondering about something."

"I might 'a knowed that you'd think of something to ask about," says Josie. Mabel sees Josie's shoulders jiggle from her quiet laugh.

"Is Grandma like the old rose?"

"She ain't quite there yet, child; hopefully, she will be one day. It's a blessing to grow old. We all have our gettin' old to look forward to," says Josie. "When that wilted rose don't have no more life, its petals start to fall away; then one day it'll be gone."

Josie's eyes constantly search for the right roses. "That's why we have to enjoy our life here while we have it, child. That's just God's way and we needs to take pleasure in these roses while we have them too." Josie snips another stem and places it in the water. "This here water will nourish them for a few more days of enjoyment."

"I know it feels good to them to get into the water. It's too hot out here," says Mabel. She picks up the vase and holds it closer to Josie. "I'm happy we'll get to see them for a while longer, Josie."

"I'm glad you like my tales, Mabel," says Josie. "My daddy use to tell me about those things when we's walking through the woods. He taught me enough to last a lifetime, child."

Josie stands up and looks at the next bush. "We just needs a few more—then we'll be finished." Josie gathers the last roses for the vases and rises to her feet with a moan. "I am one tired soul this afternoon. Let's walk around to the back and take the roses inside the house."

"We can take them in the front door, Josie," says Mabel.

"Child, you know that colored folk can't walk in the front door of a white family's house. Come on here, let's go 'round to the back—just like we's supposed to," says Josie.

As they walk along the side of the house, Mabel tries to conceal the troubled look on her face, but Josie senses Mabel's lack of understanding. She stops and turns toward Mabel. "Don't you be worrying yourself about that front door, Mabel. Them's just the rules we's got to live by these days. It just take time for things to change; and we's just gonna have to wait on time."

"Yessum," says Mabel. "When I grow up, you'll be the queen of my house and can do anything you please. I think that'll be plenty of time, don't you?"

"Now, won't that be a lovely change for us?" says Josie. "Things sure will be different by then. Yessum, I sure gonna enjoy wearin' that crown."

Josie walks up the back steps and holds the screen door open for Mabel. "Mama, we have you two vases of flowers," calls out Mabel. Mama comes to the kitchen door and opens it.

"Y'all did a wonderful job, Josie," says Mama. "Let's take the one Mabel has into the dining room and put yours in the parlor." The three of them walk back to the kitchen after placing the flowers. "I know you're exhausted, Josie; you must be ready to go home."

"Yes, Miss Lizbeth, it's been a long day," says Josie. "I'll be back in the morning so we can have everything ready for the ladies."

Mabel walks over to Josie and puts her arms around her waist. Josie gently lays her hand on Mabel's head. "Mabel sure was a big help to me with those roses, Miss Lizbeth." Mabel looks up at Josie and smiles—proud of her ability to help Josie. "You know that you girls are gonna have to stay out of my way tomorrow, don't you, Mabel?"

"Yessum, we'll have to stay outside," says Mabel.

"I believe I just might have you and Drella go blackberry picking tomorrow. Then, before the week's out, I'll make y'all a good ole blackberry cobbler," says Josie. Josie pulls Mabel closer to her. "How's that sound, Mabel?"

"That sounds like fun to me," says Mabel.

"I'll try to have Mabel outside by the time you get here, Josie—or at least well on her way," says Mama. "Mabel's gonna sleep on a pallet in the bedroom, so Mother can sleep in her bed. I don't want to make any clutter in the parlor."

"Y'all make sure to put some ice chips in those vases of roses. It'll keep them fresh for your company. Mabel, go tell Drella to come on to the kitchen so's we can get home," says Josie.

When Drella and Mabel come back to the kitchen, Josie starts walking toward the door. "See you ladies Tuesday morning," says Josie. "I've got to go get myself ready for tomorrow too, Miss Lizbeth." Josie opens the back door, steps onto the porch, and quietly shuts the door.

"Poor Josie has worked so hard today," says Mama. "She's just the finest." Mama walks over to the kitchen cabinet and begins putting the dry dishes away. "I wish I could afford to pay her for all the hard work she does around here. It makes me feel bad."

"We love Josie, don't we, Mama?" Mabel walks over and stands beside Mama at the counter. "Wonder why we love her so much."

"Josie just has a good soul. I think that's why we're both drawn to her," says Mama. "She's gentle, kind, patient, and filled with love. As far as I'm concerned, there are few people any better than our Josie. I've learned so much from her." Mama unties her apron and hangs it in the pantry. "We're going to have a light supper tonight."

"Where's Grandma?"

"She went into your room," says Mama. "I imagine she's taking a nap. She went in there right after we had our iced tea. I know Mother's tired from that long, hot ride from the country."

Mabel tiptoes down the hall to her bedroom. She quietly opens the door and peeks inside. Grandma is resting her head on Mabel's pillow on the bed. Mabel notices the gentle fluttering of the white bedroom curtains from the afternoon breeze. "Come on in, Mabel," says Grandma. "I was just resting my back for a few minutes. We haven't even had any time to talk."

Mabel slips over to the bed and sits down on the floor. "I'm glad you like my bed, Grandma. Mama says that I'm gonna sleep on a pallet in here."

"That will be nice, won't it?" says Grandma. "I heard about your sickness, but you're all well now."

"Yessum. Papa says that the Lord and Josie got me well," says Mabel. "What's Sister been doing out on the farm?" Mabel looks up at Grandma and notices how her hand under her face is pushing her cheek forward toward her lips. *That's how Grandma would look if she's fat.*

"Oh, we've been keeping her busy as a bee," says Grandma. "She's been gathering eggs and cleaning them so we can sell them. Sister has even been churning butter." Grandma laughs and moves her hand from beneath her face. "I don't think she enjoys farm work too much; but she does like the money she's making."

"Has she been helping Aunt Nell with her shroud business?" says Mabel. She looks into Grandma's eyes and waits for her answer. Grandma shuffles the pillow.

"No indeed, Mabel," says Grandma. "Nell won't be involving any of my grandchildren in that again—that's for sure."

"What's Bubba been doing?"

"I'm glad you asked," says Grandma. "He, Grandpa, and Uncle Sam have been out to the Watson farm two or three times. They've done a lot of work out there. Grandpa says that Mr. Watson is a changed man. Bubba's really a good worker. He does everything the men do." After she stops talking, her eyes seem to close a bit.

Mabel stands because she sees that Grandma is about to fall asleep. "I hope I get to go see Ruth someday," says Mabel. "I like her." Grandma closes her eyes. "I'll come back later, Grandma." She kisses her Grandma's cheek, gingerly walks out of the bedroom, and quietly closes the door.

Chapter 19

When Mabel wakes up Tuesday morning, she sits up from her spot on the pallet to see if Grandma is still asleep. *Grandma isn't even in here. She made the bed and is already in the kitchen with Mama and Josie. We're gonna have a busy day. I'd better get up and put on my clothes.* Mabel rushes through folding up her pallet. She stuffs it under her bed, gets dressed, and puts a bow in her hair. *Mama says that Josie gets all persnickety when company's coming. Josie says the same thing about Mama.* Before she leaves the bedroom, Mabel reaches up to feel for the placement of her white satin bow. Satisfied with the room, her dress, and bow, she walks into the hall leading to the kitchen.

Grandma, Mama, and Josie have their backs to the table where Mabel sits down. Mabel waits quietly—amused that they haven't noticed her. "Ahem."

Josie turns around and announces, "Well, look who's joined us, ladies." She has on a long black dress with her special apron she likes to wear for company. It has ruffles along the shoulders and around the pockets. "Mabel, you must be starving for some breakfast."

"Yessum," says Mabel. "May I have one of your ham-and-biscuits? May I have some maple syrup too?" *Josie sure looks different with all those ruffles.* Mabel can barely keep from smiling too much at Josie's outfit. *The hair around her ears has long dangly curls. That white band around her bun makes her look dressed up. Josie's trying to look prissy.*

"I'll fix Mabel's biscuit, Josie," says Grandma. "You and Lizbeth have too much to finish up." Grandma's wearing a long, navy blue skirt with a white blouse. As Grandma stands between Mama and Josie, she looks shorter than usual. "I'll fix it just the way you like it, Mabel."

"Grandma, did Josie tell you that Drella and me are going berry picking today?" says Mabel. "She said that she's gonna make us a blackberry cobbler."

"Won't that be fun for you girls," says Grandma. She puts the ham-and-biscuit on a saucer for Mabel. "I started my berry picking when I was about your age, Mabel." Grandma douses the biscuit with maple syrup and places it on the table. "Now, I know that will be good. That's exactly what I ate for breakfast."

"Do y'all have blackberries out on the farm, Grandma?" Mabel chews on her biscuit and waits for Grandma's answer.

"Lord have mercy, Mabel," says Grandma. "We've got enough berries out there to make cobblers for everybody in town." Grandma leans her head back and laughs. "There's not many a year that I haven't put up jams, jellies, and made cobblers for the family. Your grandpa's favorite dessert is cobbler."

"It'd be fun to help you pick berries, Grandma. Maybe I can go back to the farm with you and help y'all with all your work," says Mabel hopefully.

"Well, Mabel, you've had your visit and now it's Sister and Bubba's turn," says Grandma. She reaches over and pats Mabel's hand. "You got to come out there all by yourself, don't you remember?"

"Yessum, I remember," says Mabel. "I sure did like being there." Mabel forces a smile and tries to conceal her disappointment. "Maybe I can come back out there when school starts for Bubba and Sister."

"I think that'll be best, Mabel," says Mama. "Bubba and Sister need to have their time on the farm too. Having all three of you out there would be too hard on your grandma."

"I want you to come every time you can, Mabel, but your mama's right about too many all at once," says Grandma. "There's plenty of berries out there for anybody who wants to pick some."

Grandma moves over to the pantry and hangs up her apron. "I think I've done all I can in here, Lizbeth. I need to go freshen my face and hair." Grandma turns and walks into the hall.

"You need to go on outside now, Mabel," says Mama. "Drella will be here in a little while. Josie and I have got to put the finishing touches on everything." Mama keeps her back to Mabel the whole time she's talking. "Drella's coming soon, isn't she Josie?"

"Yes, ma'am," says Josie. "She should be here just any minute." Josie turns and looks at Mabel. Mabel sees the ruffles again and smiles. "Why don't you just wait out there on the back steps? We don't have no time to waste."

Mabel detects that Josie's about to get fussy. *I've seen that look in Josie's eyes. She ain't gonna be nice much longer. I'd better get out of her way. I don't want to get crossways of her—she'll start fussing.* "Yessum," says Mabel. She walks across the kitchen to the back door.

"I'll come talk to y'all about the berries when I gets a chance," says Josie. "You girls can watch them ladies coming in, but don't y'all say nothing. You only talk to them ladies if they say something to you." Josie walks over to the pantry. "You tell Drella them rules." Josie turns and watches Mabel as she walks out the door.

Mabel closes the screen door without a sound. Now safely out of reach, Mabel leans into the door and puts her hands on either side of her eyes to look into the kitchen. "May I come into the meeting, Mama?"

"No indeed—it's not a meeting for children," says Mama. "You girls just do what Josie told you to do—don't you dare come back into the house. Don't you come in under any circumstances." Mama walks over to the door. "You know that the Ladies Aid Society is for grown-ups."

Disappointed, Mabel turns and goes out to the back steps. *Mama and Josie don't want me or Drella anywhere near those ladies. I reckon I can't go back in the house until they leave. It's always like this when grown-ups come to our house.* Mabel walks down to the bottom step and sits down. *Here comes Drella. I'm glad she'll be staying out here with me.*

Mabel gets up and walks toward Drella. *Drella looks pretty in that pink dress. It makes her skin look pretty and her eyes twinkle.* "Hey, Mabel," says Drella. *She's always so nice. Her smile looks like sunshine.* "Mama Josie says your mama's having a big gathering at y'all's house. She's been talking about it for days."

"Uh huh," says Mabel. "We ain't allowed in the house until after them ladies leave."

"Well," says Drella, "that's because it's for the grown-ups." Drella holds Mabel's hand as they walk back toward the house. "I hear they's gonna have lots of good food today. Mama Josie said that she didn't think there'd be any leftovers for us."

"Don't you think it'll be fun for us to pick berries?" says Mabel. "Josie's gonna make us a great big cobbler." They stop at the bottom of the steps. Mabel turns loose of Drella's hand and sits down on the second step from the bottom. "Mama says that Josie's the best cook in Alabama."

"She is a good cook," says Drella. "She's teaching me how to make things in the kitchen, but I don't like all the cleaning up." Drella smiles at Mabel. "Mama Josie says that you help her a lot."

"I like to help her," says Mabel. "I *really* like her stories."

"Shhh—I think I hear some people talking out front," says Drella. "Bet it's some of the ladies opening the gate. Let's go and watch the parade." Without any further talk, they hurriedly sneak to the side of the house.

"We can't let them see us, Drella," says Mabel.

"Here," says Drella, "let's sit by these azaleas. We can see them, but they won't be able to see us." They sit down in the shady spot Drella selects. "Be real quiet, Mabel, so we can hear them talking."

Mabel elbows Drella. "Look how dressed up they are, Drella." Their eyes follow the first lady as she walks along the boardwalk toward the front porch. "She's wearing a hat." Just before the lady reaches the steps, she lifts the skirt of her dress so she won't trip.

"Look," says Drella, "that second lady's trying to straighten something up under her dress. Mama Josie says that's not proper in public." They snigger as quietly as possible and continue to watch the lady. She finally stops, bends over from the waist, reaches up underneath her skirt, and yanks on her slip.

"It's so hot," says Mabel, "that her slip's walking up her legs."

"Shoo wee, that's funny, Mabel," says Drella. "With all them clothes on, don't you know her legs is sweatin'?" They cover their mouths to keep from uttering a sound. Mabel gets up and mocks the lady's walk. "I think I hear Mama Josie out back," whispers Drella.

When they rush around the corner of the house, Josie doesn't look up from her seat on the back steps. She seems focused on stabbing the ice pick into the block of ice she has cradled in a white enamel pan. They walk over to Josie and sit down on the lowest step. A slight smile slides across Josie's face when Mabel chases after an ice chip that flies out of the pan. Mabel can feel Josie's hidden pleasure as they jump like crickets chasing after the ice chips.

"Drella, you girls gwan 'round front and watch all them ladies." She looks up. "Here's y'all a chunk of cool ice. Remember, don't y'all be talking to them ladies, lessen they talks to you. Be just as quiet as church mice."

As they settle back down behind the azaleas, Drella elbows Mabel to call her attention to the cluster of ladies walking up the boardwalk. Mabel hears their quiet chatter and watches them intently. "There's

Mrs. Riley," says Mabel. "She's my secret friend." The girls focus on Mrs. Riley as she tugs at the side of her skirt. "You'd like her, Drella. She's got so many nice things in her house."

"Girls? Y'all come 'round back," says Josie. Mabel tries to keep up with Drella as they run toward Josie's voice. Josie, standing on the top step, towers above the girls. Mabel's eyes follow Josie's feet as they slip out of her shoes. Josie walks down to the second step and sits down. She pushes her dress down between her legs and wiggles her toes. "Now that the ladies are kinda settled in," says Josie, "I can talk to you two about your berry picking."

"We've seen a whole parade of ladies, Mama Josie," says Drella. "They's wearing just about everything they own." The three of them laugh softly at Drella's observation.

"Well, I reckon y'all done seen all the ladies you needs to see for today," says Josie. The girls nod in agreement. A gentle smile eases over Josie's lips as she reaches down under the steps. She brings out two Rex's Jelly buckets and hands one to each girl. "Here's y'all's berry buckets." Josie lowers her feet to the ground, finds a new spot, and moves her toes around in the cool dust.

"Do you think there's enough berries to fill both of the buckets, Mama Josie?" asks Drella.

"Sure do, child," says Josie. "You two girls have to look out for one another. I don't want nobody coming back here hurt or nothing."

Josie stands up and points past the barn. "Just go down there, like I said—across the ditch—and y'all will find a heap of berries. Watch out for snakes, wasps, and thorns. Drella, you're the oldest, so you needs to be smart about where you go and what you do."

"We'll be careful, Josie," says Mabel. "We'll bring you back two full buckets; I promise."

"I's gonna fill up these two jars with some water from the well. Don't drink it all at once," says Josie as the girls follow her out to the well. She pulls the bucket to the top and dips the jars in the water to fill them up. "Carry this water in your pails, girls. Keep them lids on tight so's the water won't leak out. Now, y'all bring me back some berries."

Drella and Mabel walk toward the barn, swinging their blue-and-white-striped buckets. As they walk alongside the barn, Mabel turns and looks back at Josie. *She's putting her shoes on and going back into the house. I wish she's going with us. She'd tell us stories and we'd get more berries than Grandma's ever seen. It's hot out here.*

Drella pulls slightly ahead of Mabel. She looks back at her. "I'm taller than both of you O'Brien girls."

"Yeah," says Mabel, "but you and Sister's almost the same age." Mabel speeds up and walks beside Drella. "Y'all are in the same grade too. It's a long time before I'm gonna start school." They both look back at the house to gauge how far they've walked.

It's too hot out here to talk. I wish I had me a chunk of Josie's ice. Mabel's eyes begin to sting as salty sweat rolls down her face. In the distance, she can see the ditch Josie told them to cross. She takes a deep breath and feels the hot air burning her nostrils.

The thought of Josie's cobbler makes her feel sick to her stomach. "I think I want a sip of water. My mouth's dry," says Mabel. Drella doesn't pay any attention to her. *I wish I could sip me some iced tea with the ladies—or some sweet lemonade.* She licks her lips at the thought of the cold drinks, but all she tastes is salt.

"Come on, Mabel," says Drella. "You can't be straggling like that." Drella stops and waits for Mabel. "Let's go over yonder and sit down under the tree in the shade." The girls sit down cross-legged, face each other, and place their buckets in between themselves. "It's the hottest part of the day. We need to cool off before we try getting across the ditch." Drella and Mabel both reach for their tiny jars of water.

"We can only take sips, Drella," says Mabel. "We have to make it last for a long time." The taste of the water only makes Mabel want more, but she screws the lid back on the jar.

"Listen to those dry-flies. They's chirping today," says Drella. She reaches over and brushes a weed from Mabel's dress. "Mama Josie says that they won't let me go to the white school. She says that whites can't come to our school."

Mabel listens to Drella's talk about school. "I'll be glad when I can go to school. Maybe by then we can go to school together," says Mabel. "Wouldn't that be fun?"

"Mama Josie says that we have to go to school where they tell us to go." Drella stands up and flutters the skirt of her dress like a fan to cool off her legs.

"Our papa had to quit school when he was twelve because he had to go to work," says Mabel.

"Mama Josie ain't never been to a school, 'less she's coming to get me," says Drella. "Do you believe that teachers have eyes in the back of their heads?" Drella swishes her skirt around once again. "Mama Josie says that my teacher can see everything in front of her and in back of her."

"That's what Mama tells Bubba and Sister too," says Mabel. "Do you think that's true?"

"Let's see if we can see behind us. Maybe we'll be teachers someday." Drella steps away from the tree and turns her back to Mabel. "Now, I'm the teacher," says Drella, trying to sound like a grown-up. "I'm gonna play like I'm writing on the chalkboard. You have to do something without saying a word."

Mabel giggles as she picks some weeds and tosses them in the air. Drella can't tell her what she's doing. "Now, it's my turn," says Mabel. She takes Drella's place at the imaginary chalkboard and begins to write in the air. Drella makes faces at her back. "Drella, quit throwing those weeds," says Mabel.

"You ain't got no teacher eyes neither," says Drella. "I's making faces." They both sit back down in the shade and chuckle at their game. "I'm cooled off now. You ready to cross the ditch?"

They get up, pick up the buckets, and walk toward the ditch. As they walk, their jars roll around in their pails. "We're gonna have to run down this side to get up the other," says Drella.

"I'll go first," says Mabel. Before Drella can tell her no, she takes off, runs down the side of the ditch, and starts up the other side. She struggles with the last two steps getting up to the top. "That's not hard to do. Come on, Drella," encourages Mabel.

Drella takes off and runs down the side of the ditch. She squeals the whole time, but finally runs out of breath on the upside. "Drella, all that squealing doesn't help," says Mabel.

They walk along the ditch and find some blackberry bushes. Mabel moves her hands as fast as she can. She wants to get more berries than Drella. Then she looks over at Drella and sees her putting the blackberries into her mouth. She pops one into her mouth and enjoys the taste of its sweet juice. *These berries will keep me from being so hot. I'll put one in the bucket—then I'll put one in my mouth.* Drella and Mabel are eventually eating more berries than they're putting in their pails.

"I've got an idea," says Drella. "Let's find some other kinds of berries to eat. We can't put them in our buckets, so we have to eat them." They busy themselves looking for anything that looks like it might taste good. "Mabel, taste some of these cherries. They're juicy and sweet."

Mabel sits down in the shade of the cherry tree and puts one in her mouth. "This one tastes bitter. I like the blackberries better." She spits the pit from her mouth.

"Guess we'd better go pick some more blackberries," says Drella. "Mama Josie told us to fill up both buckets. My jar of water ain't even covered yet."

Drella walks slightly behind Mabel. "Here's some more blackberry bushes," says Mabel. Each of them continues to eat blackberries as they move along the ditch.

"Hey, Mabel, look at this big tree," says Drella. "I see some berries way up high in it."

"One time when we's out walking, Papa told me that that's a mulberry," says Mabel. "Wouldn't it be fun to climb way up there?" She points to a huge limb hanging out over the ditch. "Let's climb up there and try to get some of those berries. You're gonna have to give me a boost, Drella."

They both set their buckets beside the tree trunk. Drella cups her hands in front of her. She stands in a squatting position; Mabel puts her right foot on Drella's hands. Mabel braces herself on the tree. As Drella lifts Mabel up to the nearest limb, her body quivers under the strain of Mabel's weight.

"Shoo, Mabel, I didn't know you's so heavy." Mabel swings onto the lowest limb, pulls herself up, and works her way around until she can find a place to sit. "Here, take your bucket, Mabel." Mabel leans down, takes her bucket, and turns to weave her way up the maze of limbs. "Go on up high, Mabel," calls out Drella.

Mabel reaches a strong limb where she can brace her back and feet. "I haven't ever been up this high," shouts Mabel. "This is where the birds fly."

"Hold tight, Mabel," says Drella. "You ain't no bird. Have you tasted any of them mulberries?"

"No. I'm scared to reach over there. This is too high to be moving around much." Mabel feels unstable as she looks down at Drella. She notices her dress and sees that it's covered in berry juice. *Mama's gonna be upset about me and this dress. There's a mulberry I can grab.* "Drella, I just ate a mulberry. It sure is good," says Mabel. Drella works her way up to just below where Mabel is sitting. "I'm gonna get in trouble about my dress," says Mabel.

"Mama Josie can get the stains out," says Drella. "She's good at that. We can talk to her about it after the ladies leave."

They start singing. "Here we go 'round the mulberry bush; here we go 'round the mulberry bush, so early in the morning. …"

Mabel throws her head back and lets out a noisy laugh. Her laughter stops when she feels herself getting off balance. Mabel attempts to stop herself by grabbing for a limb—but misses. Silently, she plummets down through the branches of the tree. She hits the ground with a *thud*, rolls down the side of the ditch, and lands in the middle of some bristly weeds. Mabel can't find any air to breathe. She feels a dizziness sweeping into her head and nausea rising from her stomach. *I can't breathe.*

"Mabel?" shouts Drella. "Mabel, are you okay?" Drella balances on a limb and looks down at her.

Mabel doesn't answer. She feels too hot, too sweaty, too itchy, and too sick. Finally, capturing some air in her lungs, she rolls over into a cluster of blackberries that tumbled out of her bucket. Struggling to pull herself to her knees, she crawls to her bucket. Tears fill her eyes when she sees only one berry in it. Dragging the bucket with her, Mabel struggles up the other side of the ditch. She feels sick and wants to cry for her mama. Her lips quiver as she tries to keep Drella from knowing that tears are running down her face. She rubs her eyes and nose on the sleeve of her dress. When Mabel finally reaches the top of the hill, she gets to her feet, then turns, and walks toward the O'Brien house.

"Don't go, Mabel," yells Drella. "Wait for me. We can go to my house—I'll rub some of Mama Josie's fat drippings on your stomach. That'll make you feel better. That's what she'd do." Mabel keeps walking. "You'd better not go home with all them ladies there."

I don't want nothing on my stomach. It's too hot out here. Wish I'd picked up my water jar. Drella ought not tell me about the house—I know the rules. I'm gonna walk toward the backyard.

Now stumbling as she's walking, Mabel can feel the streams of sweat rolling down her face, arms, and legs. *It's hard for me to walk straight. I don't have far to go, but I can barely see. Maybe Mama will be outside.* Every time she licks her lips, the taste of salt clings to her dry tongue. The weeds stick to the sweat on her legs. *My shoes are cutting into my feet.*

Mabel stops, sits down, and takes off her shoes and socks. Running her finger along the deep indentations on her feet, Mabel notices how raw it feels. *My feet are so puffed up I can't get my shoes back on now. I'll just put my socks and shoes in my pail.* Drawing in a deep breath, she notices that she reeks of berry juice. *I ain't ever gonna eat another berry. Just smelling them makes me feel sick.*

Mabel considers lying down in the weeds until the ladies leave. *No, I'll just keep walking toward the house. My feet feel a lot better and I can walk faster. Hope I don't step on anything that'll cut me.* When she looks up and sees their barn in the distance, Mabel begins to feel relieved.

Drella's right about not going in the house. I sure don't want Josie to see me. I'll wait for Drella in the barn. I can cross to the back doors from here.

She reaches the barn doors and pulls only one side open. A gentle breeze floats through the air. Mabel lifts her face to let the air cool her. She closes the door tightly, walks into the shaded light of the barn, and notices Papa's horse looking at her. More interested in the oats in his bucket, the horse goes back to eating. *I wish I could have some of the horse's water, but Papa told me not to go in there by myself. He says that horses get spooked too easily—they'll kick you.*

Mabel walks across the barn to the front doors. She peeks through the space between the doors to see if she can see anyone. *About all I can see from here is the chicken coop. Reckon I'll go up to the hayloft.* She looks at the lone berry in the bottom of her bucket resting in between her shoes and socks. *Can't let anything happen to that berry.* Mabel places the wire-handled bucket over her arm and walks to the straight-up ladder Papa built. *This ladder's harder to climb than a tree.*

She struggles until she finally reaches the top and drags her body up into the loft. Mabel sets her bucket down and crawls across the straw to the two doors that stay slightly open. Exhausted, she sits there and lets the air flow through her wet hair. *That feels so good. I think I'll just lie down and watch the back porch. I don't want to miss it when Drella comes home.* Within minutes, Mabel drifts into a deep, soothing sleep.

—

"Mabel? Where are you, child?" calls out Josie. The sound of her name awakens Mabel. Without getting up, she opens her eyes and peers through the hayloft doors. She sees Josie standing on the back steps. Her eyes follow Josie as she walks toward the barn. She hears the barn door open. "Mabel? Are you in here?" Mabel feels so groggy that she lays her head back down.

In the background, she hears Josie struggling to get up the straight-up ladder. "Mabel? Come over here to me," says Josie. Mabel opens her eyes, but feels too exhausted to move.

She sluggishly watches Josie's slow crawl across the straw toward her. Josie sits down beside Mabel. She pulls her closer and lifts Mabel's head into her lap. "Lord have mercy child," says Josie, "I's scared you's lost somewhere." Josie lifts Mabel into her arms and cradles her. "We's worried to death about you, baby. I don't ever want anything to happen to you." Josie runs her long brown fingers through Mabel's hair. "Lord, you got too hot, didn't you, Mabel? I can feel the salt on your skin."

"Yessum, I fell out of the tree." She looks up into Josie's deep-brown eyes and watches a lone tear roll down her cheek. "Is Drella back, Josie?"

"She's been back a long time, Mabel. Drella's in a heap of trouble for not taking care of you. I ain't ever seen your mama so upset. Miss Drella's home by herself."

Josie runs her hands along Mabel's arms and legs. "It's a wonder you didn't break all your little bones in that fall. I'm so proud you're safe."

"I only brought one blackberry home. Mama's gonna be upset about my dress. Do you think it's ruined, Josie?"

"If I can't get them stains out, I think your Aunt Nell will make you a beautiful new dress," says Josie. "As far as the blackberries go, you brought back one more than Drella."

Josie leans over and unhitches the rope holding the hayloft doors. She lets them swing open and shouts, "Mr. Tom! Miss Lizbeth! I found Mabel up here!" Mabel looks through the opening and sees her mama and papa standing on the back steps. They hurriedly begin walking toward the barn.

They stop beneath the loft doors and look up at Josie. "Is she okay, Josie?" asks Papa.

"Yes, Mr. Tom. Your baby's just fine," says Josie. She gives Mabel a gentle hug. "Can you and Miss Lizbeth come into the barn and help me get her down the ladder? She's one tired child."

Chapter 20

As usual, on Tuesday, August 13, Mabel sits up in her bed and listens to see if she can hear Mama and Josie in the kitchen. After she makes up her bed, she puts on a short-sleeve blouse and pulls on her overalls. The cool floor feels good to her feet as she walks into the kitchen. Mama and Josie are sitting at the table drinking a cup of hot tea. "There's my girl," says Mama. "I'm glad you saw that I put out your overalls for you."

"Mabel, I made you some porridge this morning," says Josie. "I's waiting on you to get up because I'm gonna make you some toast to go with it. Does that sound good?"

"Yessum," says Mabel. She slides into a chair at the table and looks across at Josie. "Is Drella gonna be here today?"

"No, Miss Mabel, she's with her Aunt Apple. She's teaching Drella how to quilt." Josie scoots her chair back and walks over to the stove. "You know why we all call her Aunt Apple, don't you?"

"No'm," answers Mabel. She looks over at Josie. Mabel's eyes take in the floral print of the long skirt Josie is wearing. She glances at the pink of her heels just below her hemline.

"It's because Apple is her last name, isn't it Josie?" says Mama. Josie nods in agreement as she pours the porridge into a bowl.

"You forgets one thing, Miss Lizbeth," says Josie. "Most folks use they first name with 'uncle' or 'aunt' in front of it. You'd be Aunt Lizbeth—Mabel would be Aunt Mabel. I'd be Aunt Josie. You ain't Aunt O'Brien." The three of them giggle at the thought of what Josie says. "That means that Mabel's Aunt Nell would be Aunt Hood." The three of them laugh again.

"Well, tell us, Josie," says Mama, "why did they ever do that?"

Josie places Mabel's bowl of porridge and a piece of buttered toast on the table. "Blow on that some, Mabel; it's mighty hot." She walks over to the dishpan and dips the pot into the water, turns around, and then dries her hands on her apron. "The story goes that she loves being Mrs. Apple. Since she been married, she ain't ever used her first name again. You ever been in Aunt and Uncle Apple's house?" says Josie.

"No'm, I haven't," replies Mabel. Mama shakes her head showing that she's never been in the Apple house either.

"Y'all needs to go visit them. There's apple everything in that house: pictures on the wall, fruit on the table, and quilts with apples all over them. Even they bedspread is covered with apples she sewed to it. She don't care what color apple she uses—red, yellow, pink, purple, or green. So, when you go into they house, you know whose house you in, for sure," says Josie. "It even smell like apples."

"My goodness, Josie," says Mama. "I've never heard that story in all the years we've been in Shoal Crossing. Guess I never really thought about their name."

"They should be called Aunt Susie and Uncle James, but everybody just goes along with Aunt and Uncle Apple," says Josie. "It don't matter who they meet—colored, white, young or old—they introduce theyselves as Aunt and Uncle Apple. They are two fine people. That's why I allow Drella to go over there so much."

"Thank you for sharing that story, Josie," says Mama. "I would love to sit here and talk to you two all day, but I've got to get Brother and myself ready to go to my Society meeting." Mama gets up from her chair and takes her cup to the dishpan.

"When are you going, Mama?" asks Mabel.

"In just a little while, honey. We're meeting at Mrs. Delany's house. You're going to stay here with Josie," says Mama. "Mrs. Delany told those of us who have very young children that we can bring them. It seems that Mrs. Delany has enough help to watch them while we meet. Mr. Delany must be doing well with his business in Florence."

"Does that mean I get to go too?" says Mabel. She watches as Josie picks up her empty bowl.

"No, Mabel," says Mama. "I think it will be enough if I ask for her help taking care of Brother during the meeting." Mama walks over to the hallway door. "You don't know what Josie has planned for you today, do you? You're going to be happy you're here with her." Without waiting for a response, Mama walks out of the kitchen.

Josie turns from the cabinet and smiles at Mabel. "Child, you and me's gonna have us some fun today," she says. "While everybody's gone, we's gonna have ourselves a good old picnic."

A smile bursts across Mabel's face. "Oh, Josie, picnics are one of my favorite things. Where are we gonna have it?"

"Well, I's been thinking that we'd go out yonder behind the barn under the shade of the big old tree. It's nice and flat there—plenty of shade too," says Josie. "Only thing I needs for you to do is get us one of your pallet quilts and empty that bushel basket out on the back porch. That's what we'll carry everything in."

By the time Mama and Brother leave for the Society meeting, Josie and Mabel are packing the bushel basket. "I like this basket, Josie," says Mabel. "It has handles on each side so we can both carry it."

When they get to a shady spot that Josie chooses, they begin unpacking the bushel basket. "I brought this oilcloth so we won't be gettin' anything on your mama's quilt," says Josie. "Just be sure you screw the top back on your jar after you drink some lemonade, Mabel."

They spread everything out so that Josie can lean up against the tree. "Yes, ma'am, Miss Mabel, we's gonna have ourselves a pleasant afternoon out here in the shade. They's just enough breezes."

"This is fun, Josie," says Mabel. "When did you think of having a picnic?"

"Just as soon as your mama told me about the meeting last week," says Josie. "If the weather's nice, I like to eat outside. Guess that comes from the way I's raised."

"Did y'all have lots of picnics when you were a little girl?"

"Child, we didn't eat outside for fun," says Josie. "We ate outside because our old house would be blazing hot in August. My daddy did it because he had to, but I like to do it now because that's what I's used to as a child."

"This ham-and-biscuit sure is good," says Mabel. She reaches down and picks up her jar of lemonade. "Mmmm, that's so good and sweet, Josie. You know how to make good things for picnics."

"I's so glad you like it, Mabel," says Josie. "We's having us a good day."

Mabel takes another bite from her biscuit and stares at Josie as she chews. "Josie, you never did make us that blackberry cobbler. Did you forget?"

"Child, I didn't forget," says Josie. "If you'll remember, you only brought back one berry. Now, I've made some small cobblers in my day, but I thinks that would be about the smallest anybody ever made." Josie smiles and laughs. "Yes, ma'am, a one-berry cobbler sure would be little." Mabel laughs along with Josie as she imagines how a one-berry cobbler would look on the table.

"Mabel, see that redbird up on that limb?" Josie points upward.

"Yessum, I see it," says Mabel. "It's beautiful. Look Josie, its beak is orange."

"That's a male redbird. You can tell because the males are a brighter red than the females. I'm gonna tell you a secret about redbirds, child." Josie leans her shoulders forward, rests her arms on her legs, and speaks in a lower tone. "Any time you sees a redbird, you can make a wish on it. After you make your wish, you have to keep watching. If that redbird flies up, you gonna get your wish. If it flies down, you don't get your wish. You ever heard tell of that?"

"No'm," says Mabel. "Nobody's ever told me about redbirds and wishes."

"Here's what you do, Mabel. You says a little poem and then make your wish. Are you ready?"

"Yessum." Mabel leans her head back and stares at the bird.

"Redbird, redbird, way up high. Take my wish up to the sky," says Josie. "Now you make your wish, Mabel. I'm gonna make one too."

As they both sit there, watching the redbird, he seems very curious about them. Mabel is fascinated by how he quickly turns his head, sits real still, and then turns his head again. "Look, Josie," says Mabel, "he took off toward the sky." She looks back at Josie's smiling face. "I reckon we're gonna get our wishes, don't you?"

"That's right, child," says Josie. "We's gonna get our wishes for sure. You can't never tell nobody your wish though, 'cause then it won't come true. Wishes is secrets."

"That made me happy for him to fly up for us," says Mabel.

"I always like that little poem, 'cause it's showing that the redbird is carrying your wish up to heaven," says Josie. "Anything that go up to heaven gonna come back to us as good. You know God create every living thing; and I think them redbirds are just about the prettiest of all His creations."

Josie leans her back against the tree. "I'm gonna tell you another secret 'bout that redbird flying up, Mabel. Any time you watch a bird take off from wherever he is, he gotta go up first."

"What do you mean, Josie?"

"I mean a bird can't fly up or down before he hops up first. You just watch and you'll see. That's why any time you sees a redbird, you can make a wish and know it's gonna come true," says Josie. "I reckon they's just good luck every time you sees one. That'll be our secret too, Mabel."

"Josie, you tell the best stories in the whole wide world," says Mabel. "I ain't ever gonna forget to make a wish on a redbird." Mabel opens her jar of lemonade and takes a sip. "Why've you got your eyes closed, Josie? Are you sleepy?"

"No, Mabel, I ain't sleepy. I's just feeling real tired," says Josie. "Reckon I didn't get me enough sleep last night. I's having a hard time catching my breath after I went to bed, so I ended up sittin' up in a chair most of the night. Maybe it was just too hot. I don't know."

Mabel reaches over and pats Josie's leg. Josie grasps Mabel's hand without opening her eyes. "I've never seen you sleep, Josie. I've never even seen you get tired," says Mabel.

"Child, just lay your head down on my lap for a while. We can both get a rest for a few minutes," says Josie. "After we rest, we'll clean up everything and go back to the house. Your mama will be home pretty soon."

After about an hour of sitting outside in silence, Josie opens her eyes. Mabel's blue eyes are watching her. "Josie, you went to sleep. Do you feel better now?" she asks.

"Old Josie sure did nod off. We'd better get all this stuff back in our basket and head to the house," says Josie. "I don't know why I's feeling out of sorts today, Mabel. Seem like something's pressing on my chest. Right here." Josie rests her hand on the spot that's bothering her.

"Let's go tell Mama. She'll know what to do," says Mabel.

They walk up the back steps and into the house. Mama comes into the kitchen just as they are putting the bushel basket on the table. "There y'all are," says Mama. "Did you have fun on your picnic?"

"Yessum," says Mabel. "Except Josie's not feeling good today. She said that something's pressing on her chest."

"Josie?" says Mama. "Are you all right? Is there anything you need?" Mama walks over to Josie and guides her toward a chair. "Maybe a glass of water will help. It's awfully hot out there."

"No, Miss Lizbeth, I's fine," says Josie. "This started coming and going on me several weeks ago. It's decided to stay with me last night and today. Reckon I needs to just go on home and rest on my bed for a little while." She stands up and rests her hand on the table.

"Do you need for me to walk you home, Josie?" says Mama. "I've never seen you sick a day since I've known you."

"No'm, I'll be just fine," says Josie. "I'll be better by this evening. I'll see you tomorrow morning." She stops at the back door. "Mabel, it sure was fun having a picnic with you today."

Mabel walks over to Josie and puts her arms around her waist. Josie leans down and kisses the top of Mabel's head. "I love you, Josie," says Mabel. "I hope you feel better."

"Oh, I will, child. My daddy use to have these spells. I reckon it'll go away," says Josie.

"You take care of yourself, Josie," says Mama. "Send Drella for us if you need anything."

"I'll see y'all tomorrow," says Josie. "I'll be fine." Mabel and Mama watch her walk out onto the porch and down the back steps.

About two hours later, Papa comes home to find Mabel, Brother, and Mama on the front porch. After Mama checks on Papa's day at work, she tells him about Josie not feeling well. "If you can, I want you to go find Dr. Reed and see if he'll look at Josie. I'll take

Mabel and Brother to Josie's house and tell her that the doctor will be coming to see her. Bring him to her house with you, Tom," says Mama. "I'm really worried about her."

"My goodness, Lizbeth, I've never known Josie to be sick," says Papa. "I saw Dr. Reed's wagon up on the main road when I was walking home. He's at the Jefferson house most afternoons. Mrs. Jefferson is his sister, you know. I'll go find him right now. He's probably still there."

Papa puts his cap back on his head, rushes down the steps, and crosses the boardwalk to the front gate. Mabel listens as his whistle floats through the air as he begins his search to find Dr. Reed.

"Come on, Mabel," says Mama. "Let's walk through the house and go out the back door."

When they get to Josie's house, Drella is sitting out on their tiny front porch with her feet resting in a patch of dirt. "How's Josie feeling since she got home, Drella?" says Mama.

"She don't feel no kind of good, Miss Lizbeth," says Drella. "Aunt Apple just left. She's coming back this evening to sit with Mama Josie through the night."

"Is she awake now?" says Mama. "Mr. O'Brien went to find the doctor to come see about her."

"Yes, ma'am, she awake. She hurting bad in her chest," says Drella. "I don't think she can sleep."

Mabel sits down by Drella and puts her arm around her shoulder. "Dr. Reed's gonna come and help her," says Mabel. "Josie likes Dr. Reed."

Tears begin rolling down Drella's cheeks. Mama hands her a handkerchief from her dress pocket. "I know it scares you, Drella, for your mama to be sick, but we're going to see to it that she's comfortable," says Mama. "The doctor will know what to do for her."

"Yessum," says Drella. She dabs her tears from her eyes with Mama's handkerchief. Drella offers the handkerchief back to Mama. "Thank you, Miss Lizbeth."

"You can keep that as a gift from me," says Mama. She reaches down and pats Drella's hand.

"Thank you. Mama Josie's got to get better," whispers Drella. "I ain't got nobody but her."

"Don't you worry, Drella," says Mama. "You've got our whole family. You've got Aunt and Uncle Apple as well as all the people from y'all's church. You've got more than enough folks to care for you and Josie. Everyone loves her. Just think of all her church friends in Florence."

"Here comes Papa with Dr. Reed," says Mabel. "It didn't take Papa long to find him."

They all watch Dr. Reed pull his cart up to the front of Josie's house. Papa hops down out of the cart. "Hello, Mrs. O'Brien," says Dr. Reed. "Tom says that Josie's not feeling well. Where is she?"

Drella stands up. "She in the house, Doctor. Do you want me to go inside with you?" asks Drella.

"No, I think it's best that Mrs. O'Brien and I go in to see her," says Dr. Reed. "I know Josie from when she's been at the O'Brien house. So, we are acquainted with each other." He takes off his black coat as well as his hat and places them on the cart seat. "Let me just get my bag from the cart, Mrs. O'Brien."

Mama passes Brother to Papa and leads the doctor into Josie's house. Papa walks around with Brother, bouncing him in his arms and whistling. Brother claps his tiny hands and smiles.

Mabel and Drella continue to sit on the porch in silence. *I hope Dr. Reed can give Josie some aspirin and make her feel better. Maybe we'll need to put some hot blankets around her like she did for me. Mama and me can make her some broth so she'll feel better. I wonder if she has any ice in her house.*

In about thirty minutes, Dr. Reed comes outside and sits down on the porch beside Drella. He places his hand on her back and pats her. "Your mother is very sick, Drella. She has something wrong with her heart—there's nothing I can do to help her."

Drella doesn't appear to understand her mother's condition. Dr. Reed gets up, walks to his cart, and puts his bag back on the floorboard. He and Papa walk back to the porch and stand in front of Drella. "Josie told me that her daddy died from some sort of heart failure. I think she might be facing the same problem. All we can do for her is make her comfortable," says Dr. Reed.

Drella stands up and looks into Dr. Reed's face. "You mean Mama Josie's gonna die?"

Dr. Reed looks down at her. "Yes, Drella, I'm very sorry that there's nothing I can do for her. Y'all need to know that I gave her a shot so she won't be in so much pain. Mr. and Mrs. O'Brien will help you take care of her and keep her comfortable. She can't be left alone."

"Yessir," says Drella as tears begin to fall again. "Aunt and Uncle Apple will help too." Drella sits back down on the porch beside Mabel and sobs. Mabel takes the handkerchief from Drella's hand and wipes away her friend's falling tears.

A moment later, Mama steps out onto the porch. When Mabel looks up at her, she can see the redness in her mama's eyes from her tears. Mama sits down beside Drella and pulls her close.

"Drella, we're going to take care of you. I know you'd rather be with your mama, but you'll never be alone as long as we're here. Our Josie's in a lot of pain—it breaks my heart to see her so sick. She can hardly draw a deep breath." She lays her cheek down on Drella's head and they both weep. Mabel leans her head on Drella's shoulder and quietly cries with her mama and Drella.

"I'll be leaving now, Tom," says Dr. Reed. They shake hands. "I wish I could have done something for her. It won't be long. She's a fine soul. Let me know if you need something. In case she needs more sedation, I'll check on her tomorrow. She's like family to y'all. It's going to be difficult for all of you. After what she did for Mabel, she's like family to me too. It's all very sad and most unfortunate. Sometimes, the best among us leaves way too soon." Dr. Reed climbs up on his cart seat, clicks his tongue, and slowly rides away.

—

Early Wednesday afternoon, Drella comes to the O'Brien house to watch Brother while Mabel and Mama go to visit Josie. They are going to relieve Aunt Apple and Josie's other friends for several hours. "We made Josie some of her special broth," says Mama. "I hope she'll eat some of it for me."

"Yessum," says Drella. "She's been asking when you's coming back to see her. Dr. Reed came by just a while ago and gave her another shot. He say that she seem a little stronger today. He didn't have to give her so much medicine this time."

"Did she sleep last night?" asks Mabel.

"Woo, Mama Josie snored *real* loud last night." The three of them break out in smiles just talking about Josie. "Aunt Apple told her this morning that Dr. Reed owes her one of them shots after that racket she put up with all night." Drella laughs and her beautiful green eyes dance with happiness. "Maybe she gonna get well, Miss Lizbeth. Aunt Apple said that the good Lord's in charge, not the doctor."

"That's right, Drella," says Mama. "Maybe our Josie's just been worn out from taking care of everybody else. When I think of all the work she does, it really makes me feel bad." Mama carefully picks up the jar of broth she made for Josie. "We'll be back here in about two hours. Brother's taking his nap in his playpen. When he wakes up, he'll be happy to see you, Drella."

"Yessum. Me and Brother like to play," agrees Drella.

When Mama and Mabel walk up onto Josie's front porch, Mama knocks on the door. Aunt Apple comes to the door and holds it open. Aunt Apple is just as Mabel remembers her—stout, not much taller than herself, rosy cheeks, a wide smile, and an apron covering her long dress. She says, "Josie just asked me about you, Mrs. O'Brien. She'll be happy you brought Mabel. Y'all go on back to her bedroom. She's sitting up—I think she feels better. Dr. Reed came by and checked on her. He said he'll come by tomorrow too."

Mabel smiles as she notices the apples all over Aunt Apple's long apron. *She's just like Josie said she is—apples on everything.*

"If you need to go home, Mabel and I will stay with her for a few hours."

"I'll fix her some of your broth later on, Mrs. O'Brien," says Aunt Apple. "I needs to fix Uncle Apple some dinner before I come back down here. Some of the other ladies from the church will come back and relieve you. I'll be staying the night with her."

"It's so kind of y'all to take such good care of Josie," says Mama. "I know she's thankful to have all of you as friends. Josie told us the other day about how much she thinks of you and Uncle Apple." Mama hands the broth to Aunt Apple. "Let's go see Josie, Mabel."

When they walk into Josie's room, she's sitting up in bed with her back resting on stacked pillows. "Well, Lord, look who done come to see me," says Josie. "I been asking 'bout you two. I's feeling better today. Dr. Reed came by."

Mama walks across the room and goes to Josie's open arms. "I'm so glad you're feeling better," says Mama. "I'm sure Dr. Reed was surprised."

"Let me hug my baby," says Josie. Mabel steps around Mama and gently lays her head on Josie's shoulder. "Child, I sure have been missing that sweet face." Mabel stands back and smiles at Josie. Josie pats the edge of her bed. "Here, you scoot up here by me. You sure look pretty in that blue dress, Mabel."

"I put it on special for you, Josie," says Mabel. She sits alongside Josie and dangles her feet off the side of the bed. "I even put on my shoes and socks." Josie smiles and pats Mabel's arm.

Mama moves a chair close to the bed. "We're gonna be here with you for a little while, Josie," she says. "Aunt Apple's got to go cook up some dinner."

Mabel reaches over and puts her hand on Josie's hand. Josie lifts her hand and grasps Mabel's hand. *Josie looks tired. Her eyes are barely open and her skin's not shining like it does on most days. Every time she takes a breath, I can hear that noise in her chest. Wonder if Dr. Reed listened to her breathe like he did with me.*

While still holding Mabel's hand, Josie closes her eyes. "Miss Lizbeth, I've already told Aunt Apple what I wants done if I should pass." She slowly rubs her thumb back and forth over the top of Mabel's hand. "I wants Drella to stay with Aunt and Uncle Apple, but I wants her to come to your house whenever she can—maybe even live at your house some of the time. She loves you and Mabel just like I do. So, if you can see to it, I sure will appreciate it."

"Why, Josie, you know I'll do anything for you," says Mama, with tears in her eyes. "Drella is always welcome in our home. We love her too."

"If I pass, I wants you to write my sister a letter and tell her. Tell her to come down here on the train and get Drella. She needs to be with family," says Josie. "It may take my sister a little while to save up the money, but you tell her that I say that's what she should do."

"I sure will, Josie," says Mama. "I've still got her address from when we wrote her the last time."

"Now, I wants you to make sure that they put my usher's dress on me for my funeral. They's three mens I want to help carry my casket. That's Uncle Apple, Mr. O'Brien, and Dr. Reed." Josie slightly opens her eyes and looks at Mama. "None of this may never come to be, but if it does, I want you to make sure of those things. I wants you to write my death notice for the paper, Miss Lizbeth, and I wants Mr. Tom to say something at my service."

"We'll do just what you want us to do, Josie," says Mama. "It's good to make plans, Josie, but I hope that you'll get better."

"I do too. Main thing is to see to Drella until my sister can come get her," says Josie. She closes her eyes once again. "Now, Miss Mabel, I want you to help your mama take care of Drella. She loves you just like a sister."

"Yessum," says Mabel. She leans her head down on Josie's shoulder.

"I want you to always remember all the nice talks we've had, child. We's talked about just about everything, haven't we?" A slow smile crosses Josie's face. "If I pass, child, I want you to remember that I's gonna be watching over you—just like I told you I would. I's gonna be that angel up in heaven. Remember, I gets to see my mama and daddy up there too. Just always be mindful that Josie loves you and I'll always be with you." Josie grows silent and begins breathing more deeply.

"I think she's gone to sleep, Mabel," whispers Mama. "Just stay right there with her. She likes to have you close. God bless her heart; I sure do love her."

"Me too, Mama."

Chapter 21

On Friday, August 16, Dr. Reed brings word of Josie's death to the O'Brien family. He sits at the kitchen table with Mama and Mabel clinging to his every word. "Josie's heart just gave out on her. She wasn't in any pain when the end came. I was sitting beside her bed along with Aunt Apple and Drella. Josie simply went to sleep."

Tears stream down Mama's face. "Did she tell you that she wanted you to be a pallbearer, Dr. Reed?" says Mama.

"Yes, she did, Mrs. O'Brien," says Dr. Reed. Mama blows her nose into her handkerchief. "I consider it an honor to fulfill her wishes." He stands up and walks toward the back door. "We'll meet at her house at eleven in the morning—then walk with the funeral wagon to her church. Mr. O'Brien's supposed to serve as a bearer too, you know."

Mama stands and leans against the counter. She wipes her eyes. "Yes, yes, we know," she says. "I want to thank you for making Josie's last days comfortable, Dr. Reed. You're a fine man."

"Well, thank you, Mrs. O'Brien," says Dr. Reed. "When we lose people like Josie, it's difficult on all of us. Sometimes physicians can only ease the pain. We have to let go and accept that God is the one in final control. I wish I could've done more for her. I'll see you folks tomorrow." He quietly closes the door on his way out.

Mabel's face is streaked from the tears she has shed. "Mama, is Josie in heaven yet?"

"Yes, Mabel, she's already there," says Mama. "The moment she took her last breath, her soul took flight to heaven."

"Josie liked to talk about heaven. She always said that she would get to meet her mother and see her daddy again," says Mabel. "I know she's happy, Mama. She told me so."

"Yes, Mabel, there's an angel up there smiling right now. Her name is Josie," says Mama.

Saturday morning, August 17, Mama, Papa, and Mabel get dressed for Josie's funeral. Mama arranges for Mrs. Delany's teenage daughter to come stay with Brother. When Priscilla Delany arrives, Mama, Papa, and Mabel walk to Josie's house.

"My goodness, Tom," says Mama, "look at all those people gathered together for Josie."

"Yes, Lizbeth," says Papa. "She touched a lot of lives." Papa takes out his handkerchief and swipes his forehead and his eyes. "This suit and hat are mighty hot to wear today. I see Dr. Reed. I'll be walking beside the funeral wagon with the other men. You remember, Lizbeth, the pallbearers have to sit together at church too."

"Yes, I remember, Tom," says Mama. "We'll wait for you after the burial."

"Mama," says Mabel, "I'm scared. I haven't ever been to a funeral."

Mama reaches down and takes Mabel's hand. "You'll be fine, Mabel. I'll take care of you. Just remember, no talking."

As they step into Josie's yard, Mabel looks around for Drella. "Is Drella gonna be with us, Mama?"

"I'm certain she will, Mabel," says Mama. "Just stay with me and do as I do. You'll be fine."

All six of the pallbearers gather in front of Josie's porch. Papa and Dr. Reed are the only two white men. Mabel recognizes Uncle Apple and old Joe, but the other colored men are people she doesn't know.

The colored preacher, wearing a long white robe, walks down between the pallbearers; he stands on the front porch and lifts his arms up for silence. A hush falls over the crowd. The pallbearers follow the preacher into the house. In a few minutes, Drella and Aunt Apple step out onto the porch. They walk over to the funeral wagon and stand behind it.

Aunt Apple signals for Mama and Mabel to come join them. Mama leads Mabel as they weave through the crowd until they're beside Aunt Apple. They each give Drella a hug. "Drella want you two with us up front, Miss Lizbeth," says Aunt Apple. Mabel looks back and sees that all the people have lined up behind them. She notices that Drella is wearing the dress that Josie made for her—the one with pink roses all over it. She's wearing matching pink ribbons in her hair.

In a few minutes, the preacher steps out onto the porch and the pallbearers carry Josie's wooden casket behind him. They walk silently through the crowd, heave the casket upon the black floorboard of the horse-drawn funeral wagon, and position themselves on both sides of the wagon. The preacher stands behind the wagon. The crowd starts moving forward as the horse pulls Josie toward her church. Mabel hears all the footsteps following them. Drella is walking between Aunt Apple and Mama.

Mabel clings to Mama's hand and only looks up periodically to make certain that Josie is still riding on the wagon. *I know Josie's watching all of this from heaven. She's got a smile on her face because so many people are here for her. She sees Papa walking by the funeral wagon, the preacher wearing his robe, and Mama holding Drella's hand. Everything is just like she wanted it. The last time I walked to Josie's church, she was holding my hand. I wonder if I'm walking where she walked.*

As they turn off the road to go over to the church, the people behind them start humming 'Amazing Grace'. *They must know that's Josie's favorite song. Their voices sound so pretty. It's like Josie use to hum at my house. She told me that when she's humming she couldn't worry. Mama and Mabel begin humming with the crowd.* They continue humming softly as the wagon stops in front of the church. The pallbearers remove the casket from the wagon, walk up the front steps, and slowly enter the church.

Two deacons come over to walk Aunt Apple, Drella, Mama, and Mabel into the church. *Mama always said we'd visit Josie's church one day. I've never sat on the first row. Josie would be proud.* The mourners continue to hum as they file into their rows behind the pallbearers. Mama takes a hand fan from her purse and flutters it around her face. *Wish I had a fan.*

The deacons walk to the casket as the preacher continues up three steps to the platform where his opened Bible rests. One deacon raises the lid of the casket, making Josie's profile slightly visible. Mabel can see that she is wearing the white dress Josie described to Mama. Mabel slides her eyes in Drella's direction. *Drella looks pretty today, but she looks sad. She's kept her head bowed all day. I don't know what I'd do without Mama. Drella must be scared. Mama says that we're gonna take care of Drella until her aunt comes to get her. Papa mailed the letter to Josie's sister this morning. Mama says that Drella will even be spending the night with us sometimes. Wonder what will happen to Josie's house. I miss my Josie.* Mabel dabs her handkerchief around her eyes.

The humming stops as the preacher raises his arms for everyone to be quiet. "We are gathered here today to celebrate Josie Roane's beautiful life. All of us loved Josie, the beloved mother of our Drella Roane. We can all rejoice, for we know that Josie is now with her God. Knowing Josie means that you know that she believed in eternal life. Josie knew that her time here, in her earthly body, was not permanent. She is now rid of the pains of life on earth. Josie is in heaven in an eternal body created by God."

He's saying what Josie use to talk about with me. I wonder if she's seen her daddy yet. She always talked about him. I remember when she told me that she was gonna be our angel and watch over Drella, Mama, and me. Wonder if she can hear what I'm thinking. Mabel feels the breeze from Mama's fan. She looks back up at the podium.

A colored lady, dressed in black and wearing a wide-brimmed black hat, cocked to one side, goes up and sits down at the piano. Mabel watches her as she opens a hymnal and rests it on top of the piano. The piano player nods her head and everybody stands. They all start singing in unison. Their voices remind Mabel of the beauty of Josie's voice as she did her work.

Mama and Mabel do not know the song, so they just stand quietly and listen. The next song is much faster. The congregation claps, sways, and sings together. After the third song, the congregation is directed to sit down. The piano player gets up and goes back to her seat over against the wall.

"Those songs were loved by Josie," says the preacher. "They are the ones Josie asked me to make sure you sang at her funeral. They are all songs of praise. Don't you know that Josie Roane is rejoicing today? It would be unthinkable for us to be so self-centered that we wish for God to bring her back to the pain she suffered in her final days. I say to you, let her be. Let Josie be. Just let her be. Josie Roane is where her God has prepared her to be. Every deed she did, every word she spoke, every thought that crossed her mind, and every trial she went through prepared her to meet her Savior face-to-face."

Mama reaches over and pats Mabel's leg. Mabel moves closer to Mama and leans her head against her shoulder. She looks down and sees that Mama's holding Drella's hand. *I'm glad Josie is happy in heaven. The preacher says that we shouldn't wish for Josie to come back because she'd still be sick. That's gonna be hard for me to do. I want to see Josie every day. Mama's gonna miss her too.*

Mabel focuses back on the preacher. "Now, in closing, I want to ask Mr. Tom O'Brien to come forward to share his thoughts about Josie. Mr. O'Brien will dismiss the congregation to the burial site." Mabel sits up straight and watches Papa as he walks past Josie to get to the podium. He takes a piece of paper from his inside coat pocket. Mama presses her hand a little tighter on Mabel's leg. The colored preacher nods at Papa. Papa's face turns blood red.

"When we learned of Josie's death, Mrs. O'Brien and I wanted to write her obituary for her," says Papa. "It will be in the local papers next week." He looks over at Drella and attempts to smile before he begins reading. "Josie Roane went to be with her Lord on Friday, August 16, 1918. A worthy colored woman, Josie was loved by all who knew her in Shoal Crossing. She leaves one daughter, Drella Roane of Shoal Crossing. She leaves one sister, Gladys, who lives far away in Michigan. A large congregation gathered on Saturday following her death for her funeral. The size of the crowd is a mark of the respect held for her in the Shoal Crossing community."

Mabel watches as Papa refolds the paper and puts it back inside his suit coat pocket. Someone sitting in the audience breaks the silence by calling out, "Amen." Papa looks up and smiles as several more shout out "Amen!" Papa raises his hand. "Now, let's all rise for the closing prayer." Papa waits until everyone stands and silence fills the room. "You are invited to remain for the burial which will take place beside the church. There are a few chairs for those of you who might need one." Mabel watches as Papa bows his head.

"Let's bow our heads please," says Papa. "Blessed be the Lord, our heavenly Father, who has graced us all with the earthly life and presence of Josie Roane. Lord, we thank You for all the good we witnessed in Josie's life. We thank You, Lord, for all the sweet memories of Josie—her love, her joy, and her spirit she so unselfishly shared. Thank You too, Lord, for all the wisdom and witness she shared with all she met. Thank You, Lord, for allowing her to touch so many lives in such a powerful way. Thank You, Lord, for removing her from the pain within her body, but most of all, we thank You for her eternal life. We rejoice, Lord, in her joy. Let each of us know one day, Lord, the happiness Josie Roane is now living in heaven. In all things, Lord, we give thanks. Amen."

When Mabel looks up, she notices that a different person is now at the piano. The man starts playing softly as the crowd begins to move forward and walk past Josie's casket. "Mabel, we're going to have to walk in front of the casket. If you don't want to look at Josie, just bow your head as we walk by." The mourners begin humming with the piano music.

"Yessum," says Mabel. She stands on her tiptoes and whispers to Mama, "I don't want to see her in the casket, Mama. I'm not gonna look."

Mama looks down at Mabel and nods her approval. When it comes time for their row to walk past, Mabel keeps her eyes glued to the floor. Mama only stops briefly to look at Josie and begins crying again.

Mabel follows Mama back to their pew. They remain standing as Aunt Apple and Drella view Josie's body. Mabel begins sobbing as she watches her friend reach over and touch Josie's shoulder. When everyone is finished, the pallbearers move forward and Uncle Apple closes the casket. They lift the casket and slowly begin walking up the middle aisle of the church. Carrying his Bible, the preacher follows the casket. Mabel and Drella hold hands as they follow behind the preacher. Mama and Aunt Apple brace each other behind the girls. They walk down the same steps Mabel and Josie watched Drella descend that day after school. Mabel looks out toward the tree where she once stood with Josie. *Everything reminds me of her.*

The crowd begins the silent walk to the gravesite behind the casket, the pallbearers, and the preacher. Two deacons walk beside Aunt Apple, Drella, Mama, and Mabel. *I've never seen anyone get buried. Mama says that it isn't bad and that I should just keep in mind that Josie's soul's already in heaven. She says that thinking of Josie in heaven makes things better for those of us who love her down here.*

When they arrive at the gravesite, the mourners wait and watch as the pallbearers place the coffin on sturdy ropes that are strategically placed across the grave opening. Each rope is wound around a railroad spike that is driven deeply into the ground. The coffin rests on the ropes, suspended above the hole in the ground. *I wonder who dug up all that dirt.*

The preacher positions himself at the head of the coffin as the pallbearers stand along the far side. Aunt Apple, Drella, Mama, and Mabel are escorted to the front row beside the grave. Behind them, three female ushers, dressed in white uniforms like Josie's wearing, begin fanning the air around their heads. *They can fan even better than Mama. They must be ushers like Josie. She use to tell me about how ushers help people during their church services. Josie said that some people in their church got so happy about the Lord that they'd fall out on the floor. I don't reckon I've ever seen anybody fall out. I have seen people sleep at our church.*

Mama, sitting in between Mabel and Drella, holds each girl's hand. Mabel keeps her head bowed, but rolls her eyes upward so she can see Josie's grave. *That hole's deep. The preacher's white robe has red dirt all along the bottom. He's standing in dirt from the grave.*

The preacher opens his Bible and begins reading. Mabel is too distracted to hear anything he says. Her thoughts are focused on the hole, the ropes, the casket, the ushers, and Drella. *I hope Drella knows that Mama, Papa, and Aunt Apple will take care of her until she goes to live with her aunt. She's sad because Josie's gone. I feel sorry for her.*

Mabel lifts her head and looks at the preacher. "We have come here to lay Josie Roane's body in the ground, but Josie's soul went to heaven yesterday—she went immediately to be with the Lord. Her beautiful soul took flight in a miraculous way. Now we shall commit Josie's physical body into the ground."

The pallbearers step around the casket, take hold of the long ropes, unwind them from the railroad spikes, and gently lower Josie's casket into her grave. Mabel begins to hear crying from the usher behind her. *I feel sorry for Josie's friends too. There's a lot of people crying.* The lady behind Mabel stops fanning; Mabel hears her sniffling and searching the pockets of her white uniform for a handkerchief. After the usher blows her nose, the fanning resumes. *I reckon everybody loves Josie just like Mama and me.*

"Her physical body will rest here until the time of the resurrection." The preacher reaches down and picks up a handful of dirt. He holds his dirt-filled hand over the lowered casket and speaks in a loud voice. "In sure and certain hope of the resurrection to eternal life through our Lord, we commit Josie's body to the ground." Mabel watches as the preacher opens his hand to drop the dirt on Josie's casket. The sounds of the clods of dirt hitting the wooden casket make Mabel cringe. *Poor Josie. Mama told me that he'd put the first dirt on her casket. I wonder what Drella's thinking.* "May the Lord bless Josie Roane and fill her soul with eternal peace."

Now, with tears streaming down her face, Mabel struggles to listen to the colored pallbearer who has stepped over by the preacher. "It is our custom to invite the friends of the departed to step forward and drop a handful of soil on the casket. So, if you will, form a line and we shall begin." Mabel watches each person as they step forward, pick up some dirt, and drop it on Josie's casket. As the number of handfuls of dirt increases, the sound of the crashing dirt gets softer but the crying gets louder throughout the crowd. *I wonder if they're gonna let us put a handful of dirt in Josie's grave. I want to help bury her too.*

When all of those gathered have walked by and paid their respects to Drella, a deacon escorts Mabel's row to the graveside. The deacon puts them in order. First Aunt Apple, then Mama, then Mabel, and finally, Drella. Mabel feels so sad now that she doesn't want to look at anyone. She watches as Aunt Apple stoops over, picks up some dirt, and drops it into the grave. One of the ushers holds her arm around Aunt Apple and walks her back through the crowd. When it's Mama's turn, she begins sobbing, and Papa comes to brace her as she sadly adds to Josie's burial. Papa walks Mama over to stand beside Aunt Apple.

One of the ushers holds on to Mabel's arm as she stands beside the grave. When Mabel looks down into the grave, the casket is nothing more than a blur through her tears. Mabel picks up a handful of dirt and lets it flow through her fingers to Josie's casket. An overwhelming sorrow fills Mabel's chest as she realizes that she will never see Josie again. *I's gonna take care of you Josie, but now you're gone and I can't. We's gonna be together when I grew up. You're my angel now, Josie, and I still love you. I'll always watch for you.*

Mabel starts sobbing and feels Papa's arm around her shoulder. Mabel looks up at Papa—tears streaming down both of their faces. "Papa, I love Josie. Josie's my friend—but now she's gone away. I don't want her to be gone, Papa. Why'd this happen to my Josie?"

Papa pulls Mabel close to his leg. He bends over and whispers in her ear. "I know, honey. We all love Josie. We're all gonna be sad for a long, long time." As Papa straightens up, he lifts Mabel into his arms and takes her over to where Mama is standing. Mabel weeps as she lays her head down on his shoulder. "I've got to put you down and go help Drella, Mabel," whispers Papa.

He lowers her to the ground beside Mama. Papa walks over to Drella and rests his hand on her shoulder. Drella stands and looks down toward her mother's casket. Mabel leans against Mama and watches Drella pick up a handful of dirt. When the dirt begins tumbling from Drella's hand, Mabel closes her eyes from the sight of her friend burying her mother.

After the burial, Mama, Papa, and Mabel walk back home in silence. When they open the front gate, Mabel sees Priscilla Delany sitting on the front porch with Brother. Mama begins a nervous chatter as soon as she sees them. "Thank you so much for staying with Brother during the funeral. Tell your mother how much we appreciate your time."

Mabel and Papa don't hesitate for their typical niceties and continue into the house. Exhausted, Mabel goes to her room, changes into her overalls, pulls back the bedspread, and crawls into bed. After Mabel sleeps for about an hour, Papa calls her to the supper table.

As they sit at the kitchen table, Mabel watches Brother play with his food. "Lizbeth, I think it's time for us to enclose the back porch like we planned. We're going to need the space when Drella wants to stay with us," says Papa.

Mama chews her food and seems to mull over what Papa is planning. "I think that's a good idea, Tom," says Mama. "You've had the lumber out in the barn for a long, long time. Even if Drella never stays here, I think it'll be nice for the family."

"I'll get Uncle Apple and old Joe to help me," says Papa. "We'll paint it white." Papa looks at Mabel and smiles. "Would you like that, Mabel?"

"Yessir," says Mabel. "It'll really be nice when it gets cold." Mabel pushes her plate away and folds her arms on the table. "Since we's at church all day, do we still go to our church tomorrow?"

Mama and Papa laugh. "Yes, Mabel, we'll be going to our church in the morning," says Mama. "You really did a good job today. Papa and I were proud of how grown-up you acted."

"Funerals are usually long affairs, Mabel," says Papa. "I'm happy we could go for Josie. I was surprised at the number of white folks there. She lived in Shoal Crossing all of her life—I guess she knew just about everybody around this town."

"When are you gonna build that room, Papa?" asks Mabel.

"Oh, I reckon I'll talk to the men Sunday or Monday afternoon," says Papa. "If we can get started on Tuesday, then we'll be finished by this time next week." Papa leans back and stretches his back. "Since the porch is already framed, it won't be hard to do at all."

"Drella will be happy when I tell her," says Mama. "Aunt Apple and I are going to meet here at the house sometime Monday afternoon so we can discuss Drella's schedule. I think she'll be here Monday through Thursday of each week. Then she'll go back to the Apple's house on Friday afternoon after school."

"Of course, all of it depends on when her aunt can come down to Alabama to get her," says Papa.

"Do you think that'll be soon, Mama?" says Mabel.

"I don't know, honey. From the way Josie talked, she'll have to save some money," says Mama. "It seems to me that she'd want to come get her before hard winter sets in up there." Mama scoots her chair back and starts clearing the table. "We should be hearing from Gladys by the end of the month. I'm not worried about when or if she comes to get Drella. As far as I'm concerned, Drella's welcome here for the rest of her life. I promised Josie that I'd take care of her and I will."

"It'll be fun to have Drella at our house," says Mabel. "We'll have lots of time to play."

"Yes," says Mama. "You need to remember that Drella will be starting back to school and helping me do some housework. The two of you will have plenty of time to play though. You and Sister are going to be doing more around the house too. Now that Josie's gone, things are going to be different for all of us."

"Mabel, we have to remember that Drella needs to go to school just like Bubba and Sister," says Papa. "She'll have to be in school when she goes up north with her aunt. Josie thought her schooling was important and we do too."

"It'll take us a while to work out everything, but there'll be plenty of time for all of you to have your fun," says Mama. "We always found time to have our fun with Josie, didn't we? I don't look for any problems with any of it."

—

Monday morning, Mabel sees for the first time that life will be different without Josie. After breakfast, she has to dry and put away the dishes. She has to make up her bed and Mama introduces her to the dust cloth. Mabel and Mama take turns checking on and tending to Brother. After they eat lunch and clean up the dishes, Mama tells Mabel that she can go out to her sandbox and play until Aunt Apple comes.

Mabel steps out into the fresh air and takes a deep breath. As she's walking toward the sandbox, Mabel notices the rose bushes where she and Josie cut the flowers not so long ago. Mabel walks over to the bush where Josie told her about the roses being like different people. She spots a wilted rose and gently cups it in her hand. As she holds the rose, Mabel bends over and kisses it. *I'll always remember what Josie told me about the roses. I didn't think she would be the wilted one. It won't be long before they'll all be gone. I've got to remember to tell that story to Drella and Sister. They'll like it too.*

Turning away from the roses, Mabel goes over to her sandbox. While balancing her feet on the side board nearest the tree, she reaches up and swings herself onto the lowest limb. *It's been a long time since I've climbed up here.* Mabel skillfully zigzags her way up to her favorite spot. *Those men are out on the front porch of the store. One of them looks like he's nodding off to sleep. There's a lady walking up the steps. They're looking at her just like they did me. There's two colored men sitting in the shade where Josie waited for me that day. Josie said that they play checkers out there.*

Mabel leans her head back and rests it against the tree. For a moment, Mabel closes her eyes. *I'll be glad when Drella comes this afternoon. Mama said that we can play while she and Aunt Apple are talking.*

When she opens her eyes, Mabel glances up at the roof of the house. *Oh! There's a redbird! Wonder if it's the same one Josie and me wished on at our picnic.* Though no one else is around, Mabel says the poem out loud that Josie taught her. "Redbird, redbird, way up high; take my wish up to the sky." *I hope Josie knows how much I love her.* Mabel keeps staring at the redbird. *I hope that Josie's happy about Drella's special new room at our house.* Mabel keeps her eyes focused on the redbird. In a few minutes, he takes off and soars above all the trees. She watches it until it's out of sight. A smile brushes across Mabel's face. *My wish is gonna come true. Josie said it would. I'm glad Josie knows I love her.*

"Mabel?" says Mama. "You need to come on in the house. I saw Aunt Apple and Drella coming through the field." Mama pauses and her eyes search for Mabel.

"I heard you, Mama," says Mabel. "I'm up here in the tree." Mabel giggles to herself because her Mama never remembers to look up in the tree.

"Come on in, honey. I hear them knocking on the back door." Mama turns and walks back toward the kitchen.

As quickly as she can, Mabel works her way back down to the lowest limb and swings herself until her feet touch the side of the sandbox. She rubs her hands together to try to make the stinging from the rough tree bark go away. Stepping down on the ground,

Mabel stops to pull up her white socks. *I can't wait to see Drella.* She hurriedly walks over to the boardwalk, dashes up the steps, and opens the front door.

Just as Mabel closes the front door, the picture begins swirling around and quickly moves away from the O'Brien house. The picture continues to move upward and outward until the bridge over Shoal Creek is visible. Again, like a kaleidoscope, the colors in the far-off scene spin until they blend into nothingness. Within moments, the colors fade away and the shimmering white light fills the space where the pictures once appeared.

Chapter 22
Reflections

As I look around the now-silent room, I'm aware of the brightness of the light once again. I close my eyes to block out its intensity and sense that Mabel is now standing in front of her chair. Feeling the warmth of her presence, I start sending her my thoughts. "There's no way anyone could ever describe in words what we've just seen. After watching all of the people and events in your childhood, I understand why you wanted me to come here and witness this with you." Opening my eyes, Mabel smiles down at me.

"What a blessing it's been for me to be able to share a part of my review with you." Miraculously, her thoughts continue to transfer into my mind with clarity. "Since we spent so many of my final days on earth talking about my childhood, it occurred to me that seeing this would be very beneficial to you."

I close my eyes again and convey my thoughts to her. "We really enjoyed talking about your memories before you left. If you'll remember, I wanted to hear them so I could better understand my heritage. You seemed to enjoy sharing them with me, but being here with you is far more than I could've ever hoped for on earth."

When I look up, I notice how the rays of light envelop her silhouette. "Yes, I see that it's much better for both of us. I don't know if you picked up on the threads that seemed to be woven into my life from many different people." She walks back to her chair and sits down. Her silence informs me that she's waiting for my thoughts.

"I would say that the strongest thread is love—a God-like love. Because of their depth of love, other qualities come through powerfully. In them, I see happiness, kindness, and a special kind of goodness. The people and events you chose also showed a level of patience that is seldom seen today."

"Here that patience is called longsuffering. It comes from knowing that all things are based on the will of God—that our prayers and needs are answered according to God's will for our lives. It requires one to walk in total faith. Of course, that faith brings forth many of the qualities you mentioned. It doesn't mean that the people were perfect, by any means, but it does show that the foundation of their character came from their belief in God. When push came to shove in their lives, their faith always came through."

My thoughts respond to Mabel's thoughts. "For instance, the Ladies Aid Society met regularly to perform acts of goodness for people they didn't even know. They gave of their time for a cause they saw as greater than their own. I'm sure some of them had to do without so that they could contribute."

"That's true. None of the families had much of anything. Benevolence seemed to be a part of their being. All of the families were trying to get by as best they could. Mama and Papa often pointed out that some of the kindest people were the ones who had the least. They all tried to help each other. The men gave in the community too. They helped each another out by plowing the land, planting, building, and painting together. It was a part of our lives. Mama and Papa made certain that we saw love in action most every day."

"I enjoyed watching you and Drella the day of the meeting. Y'all seemed fascinated by the ladies, their clothing, and their behaviors. You two had fun together, didn't you?"

Mabel's thoughts respond to my question. "I wanted you to see how we entertained ourselves. We lived very simple lives. Josie was concerned about us that day because she knew that we had to remain in the background. She'd never sent us out to pick blackberries, but she wanted us away from the house and the ladies."

I look at Mabel and smile. "You two ate far more blackberries than you put in the buckets. As I watched it, I thought one of you was going to get sick."

"As I recall that day, I know that I felt sick long before I fell from the tree. Our behavior out there showed a total lack of self-control. Just like any other children, we soon forgot our task and began thinking only of ourselves. From childhood into adulthood, self-control is difficult to master—it's a constant problem for all people. Without it, people cannot find happiness. Mr. Watson's problems with alcohol showed us how a lack of self-control can ruin one's life."

"It's interesting that you see a connection between that and self-centeredness."

Mabel stands once again and walks over to where I'm sitting. "Self-control is a learned behavior. Our worldly lives are intended to teach us temperance. If people allow themselves to be guided by things of the flesh, they will not find the inner tranquility they constantly seek. A lack of self-control destroys their peace because they are constantly searching for more. Those who lack this trait usually seek only for themselves. If you watch and listen, you can see the lack of self-control all around you—in yourself and others. It is shown through bad tempers, criticism of others, unforgiving spirits, and indulgence in the many vices of the world."

I continue to look up at her as I send my thoughts. "We have to be constantly aware of those things that seem to come into our lives so innocently and then become a problem. I suppose the things themselves are not the problem, but rather our inability to control our behavior. It's a constant battle, isn't it?"

Mabel smiles back at me. "Yes, it's a battle and a challenge. I use to wonder why God allowed so many distractions for the human spirit. You must always remember that God will work with you to remove those flaws. The blackberries were not the problem that day with Drella. The problem came about when we took advantage of the situation and lost our self-control. That part of the review illustrates why children need parents and adults in their lives to guide them—to serve as role models. It's a constant need."

My thoughts flow back to Mabel. "What astounds me, Mabel, is how we all fall short of God's goodness. His redemptive grace allows us to fail, get back up, and try again. Through that forgiveness and kindness, we gain strength with our attempts. All of it works together to build strong character. As I told you earlier, you encouraged us to look at the learning we gained from our failures or disappointments. That was very good advice. Approaching life from that perspective made me aware that I was constantly building myself—constantly improving. It eliminates hopelessness and fear of failure."

Acknowledging my thoughts, Mabel smiles. "Now, I want you to walk with me to the review screen." I follow Mabel and am reminded of her renewed ability to walk. When we reach the screen, Mabel lifts her hand and a still picture of her and Josie appears. They are under the tree where they had their picnic. While Josie is leaning against the tree, Mabel has her head resting on Josie's lap. Josie appears to be asleep. "This was truly a wonderful time with Josie. She went to so much trouble to plan this day."

"Josie seemed to know exactly what you liked to do. Y'all look so peaceful out there, Mabel. I couldn't believe how quickly Josie got sick and died."

Mabel continues to focus on the picture. "I'm so glad Josie and I had this time together. Back then, people seemed to die very quickly from their illnesses. Dr. Reed did all he could for her; he stayed by her side until the very end. I'm sure that his presence comforted both Josie and Drella. He really seemed to care about Josie, but medicine was not like it is today." Mabel looks at me and then back at the picture. "In those days, people were usually buried within twenty-four hours of their death. I even remember some people dying in the morning and being buried that same afternoon."

"Do you remember how her death affected you, Mabel?"

"It was very difficult for me and I missed her terribly—Josie was a part of my being. However, my talks with Mama and Papa helped me to understand it all. It's ironic that Josie and I talked about heaven so much. It's as though she sensed that her life on earth was going to be short. If you'll recall some of the conversations we had, she spoke of heaven almost every time we talked. It was as though she prepared me for her death. Josie's heart was clearly focused on heaven—every single day."

"What kinds of things did Mama and Papa share with you about her death?"

"Mama explained it real well to Drella and me. She reinforced what the preacher said in his sermon about Josie being in a better place. Mama helped me to understand that life is everlasting—which supported everything Josie had told me. I truly believed Josie was still there for me. We talked openly about Josie and she continued to be a part of our daily lives. She remained very much alive within us. Each of us missed her, but we found comfort in sharing our memories of her. We kept her living in our hearts, our thoughts, and our conversations."

"When did Drella's aunt come to take her back to Michigan?"

"Well, as I recall from reviewing that earlier, she planned on coming in October, but the flu pandemic hit northwest Alabama and her arrival was delayed by about a month. It was after Thanksgiving before her aunt finally came to get her."

"Did anyone in your family get the flu?"

Mabel looks at me and then shares her thoughts. "No, we didn't get sick with the flu, but it put a quietus on our lives for about a month. We had to wear the gauze masks Papa brought home. All of the schools were closed and there were no church services. There could be no public gatherings held. The stores stayed open, but everyone was so afraid of getting sick that they stayed home. It was much worse in Florence because there were so many more people. There were thousands of deaths from the flu. Since Papa worked in Florence, he kept us updated on all of the latest information about it."

I follow Mabel as she walks back toward our chairs. "Didn't the war end around that time too?"

I remain standing and wait for Mabel's answer. "Yes, the Great War ended on November 11, 1918. Everyone was so happy that it was over, but celebrations weren't held due to the flu in the area. One of the most interesting facts about the flu and the war is that more Americans died from the flu than from fighting in the war. There were almost seven hundred thousand Americans who eventually died from the flu."

As I sit down on my chair, I look at Mabel. "Those are unbelievable facts, Mabel. It just points out how terribly hard life was in 1918. Survival must have been on everyone's mind. It's so difficult to imagine what y'all went through, but those are the things that contributed to making you such a strong person."

"Yes, all of it worked together to make me strong. If you survived back then, you came through a much better person."

Mabel gets up from her chair and begins walking toward the door. "Is it time for me to leave, Mabel?"

She continues to walk toward the door and sends me her thoughts. "Yes, I'm sorry to say that it's time for you to go. You've seen the parts of my review I needed to share with you. There may be more for you to see in the future, but I have to review many more before I can request your presence again. Follow me back to the living quarters."

As we walk back into the large open room, I see the couch where Mabel was sitting when I first saw her. We walk over to it and sit down. "This has been such a blessing to be able to spend this time with you." Mabel looks at me as I continue to share my thoughts. "Seeing the review with you made everything so real. The greatest thing I have learned is that life teaches us through our experiences—nothing happens without a purpose. I also gained a deeper understanding of our circle of influence. I'll never forget any of it, Mabel, but I really don't want to leave you. I've missed you so much."

"Yes, it's always difficult to leave the presence of those we love, but you'll find a renewed zest for life when you go back. You'll see many of the things we discussed in your own life. I believe that you're now better prepared to learn from your own experiences. You'll also have a renewed peace within your being. You'll know that I'm always with you. Now, you must go because your time here with me has run out."

We both stand and I begin walking back to the arched doorway where I first entered Mabel's living quarters. I stop, turn around, and wave. The beauty of her smile and her complete peace reassure me that all is well with her soul.

Chapter 23

WITHOUT LOOKING BACK AGAIN, I WALK through the long hallway. When I glance over to my right, I recall how the brilliance of the white light bothered me when I originally entered the living quarters. Now unaffected, I continue walking until I reach the archway and step out onto the balcony overlooking the museum. As I stand there, I see the crowd of onlookers below, but don't allow their thoughts to enter my mind or interrupt my movement toward the stairway.

The white marble steps glisten beneath my feet as I hold on to the bronze handrail to guide my descent. I look over to my right and notice the patrons gawking at me. *I know they're wondering why I would ever leave the divine quarters of my family. They don't understand yet. They don't know that I was allowed to visit and now must return to life on earth.* When I reach the bottom step, I walk out into the grand foyer. The same doorman grasps the bronze doorknob with his white-gloved hand and opens the door. He touches the brim of his black hat and nods as I walk past.

When I step outside, I look to the right and can clearly see the city below. A sense of reluctance fills me as I realize that I must go back to earth. *My dream will end soon. I have to remain optimistic that my life on earth will be revitalized through Mabel's teachings. This has been a glorious experience. She shared so many valuable lessons during her review. I now have a deeper understanding of what life's about—our earthly existence only serves to prepare us for heaven. That one lesson fills me with a new zest for life; it fills me with hope for life everlasting.*

Standing in between the two massive lions at the entrance, I turn my head to the left and look up the street. I notice that it's lined with buildings much like the one I just left. The brightness of the streetlights is subdued by the presence of a hazy fog filling the atmosphere. *Though everything is eerily quiet and I can hardly see anything, I'm not afraid to be alone here. If this were in the city, I wouldn't feel safe. There's the man who walked me up here from the city. I wonder if he's coming to escort me back down. He has on the same black felt derby hat, but is wearing a different suit. It appears that his suit and vest are black. I'll just stand here and wait until he's in front of the steps.*

As he comes closer, I smile. When he gets in front of the steps, he touches the brim of his hat to acknowledge me, walks up beside me, and offers his hand to lead me down to the sidewalk. His thoughts begin entering my mind. "I know that it's difficult for you to see in this mist after being in the light. Let me hold on to your hand as you walk down to the sidewalk."

My thoughts respond to him. "Thank you so much. The light I just left was very bright and this does take some getting used to. Aren't you the same man who walked me up here? Are you going to walk with me to the city?"

Keeping his head lowered and his face obscured, he answers my thought. "Yes, I'm the same person who brought you to this place—I'm responsible for seeing to it that you return safely. Those of us who bring people up here for visits with their loved ones have special instructions regarding their care during their stay."

I'm impressed by how polite the gentleman is to me. Though I've never seen his face, I sense his trustworthiness. I send him my thoughts again. "Coming here has been such a blessing. Do you ever go back to the city? How long have you been caring for the visitors?"

The man puts his hands into his coat pockets and looks around at the surrounding area. "I've been here since February 5, 1945, and never choose to go back to life on earth—not unless it's required. I have no desire to go back because this is truly where life exists for those who love God above all else. Everyone who comes here has the opportunity to contribute to the betterment of our divine world. I chose to escort visitors and new arrivals. It's been rewarding. How was your visit with Mabel?"

I look back up the steps at the massive doors and share my thoughts with the stranger. "It was wonderful. She took me to her review room and shared some of her childhood with me. She carried me all the way back to 1918. Through seeing her review and our conversations, Mabel reinforced the fact that all of us are children of God. Our circles of influence truly impact who we become—as children and adults."

"You'll be able to use her wisdom and others will learn from it as well." He appears to survey the city below. "Look down at the city. As you can see from the light, we don't have long to get you back. We need to begin our walk now."

As the man suggests, I turn and start walking down the sidewalk. "Can I ask you some questions while we walk?"

The stranger starts walking too, but stays slightly behind me. "I'll be happy to answer any questions you might have. We have a few more minutes."

"I'm curious about whether you know my family—namely, my mother."

"Yes, her name is Mabel. She hasn't been here very long at all. She's still going through her review. Some people don't choose to review their lives, but most prefer to examine them very closely. The reviews help them understand the twists and turns in their lives on earth more clearly."

My thoughts again turn to the stranger. "Did you choose to review your life when you entered heaven? I think Mabel is very wise in the way she's approaching her personal analysis, don't you?"

"Yes, I think she's using her time wisely here. I also took time to review my life. It's especially satisfying to be shown people and events that you tend to forget over your years on earth. When I entered my review, I had many questions about my childhood and my family as a young boy. All of the answers were played out before my eyes in the review room. After you uncover the answers, it frees you to move forward because of the understanding you gain."

"I have another question, if we have time."

"Yes, we have time."

"Do people like me ever get to come back for another visit? I mean … I mean will I be able to come again before I come here permanently?"

The gentleman slows his pace and sends me his thoughts. "You're blessed to have been able to come here before your physical death. Most people aren't allowed to have the experience you've had with your mother. She saw a need for you to be with her and sent for you. Whether you return for a visit is up to her. The visits are intended to strengthen you for your remaining time on earth. You will be reminded of what you learned here for the rest of your earthly life."

Stopping for a moment, he continues to share his thoughts. "There are those who come here, go back, and never use their experience for the betterment of their lives. That's a mistake and isn't looked upon in a favorable way. In fact, those people are placing their eternal lives in jeopardy. You should always remember the things Mabel pointed out to you. I would advise you to practice the Golden Rule as well as remain constantly mindful of the fruit of the Spirit. Look for those qualities in yourself and others."

"Mabel told me about the Golden Rule, but she didn't mention the fruit of the Spirit," I think.

The stranger looks away and then turns back to me with his thoughts. I try to make out his facial features, but the shadows obstruct my view. "The fruit of the Spirit comes to those who have turned away from their worldly desires—things of the flesh. You will recognize them as love, joy, peace, longsuffering, gentleness, goodness, faith, meekness, and temperance."

My thoughts rapidly flow back to him. "That's remarkable. I saw each of those in the people in Mabel's life as a child. I don't believe any one person had all of the fruit; some had many of them. It's funny that Mabel mentioned many of those qualities, though she never described them as fruit of the Spirit."

"If you'll recall, Mabel often taught you children through allowing you to discover the answers you sought. I'm certain she knew that you'd discern the fruit of the Spirit on your own. Mabel knew it because when you reflect about who and what you've seen with her, you'll see demonstrations of the fruit of the Spirit. Then, when you're in the presence of someone dedicated to living a spiritual life, you'll recognize it. I hope that you'll demonstrate the fruit of the Spirit in your own life. It's probably one of the reasons she brought you here—she wanted to reinforce them with you."

Thinking about the man's ideas, my thoughts turn to my own. "Mabel did encourage us to discover and work through solutions in our own way. The fruit of the Spirit communicates our depth of understanding and dedication to the laws of God. They truly reflect one's heart—their motives."

The stranger stops and his thoughts come into my mind. "That's exactly right. Surely, from what you've experienced with her, you know that your life will never be the same. Coming here should be comforting to you because it confirms how life must be lived. You know too that your mother is doing well. She has experienced a rebirth. You've seen that life is eternal and that leaving your earthly existence can be far better than anything you've ever known down there." We begin walking again.

"Are you going to walk all the way back with me?"

"No, in fact, I'm going to have to stop right here and watch you travel the remainder of the distance by yourself. You'll be safely returned to your earthly life—I'll see to that. Just remember, if you carry all you've learned in your heart and live accordingly, others will see."

I turn toward the stranger and send him my thoughts. "Thank you so much for your kindness. You have helped me understand all of this much more clearly. God bless you."

The stranger's thoughts pour into my mind. "You're welcome. You'll do fine. Keep God in your heart and always walk with the comforting knowledge you've gained. Now, you must go."

We both turn and begin walking in opposite directions. As I look down at the city, I'm keenly aware of the confusion there. In my descent, I'm aware that I have no fear and my spirit is much happier. *It really was comforting to see Mabel and heaven. What a blessing to have seen firsthand that life is eternal. There is no sting to death. If everyone could have this experience, there would be no fear of death. What's that?* I stop walking, stand very still, and hear a faint whistle. I turn and look up toward the stranger. He waves, then turns, and continues his ascent. The whistling begins again.

As I listen, I believe I recognize the sound of his whistle. I send the gentleman my thoughts and pray that he can receive them. "I heard you whistle in Mabel's review, didn't I? Are you Papa? Are you the Papa that Mabel so adored?"

I can barely see him now through the vapor as he stops and turns. He takes off his hat and bows—then his voice pours into my mind. "Yes, I'm Papa and you are my granddaughter. God truly works miracles, doesn't He? Seeing you has been a blessing. Now you know for a certainty that I'll eternally be walking and whistling. As you saw in Mabel's review, I enjoyed many happy years of preparation on earth. You must continue down now. I'll be waiting for your return. God bless you, my child."

Sensing that there is little time left, my thoughts rapidly pour out to him. "Oh, Papa, you were such a wonderful father. Mabel talked about you all of my life. Mabel was right—your whistle is beautiful. Your joy puts a song in my heart, just as it did for her."

Papa puts his hat back on and waves. He then turns and continues his climb. As I start walking back to my life, I hear his melodic whistle fading into the distance. The knowledge that I will one day return comforts me—there truly is a perfect dwelling place.